NEW

CUTTING EDGE

ELEMENTARY

STUDENTS' BOOK

sarah cunningham   peter moor

with frances eales

PEARSON

Longman

CONTENTS

Task	Further skills	Study Practise Remember
Task: Find information from documents *Preparation: reading* *Task: speaking* *Follow up: writing*	**Real life:** Answering questions *Pronunciation: Stress and intonation in questions* **WB Improve your writing:** Addresses in English	**Study tip:** Capital letters *Pronunciation spot: The sound /ə/ (schwa)*
Task: Talk about your family tree *Preparation: listening* *Task: speaking* *Follow up: writing*	**Real life:** Classroom language *Pronunciation: Sounding polite* **WB Improve your writing:** Writing about your family	**Study tip:** Learning grammar words *Pronunciation spot: The sounds /ð/ and /θ/*
Task: Find things in common *Preparation: listening* *Task: speaking*	**Real life:** Days and times *Pronunciation: Sentence stress* **WB Improve your writing:** Commas, full stops, *and* and *but*	**Study tip:** Remembering spelling *Pronunciation spot: Silent syllables*
Task: Find an e-mail friend *Preparation: reading* *Task: reading and speaking*	**Real life:** Asking politely *Pronunciation: Sounding polite* **WB Improve your writing:** A paragraph about a friend	**Study tip:** Finding spelling in a dictionary (1) *Pronunciation spot: Words ending in s*
Task: Complete a survey about transport *Preparation: reading and writing* *Task: speaking* *Follow up: writing*	**Real life:** Buying a ticket **WB Improve your writing:** Completing an immigration form	
Task: Describe the differences between two pictures *Preparation: listening* *Task: speaking*	**Real life:** Ordering food and drink *Pronunciation: international words; Sounding polite* **WB Improve your writing:** Describing food	**Study tip:** Finding grammar in a dictionary (1) *Pronunciation spot: International words*
Task: Tell your life story *Preparation: listening* *Task: speaking* *Follow up: writing*	**Real life:** Dates and other past time phrases *Pronunciation: Sentence stress* **WB Improve your writing:** Time linkers: *before, after, then*	**Study tip:** Finding grammar in a dictionary (2) *Pronunciation spot: The sounds /ɔː/ and /ɜː/*

Task	Further skills	Study Practise Remember
Task: Interview other students about arts and entertainment *Preparation: listening* *Task: speaking* *Follow up: writing*	**Real life:** Arranging a night out [WB] **Improve your writing:** A diary	**Study tip:** Checking and revising *Pronunciation spot: Stressed syllables*
Task: Choose souvenirs from your country *Preparation: listening* *Task: speaking*	**Real life:** Asking in shops *Pronunciation: Sentence stress in questions* [WB] **Improve your writing:** Describing a place	**Study tip:** Finding spelling in a dictionary (2) *Pronunciation spot: The sound /ɪ/*
Task: Complete and describe a picture *Preparation: listening* *Task: speaking*	**Real life:** Street talk *Pronunciation: Sounding polite* [WB] **Improve your writing:** Correcting mistakes	
Task: Devise a general knowledge quiz *Preparation: listening* *Task: writing and speaking*	**Real life:** Saying quantities and big numbers [WB] **Improve your writing:** Punctuation	**Study tip:** Recording new vocabulary *Pronunciation spot: The sounds /w/ and /h/*
Task: Plan a weekend away *Preparation: reading and listening* *Task: speaking*	**Real life:** Talk about the weather [WB] **Improve your writing:** Write about a holiday place	**Study tip:** Remembering collocations *Pronunciation spot: Short forms*
Task: Find the right course *Preparation: reading and speaking* *Task: speaking*	**Real life:** Applying for a course [WB] **Improve your writing:** Abbreviations (*Mr, Mrs, Dr, n/a*)	**Study tip:** English outside the classroom *Pronunciation spot: The sounds /ɒ/, /əʊ/ and /ɔː/*
Task: Analyse a questionnaire *Preparation: reading* *Task: speaking*	**Real life:** Telephoning *Pronunciation: Sounding polite* [WB] **Improve your writing:** Writing a note	**Study tip:** Revising *Pronunciation spot: The sounds /æ/ and /ʌ/*
Task: Plan a website about your town *Preparation: vocabulary and reading* *Task: speaking* *Follow up: writing*	**Real life:** Following directions [WB] **Improve your writing:** A postcard	

What English do you know?

1 a man

2 a boy

3 a teacher

4 a chair

5 a door

6 a pen

a a desk

b a student

c a woman

d a notebook

e a girl

f a window

1 Common words

T0.1 Match the pairs of words above. Listen and check, then repeat.

1 c   a man – a woman

2 Numbers 0–21

a Write the numbers.

twenty *20*	eight	nine	four
sixteen	fifteen	five	ten
three	zero	seven	two
one	seventeen	twelve	thirteen
six	twenty-one	nineteen	eleven
eighteen	fourteen		

b **T0.2** Listen and say the numbers 0 to 21.

3 Plurals

a **T0.3** Write the plurals. Then listen and repeat.

1	book	4	chair	7	boy
2	teacher	5	student	8	man
3	desk	6	girl	9	woman

b How many can you see in your classroom?

five students

4 The alphabet

a **T0.4** Listen and say the alphabet.

a b c d e
f g h i j
k l m n o
p q r s t
u v w
x y z

b Spell:
- your first name
- the name of your street
- your teacher's name
- your surname
- the name of your city

5 Pronouns and possessive adjectives

What are the pronouns in A in your language?
Match them to the possessive adjectives in B.

	A		B
a	I		your
b	you		its
c	he		our
d	she		my
e	it		her
f	we		their
g	they		his

My teacher!

6 Numbers 1–100

a **T0.5** Write the next three numbers. Listen and check, then repeat.

21 *twenty-two, twenty-three, twenty-four*

twenty-one (21)   sixty-six (66)
thirty-five (35)   seventy-four (74)
forty-three (43)   eighty-one (81)
fifty-six (56)   ninety-seven (97)

b **T0.6** Listen and write the twelve numbers.

c Say the number and the number before.

twenty-one … twenty

21	17	65	86	54	11	45
13	100	25	90	7	33	18

7 Days of the week

T0.7 Write the days in the correct place.
Listen and check, then repeat.

Friday   Sunday   Wednesday   Saturday   Tuesday

a Monday
b _____
c _____
d Thursday
e _____
f _____
g _____

8 Saying hello and goodbye

a **T0.8** Match the sentences to the pictures. Listen and check.

Bye, Kate. See you later.   Fine thanks, and you?

b Practise the conversations. Use your names.

9 Classroom instructions

a Match the teacher's instructions to the pictures.

1 Open your books at page 10, please. *f*
2 Listen.
3 Write this in your notebooks.
4 Look at the picture.
5 Put your books here, please.
6 Work in pairs.

b **T0.9** Listen and follow the instructions.

People and places

- ► *be* (positive, negative, questions and short answers): personal information
- ► Articles: *a/an* + jobs
- ► Vocabulary: Names, countries and nationalities
- ► Reading and listening: *General knowledge quiz*
- ► Task: Find information from documents
- ► Real life: Answering questions

Language focus 1
be: names and countries

1 Work in pairs. Practise this conversation.

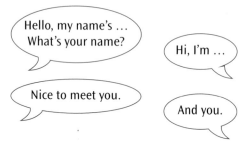

> Hello, my name's …
> What's your name?

> Hi, I'm …

> Nice to meet you.

> And you.

2 a **T1.1** Put the sentences in the box in the conversation on the right. Then listen and check.

> No, no! I'm from Buenos Aires.   ~~Hi. How are you?~~
> Nice to meet you, Carla.   Nice to meet you, too.
> Really? Manchester's a fantastic city.

b Are these sentences true (✔) or false (✗)?

1   Carla's from Italy.   3   Ben and Emily are English.
2   Ariel's from Italy.   4   They're from London.

EMILY: Hi, Carla.

CARLA: (1) *Hi. How are you?*

EMILY: Fine, thanks. Carla, this is Ben. Ben, this is Carla, from my class. She's from Milan.

BEN: (2) _____

CARLA: Hello, Ben. Nice to meet you. This is my friend Ariel.

EMILY: Hello, Ariel. Where are you from? Are you from Italy, too?

ARIEL: (3) _____

EMILY: Well, nice to meet you.

ARIEL: (4) _____

CARLA: Emily and Ben are from Manchester.

ARIEL: (5) _____

EMILY: Thank you.

Grammar

1 *be*: positive forms

Complete the gaps.

I	I'_____ from Milan. (= I am)
You	_____ you from Milan too?
He	He'_____ from Buenos Aires. (= He is)
She	Carla'_____ from Italy. (= Carla is)
They	Ben and Emily _____ from Manchester.

2 Questions

_____'s your name?
_____ are you from?

► Read Language summary A on page 150.

Practice

1 a Walk around the class. Ask and answer these questions.

> What's your name?

> Where are you from?

b Introduce a student to the class.

> This is Ramon. He's from …

Pronunciation

T1.2 Listen and practise saying these countries.

• • •	• • •	• •	• • • •
Italy	Mexico	Britain	the USA

• • • •	• •	• •	• •
Argentina	Russia	China	Egypt

• •	•	• • •	• •
Poland	Spain	Germany	Thailand

---

2 Work in pairs. Point to the photos. Ask and answer questions like this.

> Where's he from?

> He's from the USA.

> Where are they from?

> They're from Argentina.

3 a Where are these cities? Which are capital cities? Ask and answer with your partner.

Hamburg	Bangkok	San Diego	Liverpool
Warsaw	St Petersburg	Beijing	Buenos Aires
Cairo	Barcelona	Rome	Monterrey

> Where's Hamburg?

> Hamburg's in Germany.

> Where's Bangkok?

> Bangkok's the capital of Thailand.

b **T1.3** Listen and check.

9

Vocabulary
Nationalities

a Match the nationalities to the countries.

	Country	Nationality
1	Spain	British
2	China	American
3	the USA	Japanese
4	Turkey	Chinese
5	Italy	Polish
6	Britain	Italian
7	Poland	Korean
8	Australia	Russian
9	Japan	French
10	Korea	Spanish
11	France	Turkish
12	Russia	Australian

b **T1.4** Listen and check.

> ### Pronunciation
>
> **T1.5** Listen. Can you hear the stress?
>
> ●
> Bri-tish
>
> ●
> A-mer-i-can
>
> ●
> Ja-pa-nese
>
> Mark the stress on the other nationalities in exercise 1. Listen, check and repeat.

Reading and listening

a Work in pairs. Do the general knowledge quiz.

b **T1.6** Listen and check your answers. Count your marks.

GENERAL KNOWLEDGE QUIZ

A Match the currencies to the countries. (4 marks)

Australia   Japan   France   Turkey

euro

lira

dollar

yen

B Match the stamps to the countries. (4 marks)

Poland   Egypt   Thailand   Britain

C Which of these companies is: (4 marks)

Italian?   Korean?   German?   Japanese?

D Which word below is in: (5 marks)

Arabic?   Chinese?   Russian?   Italian?   Spanish?

1 Hola   2 ٱلسَّلَامُ عَلَيْكُمْ   3 Здра́вствуйте   4 你好   5 Ciao

E What nationality are these actresses? (3 marks)

Nicole Kidman

Penélope Cruz

Jennifer Lopez

Language focus 2
be: personal information

1 **MD** Look at photos 1–3. Match the sentences below to the people.

1 — Andrei

2 — Toshi and Mariko

3 — Marisol

a His name's Andrei. **1**
b Her name's Marisol.
c Their names are Toshi and Mariko.
d They're from Tokyo.
e He's from Russia.
f She's from Valencia in Spain.
g He's twenty-two.
h He's a student at Moscow University.
i He's nineteen.
j She's at the airport.
k She isn't on holiday. She's on business.
l They're tourists.
m She's thirty-five and she's married.
n He isn't married. He's single.
o They aren't married. They're friends.

2 **T1.7** Listen to Andrei, Marisol and Toshi. Check your answers.

Grammar

be: positive and negative short forms.

T1.8 Complete the table. Then listen and check.

➕	short form	➖	short form
I am	_____	I am not	I'm not
you are	you're	you are not	_____
he is	_____	he is not	_____
she is	_____	she is not	_____
it is	it's	it is not	_____
we are	we're	we are not	we aren't
they are	_____	they are not	_____

▶ Read Language summaries A, B and E on page 150.

▶ Read Language summaries A, B and E on page 150.

Pronunciation

Look at the tapescript for recording 8 on page 164. Listen again. Practise saying the short forms in sentences.

Practice

1 **a** Write four true and four false sentences about the people in the photos.

b Work in pairs. Read out your sentences. Your partner corrects the false ones.

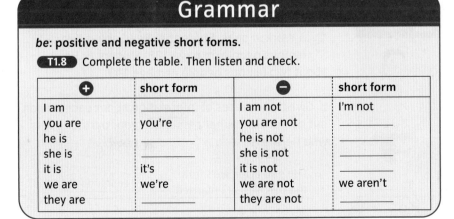

Toshi's from Tokyo.

True.

Toshi and Mariko are married.

False. They aren't married. They're friends.

2 **MD** Tick the sentences that are true for you. Correct the false ones.

a You're in an English lesson. ✔
b You're from China.
   I'm not from China. I'm from …
c You're Italian.
d Your school's in New York.
e Your classroom's very small.
f Your teacher's from Scotland.
g Your teacher's married.
h Your father's a politician.
i Your parents are on holiday.
j Your English lessons are in the evening.
k You're thirty-five years old.
l You're at work.

Language focus 3
Articles (1): *a/an* + jobs

1 **T1.9** Match the jobs to the pictures. Then listen and check.

a footballer   a musician   an engineer   a lawyer
a police officer   a PA (personal assistant)   a singer
an electrician   a shop assistant   a doctor and a nurse
an actor and an actress   a waiter and a waitress
a businessman and a businesswoman

Pronunciation

T1.10 Listen and mark the stress on the words in exercise 1. Practise saying the words.

● footballer ● musician ● engineer

2 Work in pairs. Ask and answer questions about the people in the pictures.

What's his job?   He's an actor.

Grammar

With jobs we use the articles *a/an*.

an + vowel (a, e, i, o, u)   **a + other letters**
He's **an** engineer.   I'm **a** waiter.
She's **an** actress.   He's **a** police officer.

▶ Read Language summary F on page 150.

Practice

1 Make four true sentences. Compare sentences with a partner.

Examples:
I'm a law student.   My mother's a doctor.
My father's an electrician.   My friend Yusef's a student.

2 Write a short paragraph about yourself.

My name's ...
I'm ... years old.
I'm a ...
I'm from ... in ...
I'm ... (married).
My mother/husband is a ...

3 a Work in pairs. Student A: Read about two famous people on page 138. Student B: Read about two famous people on page 140.

b Give three pieces of information about each person but do not say his/her name. Can your partner guess who he/she is.

He's an actor. He's from the USA. He isn't married.   Leonardo DiCaprio?

c Play again. This time you think of the famous people.

Language focus 4
be: personal questions

1 **a** **MD** Read the market research interview. Which is the best answer to each question?

1 What's your full name?
  a My name's Will.
  b It's William Anthony Barker.

2 Where are you from?
  a I'm from Wellington in New Zealand.
  b I'm French.

3 Are you here on holiday?
  a No, I'm a tourist. **b** Yes, I am.

4 How old are you?
  a It's thirty-two. **b** I'm twenty-six.

5 What's your job?
  a I'm a musician. **b** You're a student.

6 Are you married?
  a Yes, I'm single. **b** No, I'm not.

7 What's your address in England?
  a It's 25 Manor Road, London N10.
  b It's willbarker@blc.com.

8 What's your telephone number?
  a It's 020 7535 3555. **b** No, it isn't.

b **T1.11** Listen to the interview and check.

Grammar

1 **Questions with be**
Notice the word order.

answer	question
I'm twenty-six.	How old **are you**?
My phone number's 0171 53355.	What's **your phone number**?

2 **Short answers to yes/no questions**

Are you married?	Yes, **I am.**
	No, **I'm not.**
Is he on holiday?	Yes, **he is.**
	No, **he isn't.**

▶ Read Language summaries C and D on page 150.

2 Work in pairs. Ask and answer the questions from exercise 1. Answer for yourself.

Pronunciation

1 **T1.12** Look at the tapescript on page 164. Listen to the stress in the questions and short answers.

Are you on holiday?   Yes, I am.

Are you married?   No, I'm not.

2 Listen and practise the questions and answers.

Practice

1 Put the questions into the correct order.

a you / a student /are? *Are you a student?*
b you / are / twenty-one?
c from / is / Britain / your teacher?
d what / your / e-mail address / 's?
e old / how / is / your mother?
f where / from / Jennifer Lopez / 's?
g where / Manchester / 's?
h you / single / are?
i you / from / are / a big city?
j your father / a businessman / is?

2 Work in pairs. Choose five questions to ask your partner.

What's your full name?   Are you from …?

Task: Find information from documents
Preparation: reading

1 **MD** Read Hana's employee card. Mark the sentences true (✔) or false (✘).

a Her first name's Antonia.
b Her surname's Vincent.
c Her mobile number's 07711 681609.
d She's thirty-three years old.
e She's from Britain.
f Paul Vincent is her husband.
g His work number is 776544.
h Her doctor's name is Dr Elm.

2 Work in pairs. Look at the questions in the Useful language box. Then ask and answer about Hana.

Employee Personal Data

Full name Hana Antonia Vincent
Address 78A Elm Road, York, YO19 5US
Home phone number (01904) 8763973
Mobile ~~07711681609~~ 0795 323561
Date of birth 22.11.79
Place of birth Prague, Czech Republic

Contact in an emergency Paul Vincent (husband)
Home number as above
Work number (01904) 776 544
Mobile 0795 768879

Doctor's name, address and telephone number
Dr Jo Boxer, Elm Medical Centre, 3 Elm Road, York, YO6 4EJ
01904 998 788

Task: speaking

1 Work in pairs. Student A: Look at Jamie's documents on page 15. Complete the table about Jamie. Student B: Look at Chrissie's documents on page 139. Complete the table about Chrissie.

	Jamie	Chrissie
Full name		
Age		
Address		
Job		
Where from?		
E-mail address		
Telephone number		
Married / Single?		

CURRENT ACCOUNT STATEMENT

Account name   JS Burden
Account number   89387239
Branch   Glasgow, Dumbarton Road
           Tel 0141 663 1890

2251 of 3   W042 UPA3 57033   006383

Mr J S Burden
33b Park Street
Glasgow
G12 8AG

student card

NAME	Jamie Stuart Burden
PLACE OF STUDY	University of Glasgow
COURSE OF STUDY	Art History
CONTACT TELEPHONE NUMBER	0141 228 4275
E-MAIL ADDRESS	j.burden@glas.ac.uk

This card entitles you to use the facilities of the Students' Union, including the library, the computer centre, and the bar.

United Kingdom of Great Britain and Northern Ireland

Passport Passeport   **Type / Type**   **Code of Issuing / Code de l'Etat**   **Passport No / Passeport No**
                 P   GBR   700253853

Surname / Nom (1)
BURDEN
Given names / Prénoms(2)
JAMES STUART
Nationality / Nationalité (3)
BRITISH CITIZEN
Date of birth / Date de naissance (4)   **Children / Enfants(5)**
24 AUG / AOUT 86   0
Sex / Sexe(6)   **Place of birth / Lieu de naissance(7)**
M   GLASGOW

2 Student A: Ask Student B questions about Chrissie. Student B: Ask Student A questions about Jamie. Write the information in the table.

▶ Useful language a and b

Follow up: writing

Write a short paragraph about Hana, Chrissie or Jamie.

His/Her name's ...
He's/She's ... years old.
He's/She's from ...
His/Her address is ...
He's/She's ...

Useful language

a Questions

What's his first name / surname / full name?

How do you spell it?

What's her work / home / mobile number?

What's his job?

How old is she?

Where's he from?

Is she married?

b Other useful phrases

I don't know.

Sorry, I don't understand.

Real life
Answering questions

1 Do you remember how to say the alphabet and numbers? Look back at page 6, if necessary.

2 **T1.13** Listen and match the conversations to the pictures. Where are the people?

3 **a** Look at the forms. What questions can you ask to find the missing information?

b Listen again and complete the forms.

Full name: Shireen (a) _____

Address: (b) _____ Abbot's Road, Colchester

CO2 (c) _____

Phone numbers: home (d) _____

work (e) _____

E-mail: s.rahman@firstserve.com

Nationality: (f) _____

Married: (g) Yes _____ No _____

Occupation: (h) _____

Age: (i) _____

4 a **T1.14** Listen and stop after each question. Answer for yourself.

b Practise the questions.

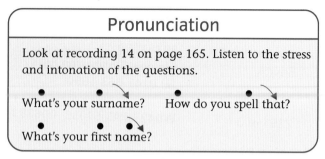

Pronunciation

Look at recording 14 on page 165. Listen to the stress and intonation of the questions.

What's your surname? How do you spell that?

What's your first name?

5 Work in pairs. Act out the conversations in the pictures. Use your own name, address, etc.

The Royal Spa

Name: (j) Emma _____

Passport number: (k) _____

Room number: (l) _____

STUDY...

Capital letters

1 Which underlined letters need capital letters? Look back through Module 1 to help you correct the sentences.

a w̲hat's your n̲ame?

b i̲'m here on b̲usiness.

c t̲his is e̲mily.

d a̲re you m̲rs r̲eam?

2 MD Use your mini-dictionary to find which of these need capital letters.

english   arabic
poland   teacher
saturday   notebook
december

▶ Read Language summary G on page 150.

Pronunciation spot

The sound /ə/ (schwa)

a **T1.15** /ə/ is a very important sound in English. It isn't stressed. Listen and repeat.

/ə/ ●   /ə/   ● /ə/
American   German

/ə/ ● /ə/   /ə/   /ə/ ●
a doctor   an engineer

●/ə/
holiday

b **T1.16** Listen and mark the stress. Then listen again and mark the /ə/ sounds.

Britain   London   Russia

Australian   Italian

a waiter   an actor   a student

a businessman   an electrician

PRACTISE...

1 Short forms of *be* ☐

Rewrite the sentences using short forms.

She's
a ~~She is~~ on business.   d You are on holiday.   g We are from Malaga.

b He is a student.   e I am not married.   h She is not at school.

c I am Marta.   f We are not from Madrid.   i They are not American.

▶ **Need to check? Language summaries A and B, page 150.**

2 *be* ☐

Put the correct form of *be* in the correct place. Use short forms, where possible.

Are
a ^ you married?   d Where you from?   g She twenty-three years old.

b This Pablo.   e They Italian.   h We on holiday.

c What your name?   f I not a student.   i How old he?

▶ **Need to check? Language summaries A, B and C page 150.**

3 Countries and nationalities ☐

Write the country and nationality for each capital city.

a Paris   _France, French_   e Madrid   _____

b London   _____   f Beijing   _____

c Moscow   _____   g Warsaw   _____

d Rome   _____   h Tokyo   _____

▶ **Need to check? Vocabulary, page 10.**

4 *a/an* + jobs ☐

Complete the jobs and add *a* or *an*.

a _an_ a c̲t o̲r   e ____ w _ i _ e _

b ____ b _ s _ n _ ss ___   f ____ e l ___ r ____ n

c ____ n u ___   g ____ p _ l ___ o ___ c _ r

d ____ e _ g i n ___   h ____ l __ y __

▶ **Need to check? Language focus 3, page 12.**

5 Question words ☐

Complete the questions with *How*, *Where* or *What*.

a _What_'s your name?   d _____ are you from?

b _____ old are you?   e _____ do you spell your surname?

c _____'s your job?   f _____'s your work number?

▶ **Need to check? Real life, page 16.**

REMEMBER!

Look back at the areas you have practised.
Tick the ones you feel confident about.
Now try the MINI-CHECK on page 160
to check what you know!

You and yours

▶ *this, that, these, those*
▶ *have got*
▶ Possessive *'s*
▶ **Vocabulary:** Everyday objects, Family vocabulary
▶ **Reading and listening:** *My favourite thing*
▶ **Task:** Talk about your family tree
▶ **Real life:** Classroom language

Language focus 1
this, that, these, those

T2.1 Circle the correct words. Then listen and check.

① Ahmed, this / that parcel's for you.

Oh right, thanks.

Grammar

this book	these books	that book	those books

▶ Read Language summaries A and B on page 150.

Pronunciation

1 **T2.2** Listen to the pronunciation, then repeat.
this /ðɪs/ parcel   these /ðiːz/ children
that /ðæt/ man   those /ðəʊz/ keys

2 **T2.3** Listen and write the eight sentences. Then listen again and repeat.

② Who's that / this over there? He's lovely!

That's / This is Marco, my new boyfriend.

Oh, right.

③ Are these / those your car keys, sir?

Oh, yes! Thank you very much!

④ Hi, Suzanna!

Hi, Philip. How are you? These / Those are my children. This / That is Tomas, and this / that is Anna.

Hi, Tomas. Hi, Anna.

Hi.

Practice

Choose the correct alternatives.

1 Look! This / That letter's from Jon.
2 Marianne, this is / that's Katie.
  Katie, this is / that's Marianne.
3 Look at this / that man over there!
4 Who are that / those people
  with Julia?

5 Excuse me, what's this / that
  word here?
6 Are this / these your books,
  Charlie?

7 Is this / that Tanya in that car?
8 Look at these / those photos
  over here.

Vocabulary
Everyday objects

1 Find these things in the photo. Then test your partner.

photos	a camera	a bottle of water	a credit card	keys	stamps
a mobile phone	a brush	a diary	coins	a packet of chewing gum	
a watch	a cheque book	a phone card	postcards	a dictionary	
an identity card	a packet of tissues	a wallet	sweets	glasses	

What's this in English?

It's a credit card.

What are these?

I don't know.   They're coins.

Pronunciation

T2.4 Look at the words in the box above. Listen and mark the stress. Then listen and repeat.

● photos   ● camera   ● ● bottle of water

2 Work in pairs. Point to things in the classroom and ask your partner.

What's that in English?

A cassette player, I think.

What are those?

Chairs.

Language focus 2
have got

1 [T2.5] Listen and complete the gaps with the phrases.

| I've got   Have you got   I haven't got |

What's the matter?

(a) _____ a phone card with me.
(b) _____ one?

PAYPHONE

No, but (c) _____ my mobile – here.

Oh, thanks.

2 [T2.6] Listen and answer the questions for yourself with a ✔ or a ✗.

a ☐   c ☐   e ☐   g ☐   i ☐
b ☐   d ☐   f ☐   h ☐   j ☐

3 a Work in pairs. Guess what your partner has got in his/her pocket or bag.

Have you got a dictionary with you?

Yes, I have. Here it is.

No, I haven't. It's at home.

b Tell the class about your partner.

Paulo's got a mobile in his bag, but he hasn't got a pen.

Grammar

1 Complete the gaps.

➕ I've _got_ my mobile phone with me.
He's/She's _____ his/her credit card.
We've/They've _____ the bag.

➖ I haven't _____ my watch with me.
He/She hasn't _____ his/her money.
We/They _____ the keys.

❓ _____ you _____ a phone card?
_____ he/she _____ her camera?
_____ we/they _____ the photos?

2 Notice:

He's French. (= he is)
He's got a French car. (= he has)

▶ Read Language summary C on page 151.

Practice

1 Complete the gaps with the correct form of *have got*.

a   I think her parents are rich – they _____ four cars.
b   Sorry, I _____ a pen with me.
c   We _____ a dog. His name's Alfie.
d   Annie's from a very big family. She _____ six brothers.
e   '_____ you _____ your cheque book with you?' 'No, but I _____ my credit card.'
f   _____ your brother _____ a new motorbike?

2 a Match the questions with the answers. Then complete the gaps.

1   _____ you got a car? ☐
2   How old _____ it? ☐
3   What colour _____ it? ☐
4   What make _____ it? ☐

a   It's a Fiat.
b   It's red.
c   Yes, I have.
d   It's very old – about ten years old.

b Work in pairs. Use some of the questions above to ask about these things.

a car	a TV in your bedroom	a bicycle
a pet	a mobile phone	a computer
a piano	a DVD player	a camera

Reading and listening
My favourite thing

1 **MD** **T2.7** Look at the photos. What are Kemal, Lisa, Tom and Mo's favourite things? Listen and read to check your answers.

Kemal

❛This is my car and I love it! It's a German car and it's my favourite colour, silver. It's really, really fast, really comfortable and it's got a fantastic CD player – it's just great. ❜

❛My favourite thing isn't really a thing, it's our pet cat, Billy. We've got four cats in our family, but Billy's my favourite. He's black and white and he's got beautiful green eyes. He isn't very friendly with other people, but he loves me! ❜

Lisa

Tim

❛I'm a professional musician, so my trumpet's really important to me. Actually, I've got three, but this one's my favourite: it's a Bach trumpet made in America – and it's about forty years old! ❜

❛My favourite thing is my computer – my laptop. It isn't new but I really like it. I really like the orange colour. And it's got everything I want – e-mail, the Internet, a DVD player and I've got some really good games on it. I love my laptop! ❜

Mo

2 Work in pairs. Answer the questions.

a What is …
• German?
• orange?
• about forty years old?
• fast and comfortable?

b Who is …
• black and white?
• a musician?
• not very friendly?

c Who has got …
• green eyes?
• three trumpets?
• four cats?

d What has got …
• a great CD player?
• good games?

3 Cover the texts. Talk about each person's favourite thing.

> Kemal's favourite thing is his car. It's German. It's really fast and it's got a fantastic CD player. It's silver and it's comfortable.

Pronunciation

1 Look at Kemal and Lisa's section of the tapescript on page 165. Change the full verbs to short forms.

's
It ~~is~~ a German car.

2 **T2.8** Listen and check. Practise saying the short forms.

---

4 **a** Write about your favourite thing(s).

My favourite thing is my …
It's (American / a Honda / very old).
It's (fantastic / very important to me / beautiful).
It's got …

b Work in small groups. Tell other students about your favourite thing.

▶ Read Language summaries D and E on page 151.

Language focus 3
Family vocabulary; Possessive 's

1 Put the family words in the box into the correct column of the table. (Write each word only once.)

brother and sister   husband and wife   sisters   cousins
boyfriend and girlfriend   grandmother and grandson
mother and daughter   mother and son   father and daughter

male	female	both
brother	sister	cousin

2 **a** Look at the famous people and their relations. Can you guess the relationship? Use the ideas in the box in exercise 1.

> They aren't husband and wife!

> Maybe they're cousins.

> I'm sure they're brother and sister.

b **T2.9** Listen and check your ideas.

Grammar

Notice:
William is Queen Elizabeth's grandson.
NOT: ~~the grandson of Queen Elizabeth~~

▶ Read Language summary F on page 151.

Practice

1 Write five sentences about the people in the photos.

Queen Elizabeth is Prince William's grandmother.

2 Add these words to the table at the top of the page.

children   parents   grandparents
grandfather   granddaughter   aunt
uncle   nephew   niece

3 **a** Study the family words. Then try the puzzle on page 144.

b Work in pairs. Test your partner like this.

> Who's your mother's father?

> Your grandfather.

4 Do you know any more famous people who are related? Tell the class.

22

Actress Liv Tyler and and rock guitarist Steve Tyler

Footballer David Beckham and Lynne Beckham

Actresses Goldie Hawn and Kate Hudson

The British Queen and Prince William

Task: Talk about your family tree
Preparation: listening

1 a Find Alex above and look at the photos of his family. What are the relationships between the people, do you think?

b Look at the family tree on page 146 and check your ideas.

2 [T2.10] Listen and number the people above in the order that Alex talks about them.

3 Check the words in bold. Then listen again and answer the questions. Who …

a	is an **economics** student?	f	is a lawyer?
b	is forty-one?	g	is very **clever**?
c	has got a **computer business**?	h	hasn't got children?
d	is at school?	i	is quite **rich**?
e	is really **funny**?	j	is really **nice** and funny?

Task: speaking

1 *Either* Make a family tree for your family. Write in the names of at least six people.

Or Bring in some photos of your family to show other students.

2 Decide what information to give about each person in your family tree / photos. Ask your teacher for any words or phrases you need.

▶ Useful language a

3 a Work in small groups. Show your family tree / photos to other students. Tell them about your family.

b Ask questions about the people in other students' family trees.

▶ Useful language b

Useful language

a Describing your family

I've got (two sisters / five cousins).

This is my niece/uncle.

She's (five) years old.

He's (not) married.

His wife's name's (Sara).

Their names are (Ann and Ben).

b Asking questions

Who's this?

How old is (Karina)?

What's (your uncle's) job?

Follow up: writing

1 Write a paragraph about your family.

I've got (three sisters).
My older sister's name is … She's …
My mother's got one brother.
His name's … He's married to …
They've got … children.

2 Put it on the wall or a table for the class to read, together with your photos / family tree. Answer other students' questions.

Real life
Classroom language

1 **MD** Read the classroom conversations and tick (✔) the best reply.

a STUDENT: Excuse me, how do you say this word?
TEACHER: 1 I understand.
2 Erm … it's 'uncle'.

b STUDENT: Can you say that again, please?
TEACHER: 1 Yes, it's 'uncle'.
2 No, thank you.

c STUDENT: How do you spell 'cousin'?
TEACHER: 1 She's fine, thank you.
2 C-O-U-S-I-N.

d STUDENT: Can you write it on the board, please?
TEACHER: 1 Yes, sure.
2 I don't understand.

e STUDENT: What does this word 'aunt' mean?
TEACHER: 1 I don't remember.
2 Your aunt is your mother or your father's sister.

f STUDENT: What's the English word for 'calcio'?
TEACHER: 1 I don't know.
2 It's 'football'.

g STUDENT: Can you play the recording again?
TEACHER: 1 Yes, please.
2 Yes, of course.

h STUDENT: Excuse me, what page are we on?
TEACHER: 1 Twenty-four.
2 Open your book and look at this picture.

2 **T2.11** Listen and check your answers. Cross out the wrong replies.

> ## Pronunciation
> **1** **T2.12** Look at the tapescript on page 165. Listen to how we say these things politely.
>
> **2** Listen again and practise the polite intonation.

3 **a** Work in pairs. Student A: You are a student. Student B: You are the teacher. Make four short classroom conversations, like the ones in exercise 1.

b Now swap roles. Make four more conversations.

STUDY...

Learning grammar words

1 Use a monolingual dictionary to match the grammar words in A with the examples in B.

	A	B
a	nouns	from, on
b	verbs	beautiful, rich, important
c	adjectives	an uncle, a cat
d	pronouns	. , ?
e	prepositions	I, you, we
f	syllables	dic-tion-a-ry
g	short forms (contractions)	say, write
h	question words	What? Where?
i	the stress	com•fortable
j	punctuation	I've, he's, they're

2 Look through Modules 0 to 2 and find at least one more example of a–h above.

nouns: teacher, family

Pronunciation spot

The sounds /ð/ and /θ/

a **T2.13** Listen and notice the two 'th' sounds /ð/ and /θ/.

/ð/ this, that, these, those, there, they, the, mother, father, brother

/θ/ thank you, three, thirty, thirteen, thing, Thursday

This is how you make the sounds.

b Listen again and repeat the words.

c **T2.14** Listen and repeat the eight sentences.

PRACTISE...

1 Word groups ☐

Add three words or phrases from the box to each group.

a daughter	an aunt	a niece	beautiful	cousins
a computer	a DVD player	friends	a mobile phone	a son
friendly	a grandfather	a nephew	grandparents	clever

a a TV, a stereo _____   d a father, an uncle _____

b rich, fantastic _____   e children, parents _____

c a mother, a sister _____

▶ **Need to check? Vocabulary, pages 19 and 22.**

2 *this, that, these, those* ☐

Complete the gaps with *this, that, these* or *those*.

a Look at <u>these</u> photos of my holiday.

b Is _____ man over there okay?

c Sonia, _____ is my friend Mariko.

d Are _____ your keys?

e Are _____ glasses here yours, Samia?

f What's the English word for _____ ?

▶ **Need to check? Language summary A, page 150.**

3 *have got* ☐

a Write questions with *you* and the correct form of *have got* or *be*.

1 <u>Have you got</u> a car?   5 _____ at university?

2 _____ married?   6 _____ a job?

3 _____ a big family?   7 _____ a garden?

4 How old _____ ?   8 _____ a pet?

b Ask and answer the questions in pairs, or write answers for yourself.

▶ **Need to check? Language summary C, page 151.**

4 *'s* ☐

Put in apostrophes (') before the 's', where necessary.

a Are these your keys?   c Shes got three sisters.   e Hes Lauras cousin.

b Thats Annas bag.   d Whats the matter?

▶ **Need to check? Language summary G, page 151.**

5 Classroom language ☐

Put the words in the correct order.

a do you spell / how / 'nephew'? *How do you spell 'nephew'?*

b again / say that / can you?

c what / mean / does this word?

d do you say / how / this word?

▶ **Need to check? Real life, page 24.**

REMEMBER!

Look back at the areas you have practised. Tick the ones you feel confident about. Now try the MINI-CHECK on page 160 to check what you know!

Everyday life

- ▶ Present simple (positive, negative, questions and short answers): *I, you, we, they*
- ▶ Vocabulary: Common verbs
- ▶ Reading and vocabulary: *Life in Britain*
- ▶ Listening: Life in Australia
- ▶ Real life: Days and times
- ▶ Vocabulary and speaking: Daily routines
- ▶ Task: Find things in common

Vocabulary
Common verbs

1 **MD** Write the verbs in the circles below. Which verbs in the box do the photos show?

work   go   ~~live~~   speak   study   eat   drink

a I (*live*) — in a flat.
— in a big city.
— in London.

b I ( ) — for a big company.
— long hours.

c I ( ) — English.
— Russian.

d I ( ) — to English classes.
— out a lot.

e I ( ) — at university.
— a lot.
— economics.

f I ( ) — fish.
— a lot of chocolate.
— in restaurants a lot.

g I ( ) — tea.
— coffee.

2 **T3.1** Listen and check. Practise saying the sentences.

3 **MD** Add these words and phrases to the diagrams in exercise 1.

Chinese   meat   law   with my parents   in an office
beer   lemonade   in a small town   to the cinema a lot

26

Language focus 1
Present simple questions

T3.2 Listen and answer the questions for yourself.

✔ = Yes, I do.   ✘ = No, I don't.

a ☐   c ☐   e ☐   g ☐
b ☐   d ☐   f ☐   h ☐

Grammar

1 Present simple: *I, you, we, they*

I	**live** in Dubai.
You	**work** long hours.
We	**go** to English classes.
They	**speak** Italian.

2 Questions and short answers

To make questions and negatives we use *do/don't*.

Do	you	**speak** English?	Yes, **I do**.
		live in a flat?	No, **I don't**.

▶ Read Language summary A on page 151.

Practice

Pronunciation

1 Listen to the questions in Recording 2 again. We stress the important words. *Do you* /djə/ is weak.

/djə/ ●   ●   ●
Do you live in a big city?

/djə/ ●   ●   ●
Do you go to English classes?

2 Look at the tapescript on page 166. Practise saying the questions.

1 Work in pairs. Ask and answer the questions.

> Do you live in a big city?   No, I don't.

2 a Look back at the diagrams on page 26. Write five more questions.

Do you go to the cinema a lot?

b Walk around the class. Ask and answer your questions.

3 **T3.3** Can you complete the questions and answers? Listen and check.

a A: _____ you _____ meat?
   B: No, _____ _____ . I only _____ fish.
b A: _____ _____ and your family _____ _____ _____ house?
   B: No, _____ _____ . We _____ _____ a flat.
c A: _____ your parents _____ English?
   B: Yes, _____ _____ .
d A: Do you _____ _____ a big company?
   B: No, I _____ . I _____ _____ a small company.
e A: _____ _____ and your friends _____ _____ _____ cinema a lot?
   B: Yes, _____ _____ . We love the cinema.

4 a Write eight true sentences about yourself, your parents, your family, or you and your friends.

I study economics at university.
We live in a flat.
My parents work long hours.
We go out a lot.
They eat a lot of chocolate.

b Compare your sentences with a partner.

Reading and vocabulary

1 a **MD** Which things can you see in the photos?

the beach	a flat	a pub	a shop	the city centre
a house	a garden	an office	a swimming pool	
a school	a restaurant	a supermarket		

b **T3.4** Listen and practise the words.

2 Do the places in the photos look the same or different in your country?

> The school is the same.

> The house is very different.

3 **MD** Match the words and phrases in A and B.

A	B
a start	a snack
b open	in the morning
c a big meal	go home
d in the evening	close
e go to work	finish

4 Read about life in Britain. Complete the text with a word or phrase from exercise 3.

Life in Britain

HOMES

Most British people live in houses not flats. Most houses have gardens.

DAILY LIFE

Most office workers (a) _go to work_ at about nine o'clock in the morning and finish at about five or six (b)_____ . People don't go home for lunch. People usually eat a big meal in the evening – they just have (c) _____ at lunchtime.

SCHOOL LIFE

Children start school at about nine o'clock and (d) _____ at about half past three. Most children have lunch at school. Children (e) _____ school when they are four or five years old and leave when they are sixteen or eighteen.

SHOPS AND RESTAURANTS

Shops (f) _____ at about nine o'clock in the morning and (g) _____ at about six in the evening. Normally, they don't close for lunch. Most shops open on a Sunday, too. Many supermarkets stay open twenty-four hours, but most pubs and restaurants close at about eleven o'clock in the evening.

Listening
Life in Australia

1 **T3.5** Nicky is asking about daily life in Australia. Listen and number the questions.

a Do most people live in flats or houses?

b What time do children go to school?

c What time do people start work?

d Do they go home for lunch?

e When do shops open and close in Australia? 1

f What time do pubs and restaurants close?

g What do people do at the weekend?

2 Listen again. Tick the sentences which are true.

a Shops open at 9.00 and close at about 5.00. ✔

b Supermarkets close at midnight.

c Pubs and restaurants close at about eleven o'clock.

d Most people go home for lunch.

e People have lunch in cafés.

f Children finish school at half past eight.

g At the weekend most people go to the beach.

h In the city centre, people live in houses.

i A lot of people have got swimming pools.

Language focus 2
Present simple (positive and negative)

Look back at the text about life in Britain. Find three positive sentences and two negative sentences.

Grammar

Complete the gaps.

⊕	I	live in a house.
	You	go to work at about 9.00.
	We	have lunch in a café.
	They	start school at about 9.00.
⊖	I	_____ have a big lunch.
	You	_____ work in an office.
	We	_____ live in a flat.
	They	_____ go to school.

▶ Read Language summary B on page 152.

Practice

1 Complete the sentences for your country. Use either the positive or negative form. Correct the information, where necessary.

Most people don't live in houses. They live in flats.

Life in my country

A	Most people _____ (live) in houses.
B	Most people _____ (have) gardens.
C	Most office workers _____ (start) work at 9.00.
D	Most people _____ (go) home for lunch.
E	Most people _____ (have) a big meal in the evening.
F	Children _____ (go) to school in the afternoon.
G	Most young people _____ (leave) school at sixteen.
H	Most shops _____ (stay) open twenty-four hours.
I	Most shops _____ (close) at lunchtime.
J	Most shops _____ (open) on Sundays.
K	Restaurants _____ (close) at eleven in the evening.

2 **a** Write about three things that are different between your country and Britain.

In Britain children start school at about nine o'clock, but in Poland they start at eight o'clock.

b Write about three things that are the same in Britain and Australia.

Children finish school at half past three.

3 Use the ideas below to make six true sentences about yourself. Compare sentences with a partner.

live in a house	have a swimming pool in my garden
have lunch at home	have a big meal in the evening
eat a lot of meat	drink a lot of coffee
speak Spanish	study a lot at the weekend
go to restaurants a lot	work in an office

> I don't have lunch at home.
> I have lunch in a café.

Real life
Days and times

1 a **T3.6** It's four o'clock in London. Listen and mark the time around the world on the clocks.

b Work in pairs. Ask and answer.

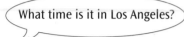

What time is it in Los Angeles?

It's nine o' clock.

2 Match the times with the watches.

a It's twenty to eleven.
b It's quarter past eight.
c It's five past six.
d It's twenty-five past three.
e It's half past nine.
f It's ten to four.

3 **T3.7** Write the times. Then listen and check.

a 9.55 _five to ten_   g 2.45 _____
b 7.15 _____   h 3.10 _____
c 9.30 _____   i 9.25 _____
d 8.40 _____   j 7.50 _____
e 6.45 _____   k 2.55 _____
f 12.05 _____   l 9.35 _____

Pronunciation

1 Listen again and notice the stress. *to* is weak.

● /tə/ ●   ●   ●
five to ten   quarter past seven

2 Practise saying the times.

---

4 Work in pairs. Student A: Look at the TV guide on page 140. Student B: Look at the TV guide on page 142.

5 Work in pairs. Discuss the questions.

a Do banks open at the weekend in your country?
   What time do they normally open and close?
b Do shops in your country open on Sunday?
   What time do they open and close?
c Do people have a big lunch on Sunday?
   What time do they normally have lunch?
d Which days do you have English lessons?
   What time do your lessons start and finish?

▶ Read Language summary C on page 152.

1 Los Angeles
2 São Paulo
3 London
4 Moscow
5 Tokyo
6 Auckland

Vocabulary and speaking
Daily routines

1 **MD** Tick (✔) the things below that you do every day. Cross out the things you don't do.

sleep ✔	go to school/university
get up early	catch the bus
go to bed late	go to work
have breakfast	come home
have lunch	watch TV
have dinner	have a bath
read the newspaper	have a shower

2 Write the activities in exercise 1 in the correct place for you on a 24-hour clock.

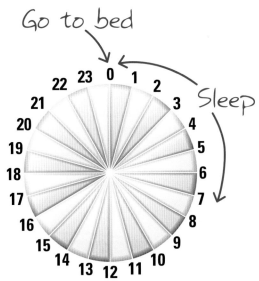

Go to bed

Sleep

3 Work in pairs. Ask and answer about your typical day.

> What time do you get up?   At about seven o'clock.

4 Work with a new partner. Use the prompts on the right to make questions. Ask and answer.

> Do you have breakfast at home?   Yes, I do.   Sometimes.

5 Write a paragraph about yourself and your life.

I study/work ... (economics / for a big company)
I get up at ...
I have breakfast/lunch/dinner ... (at home / at work)
I come home at ... (about six o'clock)
I go to bed at ...
I go to English classes on ... (Tuesday)
I study a lot ... (in the evening / at the weekend)

Do you ...

go to bed early or late?

have dinner early or late?

get up early at the weekend?

watch a lot of TV in the evening?

have a bath or a shower?

have breakfast at home?

go out a lot in the evening?

Task: Find things in common
Preparation: listening

1 (T3.8) Listen and number the topics your hear 1–7.

nationality ☐   brothers and sisters ☐   age ☐
where you live ☐   meat ☐   breakfast ☐
married or single? ☐

2 Listen again and tick (✔) the topics if the speakers have something in common and write a cross (✘) if they are different.

3 Look at the four conversations. Which speakers are the same? Which are different?

a   A: I'm a student.
     B: Me, too.
b   A: I don't have breakfast.
     B: Really? I do.

c   A: I'm not married.
     B: Me, neither.
d   A: I get up very early.
     B: Oh, I don't.

Task: speaking

1 Work in pairs. Use the prompts below to write eight questions to ask another student.

– family
– age
– school/university/work
– where he/she lives
– languages
– daily routine

▶ Useful language a

2 Work with a new partner. Ask and answer your questions. Try to find five things in common.

▶ Useful language b

3 Tell the class three things you have in common with your partner.

▶ Useful language c

Useful language

a Asking questions

Are you (a student)?

Have you got (a pet)?

Do you (go to bed late)?

Do you work (long hours)?

Do you eat (meat)?

Do you speak (German)?

What time do you (get up)?

b Finding things in common

Me, too.

Me, neither.

How about you?

c Telling the class

We both live with our parents.

We don't get up early.

STUDY...

Remembering spelling

1 Many words in English have double consonants, but you can't hear the difference between double and single consonants. Underline the double consonants in these words.

off<u>i</u>ce	holiday
wa<u>ll</u>et	address
business	normally
cousin	camera
dinner	tissues
married	parents
bottle	waitress

2 You have two minutes to study the words and remember the double consonants.

3 **T3.9** Listen and write down the fourteen words you hear. Be careful with the spelling!

Pronunciation spot

Silent syllables

a **T3.10** Listen and count the syllables you hear.

chocolate 2	favourite
breakfast	Saturday
camera	business
different	comfortable
restaurant	dictionary

b Cross through the silent syllables like this:

choc~~o~~late

c Listen again and repeat.

PRACTISE...

1 Common verbs ☐

Match the pairs of verbs.

finish	~~drink~~	have breakfast	~~close~~
go home	read a book	study	go to bed

a eat ___*drink*___   e start _____
b open ___*close*___   f get up _____
c go to work _____   g have lunch _____
d work _____   h watch TV _____

▶ **Need to check? Vocabulary, pages 28 and 31.**

2 Verb forms ☐

Complete the gaps with *do/don't*, *are/aren't* or *have/haven't*.

a '___*Do*___ you live in a big city?' 'No, we _____ .'
b '_____ you got brothers and sisters?'
   'I've got a brother but I _____ got a sister.'
c Where _____ you work?
d How old _____ your children?
e Marek and Monica _____ married. They're just friends.

▶ **Need to check? Language summaries A and B, pages 151 and 152.**

3 Vocabulary ☐

Circle the odd one out.

a coffee / (meat) / tea   d a newspaper / a school / a university
b a flat / a house / an office   e a city / a shop / a town
c a bath / a garden / a shower   f a beach / a café / a restaurant

▶ **Need to check? Reading, Vocabulary and Listening, pages 28 and 29.**

4 Times ☐

Write the times.

a 1.25 *twenty-five past one*   e 11.00 _____
b 3.30 _____   f 5.45 _____
c 6.15 _____   g 9.35 _____
d 5.10 _____   h 3.55 _____

▶ **Need to check? Real life, page 30.**

5 Prepositions ☐

Complete the gaps with *in*, *at* or *on*.

a Do you catch a bus *in* the morning?
b Where are you normally ___ four o'clock ___ the afternoon?
c Do you study ___ the weekend?
d What time do you get up ___ Sundays?
e Do you read in bed ___ night?

▶ **Need to check? Language summary C, page 152.**

REMEMBER!

Look back at the areas you have practised.
Tick the ones you feel confident about.
Now try the MINI-CHECK on page 160
to check what you know!

Loves and hates

- ▶ **Present simple:** *he* and *she*; *like ...ing, questions*
- ▶ **Activity verbs and adverbs of frequency**
- ▶ **Listening:** Celebrity loves and hates
- ▶ **Vocabulary:** Activities
- ▶ **Reading:** *An American star in London ... and a British star in Hollywood*
- ▶ **Task:** Find an e-mail friend
- ▶ **Real life:** Asking politely

Listening
Celebrity loves and hates

1 Match the things in the box to the pictures. Which do you like / do you hate / are you frightened of?

dog	doll	clown	crowd	spider
TV	flying	doing housework		

2 **T4.1** The people in the photos love or hate these things. Listen and match the people to the things.

3 Listen again. Tick (✔) the things they love and write a cross (✗) next to the things they hate. (One person hates three of the things!)

4 Complete the sentences with the verbs in the box.

loves	hates	goes	has
doesn't have		~~doesn't watch~~	

a Cameron Diaz <u>doesn't watch</u> TV.
b She _____ a TV in her house.
c Johnny Depp _____ clowns.
d Harrison Ford _____ doing housework.
e Dean Cain never _____ on planes.
f Britney Spears _____ hundreds of dolls.

Singer Britney Spears

Indiana Jones actor Harrison Ford

Actress Cameron Diaz

Film director Woody Allen

Superman actor Dean Cain

Actor Johnny Depp

Language focus 1
Present simple: *he* and *she*; *like ...ing*; Activities

▶ Read Language summary A on page 152.

Practice

1 **a** Work in pairs. Close your books. Test your partner.

> Cameron Diaz.

> She doesn't like TV.

b **T4.2** Look at the tapescript on page 166. Listen and practise the positive and negative verbs in sentences.

2 **a** **MD** Match the words to the pictures.

| cats | computer games | cooking | cycling | driving |
| reading | running | salad | swimming | |

b Work in pairs. Ask and answer what your partner likes and doesn't like. Use the pictures on these pages.

> Do you like cooking?

> No, I don't. I hate it.

3 **a** Use the ideas below to write about yourself on a piece of paper. Give your paper to the teacher.

> **FACT FILE**
>
> **Food and drink**
> I love ... I also like ... I don't like ...
>
> **Sports and activities**
> I love ... and ... I think ... is okay I hate ...
>
> **Other things**
> I love ... I hate ...
>
> NAME: _____

b Your teacher will give you another student's paper. Tell the class about this person. The other students guess who it is.

> This person loves Italian food. She also likes playing basketball and watching football. She doesn't like dogs and she hates spiders. Who is it?

Pronunciation

1 **T4.3** Look at the tapescript on page 166 and listen to some third person forms in sentences. How many syllables are there: 1, 2 or 3?
likes 1   watches 2

2 Practise the verb forms. Then practise the sentences.

Reading

1 Look at the photos. Do you know who they are?

2 Read the text quickly. What nationality is each person? Where do they live?

3 a **MD** Check the words in bold. Then read the text again. Who ...

1 goes to the pub a lot?
2 comes from an **ordinary** town?
3 likes cycling with her children?
4 loves **rugby**?
5 thinks Americans work very hard?
6 **enjoys** the **art** and **theatre** in Britain?
7 **misses** her family?
8 misses her friends?

b Compare your answers with a partner.

An American star in London ...

There are many Americans in Britain, but the most famous is pop singer Madonna. She lives in London with her British husband, film director Guy Ritchie, and sends her children to school in Britain, too.

So what does she like about London? 'The theatre, the art, the architecture ... and I love the pubs. We often go to our local pub with friends. It's really fun.' She also loves cycling in London parks with her children.

And what does she think about British people? 'Americans work more than the British, but Europeans enjoy their free time more than Americans, and I really like that.' So does she miss the USA? 'I miss friends,' she says.

... and a British star in Hollywood

Actress Catherine Zeta Jones comes from an ordinary family and a very ordinary town – Swansea in Wales. But these days she enjoys the life of a Hollywood film star. She lives in a big house in Beverly Hills with her husband, billionaire Hollywood actor Michael Douglas and their two children. The couple also have homes in Los Angeles, Colorado, New York, Bermuda and Majorca.

So with all this, does she miss Wales? The answer is yes. 'Catherine's a big star these days, but she still loves Welsh rugby,' says an old friend. She also misses her family and often goes back to see them. So now she and her husband have got another house ... this time in Swansea!

Language focus 2
Present simple questions: *he* and *she*

Grammar

1 **Questions and short answers with *he* and *she***

   Does she ***like*** London?
   Yes, she ***does***.
   Does she ***miss*** the USA?
   No, she ***doesn't***.
   (NOT: Does she likes?)

2 ***Wh-* questions**

   What ***does*** she ***think*** about British people?
   Where ***does*** she ***come*** from?

▶ Read Language summary B on page 152.

Practice

1 a Use the prompts to make questions.

1 where Madonna live?
   Where does Madonna live?
2 what her husband do?
3 she like Britain?
4 what she love?
5 she miss the USA?
6 where Catherine Zeta Jones come from?
7 where she live now?
8 she go back to Wales?
9 why she miss Wales?

b Work in pairs. Ask and answer the questions.

> Where does Madonna live?

> She lives in London.

2 a **MD** Choose the correct verb form.

This (1) is / are my friend Sarinder. He (2) 's / 're at college with me. He (3) come / comes from Delhi in India, but now he (4) live / lives in Brighton with his parents and brother. His parents (5) is / are both doctors at our local hospital. After Sarinder (6) finish / finishes college, his parents (7) want / wants to go back to India because Sarinder's grandfather (8) own / owns a small children's hospital near Delhi, and they (9) want / wants to work there.

Every year they (10) go / goes back to India and (11) stay / stays with Sarinder's grandparents. Sarinder (12) love / loves Brighton because he (13) 's got / 've got lots of friends here, but he (14) live / lives in a very small house here and sometimes he (15) miss / misses his grandparents' big house in Delhi. They (16) 's got / 've got a fantastic garden with monkeys in it!

b **T4.4** Listen and check your answers.

3 a Think of a person from another country, city or culture (a person you know or a famous person).

b Work in pairs. Use the prompts to ask your partner questions about the person.

> What's his name?

> It's David.

a What … his/her name?
b Where … he/she come from?
c Where … he/she live (in your country)?
d … he/she here with his/her family?
e … he/she work in your country?
f … he/she like (your country)?
g … he/she like the weather and the food?
h … he/she miss his/her own country?

4 Write a paragraph about the person in exercise 3a.

Language focus 3
Activity verbs and adverbs of frequency

1 **MD** Write the verbs in the circles below.

| play listen to write watch have do |

a (read)———— a newspaper

b (go)———— swimming

c ( )———— football

d ( )———— a letter

e ( )———— the radio

f ( )———— television

g (go to)———— school

h (visit)———— friends

i ( )———— nothing

j ( )———— a meal

2 **a** **MD** Add these words to the diagrams in exercise 1. (There may be more than one possibility.)

shopping	a magazine	the cinema	an e-mail
the guitar	CDs	a video	computer games
a restaurant	a shower	your relatives	your homework

b Practise saying the phrases above. Then work in pairs and test each other.

(play) (play football … play the guitar … play computer games)

3 **a** Put the adverbs in the correct place.

| usually   often   sometimes   not … often |

0% ←———————————————→ 100%
never   always

b Which sentences are true for you?

1 I often go shopping on Saturday.
2 I always read the newspaper in the morning.
3 I never watch football on television.
4 I don't often write letters.
5 I usually listen to the radio in the car.

Grammar

Look back at the sentences in exercise 3b and complete the rules.

Adverbs of frequency (*always, often, never,* etc.) come before / after the verb in positive sentences and come before / after *don't* in negative sentences.

► Read language summary C on page 152.

Practice

1 Write sentences about something …

- you never do.
- you sometimes do in the evening.
- you often do at the weekend.
- you usually do in the morning.
- you always do on Sunday.

2 Work in pairs. Ask and answer the questions below.

(Do you ever go to concerts?)   (Not often. How about you?)

Do you ever ...

- go to concerts?
- visit relatives at the weekend?
- read poetry?
- listen to the radio at night?
- go swimming in the sea?
- play tennis?
- read computer magazines?
- do your homework on the bus?

Findmeafriend.com

friends | **e-mails** | dating | family tree

Hi! My name's Teresa and I'm from Cork, a city in Ireland. I'm a music student at the university here, and I'm twenty-one years old.

I LOVE all types of music, of course! I like both writing and playing. I play the piano and guitar and write songs, too. I also like going to the cinema, reading, the Internet, dogs, driving my car, going out with my friends, travelling, speaking Spanish. (I study Spanish at university, too.)

I HATE football (and all types of sport), spiders, cats, eating meat and doing nothing!

I love writing and receiving e-mails and I want to make friends from all over the world. Please write!

MAKE MORE ROOM FOR FRIENDS AND MEMORIES

◀ ◀ ◀ ◀ ◀

Task: Find an e-mail friend
Preparation: reading

Teresa wants to find friends from other countries. Read what she writes about herself on the Internet. Answer the questions.

a   Where is Teresa from?
b   Is she a student?
c   How old is she?
d   Does she like music?
e   Does she enjoy reading?
f   Does she have any hobbies?

Task: reading and speaking

1 Four people write to Teresa. Work in pairs.

Student A: Look at page 138.
a   Ask Student B about Peter and Sofia. Complete the table.
b   Answer Student B's questions about Marina and Joao.

Student B: Look at page 140.
a   Answer Student A's questions about Peter and Sofia.
b   Ask Student A about Marina and Joao. Complete the table.

▶ Useful language a

	Peter	Sofia	Marina	Joao
nationality/city				
age				
occupation				
interests				
languages				

Useful language

a Asking for information

Where is ... from?

How old is ...?

Is ... a student?

What ... like?

What languages ... speak?

b Discussing

I think ... is best because (he likes music, too).

... isn't good because (he doesn't like classical music).

I agree. / I don't agree.

Maybe ...

Yes, but ...

2 Who is the best e-mail friend for Teresa? Compare answers with other students. Do you agree?

▶ Useful language b

Real life
Asking politely

1 **T4.5** Look at the five conversations in a café. Match the first lines of each to the pictures. Then listen and check.

1 Excuse me. I'd like the bill, please.   4 I'd like one of those, please.
2 Do you want milk?   5 Do you want a drink?
3 Excuse me. I'd like three lemonades, please.

Pronunciation

1 **T4.6** Listen to the sentences from exercise 1. Notice how the speakers use intonation to sound polite.
Excuse me. I'd like the bill, please.
Do you want milk?

2 Practise the sentences, copying the intonation.

2 Work in pairs. Practise the conversations.

3 Imagine you are in a café. Take turns to ask and answer politely, using the ideas below.

Tell the waiter you want:
- an ice cream
- another drink
- more milk
- a clean spoon

Ask if your partner wants:
- sugar
- another coffee
- a sandwich
- a tissue

STUDY...

Finding spelling in a dictionary (1)

1 **MD** You can use your mini-dictionary to find the spelling of *he/she* Present simple forms.

vis·it /'vɪzɪt/ *verb* (visits) visiting, visited, have visited
1 to go and spend time with someone: *Granny is visiting us next weekend.* | *I went to visit Simon in hospital.* | *You must **come and visit** me some time.*

2 Use your mini-dictionary to find the *he/she* forms of these verbs.

a run   e work
b finish   f fly
c swim   g say
d miss   h watch

3 Complete the rules with the phrases in the box.

> take 's'   take 'es'   change to 'ies'

a Most verbs (e.g. *work*) _____ .
b Verbs that end with -ss, -sh, -ch (e.g. *watch*) _____ .
c Verbs that end with consonant + y (e.g. *fly*) _____ .
d Verbs that end with vowel + y (e.g. *play*) _____ .

4 Use the rules to write the *he/she* forms. Use your mini-dictionary to check.

a eat   d stay
b leave   e catch
c study   f carry

Pronunciation spot

Words ending in *s*

a **T4.7** Listen to the three different pronunciations of words that end with *s*.

/s/ books, likes, Mark's
/z/ newspapers, loves, Anna's
/ɪz/ places, watches, Tomas's

b **T4.8** Listen and add the words to the categories above.

c Practise saying all the words.

PRACTISE...

1 Present simple *he/she* forms ☐

Write the *he/she* forms of these verbs.

a know _knows_   d watch _____   g go   _____
b study _____   e do   _____   h work _____
c listen _____   f hate   _____   i have _____

▶ **Need to check? Language summary A, page 152.**

2 Present simple auxiliaries ☐

Complete the gaps with *do/don't* or *does/doesn't*.

a '__Do__ you like swimming?' 'No, I _____ .'
b What time _____ the film finish?
c '_____ your parents live near here?' 'Yes, they _____ .'
d Where _____ your boyfriend work?
e '_____ your mother speak English?' 'No, she _____ .'

▶ **Need to check? Language summary B, page 152.**

3 Words that go together ☐

Match words to make phrases.

a play   dinner   e go   a restaurant
b visit   the violin   f go to   a CD
c have   your aunt   g listen to the newspaper
d do   your homework   h read   shopping

▶ **Need to check? Language focus 3, page 38.**

4 Adverbs of frequency ☐

Put the words in the correct order.

a in the evening / never / Ellen / studies *Ellen never studies in the evening.*
b me / you / listen to / never
c I / catch / don't / the bus / often
d me / usually / on Sunday / my sister / visits

▶ **Need to check? Language summary C, page 152.**

5 Activities ☐

Unjumble the letters to make activities.

a PISOPHNG   _shopping_   d MMNIISWG   s_____
b GOKONCI   c_____   e VRDIING   d_____
c NNNIRGU   r_____   f IEARDNG   r_____

▶ **Need to check? Language focus 1, page 35.**

6 *Do you want ...? / I'd like ...* ☐

Match the two lines of the conversations.

a Do you want the sugar?   1 Of course. Just one minute.
b Do you want a dictionary?   2 Yes, please.
c I'd like another coffee, please. 3 Large ones or small ones?
d I'd like two chocolate ice creams. 4 It's okay, I've got one, thank you.

▶ **Need to check? Real life, page 40.**

REMEMBER!

Look back at the areas you have practised. Tick the ones you feel confident about. Now try the MINI-CHECK on page 161 to check what you know!

Getting from A to B

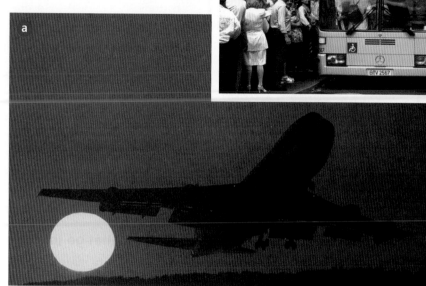

- ▶ *can* and *can't*
- ▶ Articles: *a/an, the* and zero
- ▶ Vocabulary and reading: Transport
- ▶ Listening and vocabulary: At the airport
- ▶ Task: Complete a survey about transport
- ▶ Real life: Buying a ticket

Vocabulary and reading
Transport

1 Find these types of transport in the photos.

a motorbike	a bus	a train	a tram
a taxi	an aeroplane	a car	a ship
a scooter	a ferry	a bicycle	
an underground / a subway train			

2 Put the types of transport in order from fast to slow. Then compare your answers with another student.

1 = aeroplane

3 How do these people usually travel in your town?

- schoolchildren
- students and young people
- businesspeople
- old people
- police officers

by car   by bus   on foot

4 Find these things in the photos.

people waiting in a queue	passengers
a crowded train	travelling fast
travelling slowly	bad traffic

↓ Transport facts!

→ People in most countries drive on the right – but people drive on the left in (a) _____ countries, including Japan, India, Australia and Britain.

→ In the USA (b) _____ people in every thousand drive a car. In Japan, it's 640 and in Germany it's 570. More than (c) _____ people in the world ride a bicycle!

→ In Tokyo, people never wait for more than (d) _____ minutes for an underground train. The only problem is it's often difficult to get on or off a train because they're so crowded!

→ (e) _____ people fly to Hartsfield Airport in Atlanta, USA every year! (That's about one hundred and fifty people every minute!)

→ In China, the 30 km journey from Shanghai city centre to Pudong Airport takes only (f) _____ minutes on the new Magnetic Levitation (Mag Lev) train.

→ Most people in Moscow go to work by underground. The Moscow Metro has 165 stations and about (g) _____ passengers every day. The stations in the city centre are very beautiful.

→ Every day more than (h) _____ people travel into the centre of London. About 20% drive, 77% take the train or the bus, and only (i) _____ % walk to work!

→ In Italy, a country of 57 million people, 9 million people have scooters. In Rome, (j) _____ people ride scooters so they can travel fast in the city traffic.

5 **MD** **T5.1** Read the text. Can you guess which numbers go in the gaps? Listen and check.

1,000,000 (one million)	100,000,000 (one hundred million)	8	9,000,000
3	59	77,000,000	5	740	500,000 (five hundred thousand)

6 **a** Look back at the text and choose the correct words to go together.

1 drive / ride a car
2 drive / ride a bicycle
3 wait / wait for a train
4 get on / in a train
5 get off / out a train

6 fly in / to Atlanta
7 go with / by underground
8 take / go a train or a bus
9 walk to / in work

b Work in pairs. Test your partner.

drive   drive a car

7 Which sentences are true for your country? Correct the false ones. Then compare with other students.

a Most people drive small cars. *False. Most people drive big cars!*

b People always wait in a queue to get on a bus.

c People often fly from one city to another.

d Not many people walk to the shops.

e A lot of people ride bicycles to work.

f Traffic is a problem all day.

g The buses are very crowded.

h Taxis drive very slowly.

▶ Read Language summary A on page 152.

Language focus 1
can and *can't*

Karen is at the Metropolitan Museum of Art in Manhattan, New York. She has $25 and it's ten past three. She wants to be at JFK Airport at half past four.

1 Look at the photos and read about Karen. Where is she? Where does she want to go?

2 Read about four ways to get to JFK Airport and complete the table.

type(s) of transport	time (in hours/ minutes)	cost
1		
2		
3		
4		

3 Work in pairs. Decide the best way for Karen to go to the airport.

4 **T5.2** Listen to someone working out how she should travel. Was your answer the same?

Grammar

Complete the gaps with *can* or *can't* (*cannot*).

➕ She _____ take a bus at twenty past three.

➖ She _____ take a taxi because she's only got $25.

❓ _____ she take the subway to the airport?

▶ Read Language summary B on page 153.

Pronunciation

T5.3 Listen and mark the ten sentences +, – or ? Look at the tapescript on page 167 and practise saying the sentences.

1 You can take a taxi but it is often slow because of the traffic. The journey takes about an hour and costs $35 (and also a tip of 15–20% for the driver!).

2 You can take a subway (the 'A' train) to Howard Beach-JFK Station and then a bus to the airport terminal, a journey of about 90 minutes. The subway costs $2 and the bus is free.

3 You can walk through Central Park to the Museum of Natural History (about twenty minutes). From there, you can take the subway to Howard Beach-JFK Station ($2) and then an AirTrain to JFK Airport Station ($5). It takes about an hour on the subway and another twelve minutes on the AirTrain.

4 You can take the subway to Grand Central Station. It takes five minutes and costs $2. From there you can take the New York Airport Express bus. The journey takes about an hour and costs $13. In the afternoon, the buses leave every twenty minutes at three o'clock, twenty past three, twenty to four, etc.

Practice

1 [T5.4] Gina is asking about things you can and can't do in New York. Listen and mark the sentences …

✔ if you can do this.

✗ if you can't.

? if it depends.

a   travel by tram ✗
b   smoke in the subway
c   eat on a train
d   find a taxi easily
e   have five people in a taxi
f   drive at sixty kilometres an hour
g   ride a bicycle safely
h   eat in a restaurant at midnight
i   smoke in a restaurant

2 Work in pairs. Ask and answer about the things in exercise 1.

Either Ask and answer about New York.

Or Ask and answer about your city/town.

> Can you travel by tram in New York?

> No, you can't.

> Can you find a taxi easily in Hamburg?

> It depends.

3 Write eight sentences about things you can and can't do in your city.

You can't smoke on buses.
You can drive in the city centre.

Listening and vocabulary
At the airport

1 Karen is at JFK Airport. Look at her travel itinerary and answer the questions.

a   What times are her flights?
b   Which airports do they go to?
c   What are the flight numbers?

Travel Itinerary Ms Karen Davis		
Sun 02 Nov Flight AA100	Check in by 16.30 American Airlines Desk Scheduled departure: 18.30 JFK Scheduled arrival: 07.25 London Heathrow (LHR)	Terminal X
Mon 03 Nov Flight BA0572	Check in by 08.00 British Airways Desk Scheduled departure: 09.35 LHR Scheduled arrival: 12.30 Milan: Malpensa MXP	Terminal 1

2 **MD** Match the phrases in A with the meanings in B.

A
a   in transit
b   check in
c   boarding
d   is delayed
e   last call
f   proceed to

B
1   is late
2   go to
3   changing from one plane to another
4   final call
5   show your ticket and passport at a desk
6   getting on (a plane)

3 a [T5.5] Listen to the announcements at JFK Airport and answer the questions. (You do not need to understand every announcement.)

1   Where does Karen check in?
2   What is the problem with her flight?
3   What is the gate number for her flight?

b [T5.6] Listen to the announcements at Heathrow Airport and answer the questions.

1   At Heathrow Airport, where does Karen go?
2   What is her gate number?

Salem Al-Romeithi is twenty-three years old. He's an (a) _____ and he lives with his family in a large house in (b) _____ , a large city in (c) _____ . He works for an international company from (d) _____ to (e) _____ , but at the (f) _____ he spends all his time playing (g) _____ .

Language focus 2
Articles (2): *a/an*, *the* and zero

T5.7 Look at the photos and complete the text about Salem Al-Romeithi with the words in the box. Then listen and check.

weekend	golf	the United Arab Emirates
engineer	Saturday	Dubai	Wednesday

Grammar

1 Underline the articles *a/an/the* in the text about Salem. When do we use *an*?

2 Complete the gaps with *a/an*, *the* or zero (no word).

   a we've got __a__ new car, he lives in ___ apartment in ___ big city
   b ___ Salem, ___ Mrs Wilson, ___ Doctor Singh
   c he's ___ politician, she's ___ teacher, I'm ___ artist
   d it's ___ capital city, it's in ___ city centre, it's on ___ right/left
   e in ___ Bangkok, in ___ Dubai, in ___ Spain
   f in ___ UAE, in ___ USA, in ___ UK
   g in ___ morning, in ___ afternoon, at ___ weekend
   h on ___ Saturday, from ___ Monday to ___ Friday
   i go to ___ work, go ___ home, at ___ school
   j by ___ bus, by ___ car, on ___ foot

▶ Read Language summary C on page 153.

Practice

1 a Complete the gaps with *a/an*, *the* or – (no word).

I live in (1) __–__ Dubai. It's (2) _____ fantastic city but we have (3) _____ real problem with traffic. Most people come to work by (4) _____ car so it's very busy in (5) _____ morning when they come into (6) _____ city centre, and in (7) _____ evening when they go (8) _____ home. I'm (9) _____ engineer and I have (10) _____ company car. My journey to (11) _____ work takes about twenty-five minutes. I also use my car at (12) _____ weekend when I play golf.

b **T5.8** Listen and check.

2 a Write the answers to these questions using a phrase with *a/an*, *the* or zero (no word).

1 What's your father's job?
2 What's your mother's job?
3 Where do your parents live?
4 How do you come to school?
5 What other ways can you travel to school if you want to?
6 Which day(s) do you usually do your English homework?
7 When do you usually watch TV?
8 Which things do you usually carry in your bag?
9 What is your favourite day of the week? Why?
10 What do you usually do in the morning, in the afternoon and in the evening?

b Work in pairs. Ask and answer the questions.

3 Work in small groups or teams. Answer the quiz questions with *a/an*, *the* or – (no word). Then check your answers on page 147.

Quiz

1 **What are the capital cities of these countries?**

   a Korea   **b** Argentina   **c** Poland   **d** Canada

2 **What are these people's jobs?**

   a Vladimir Putin   **b** Jackie Chan   **c** JK Rowling

3 **On which side of the road do people drive in these countries? (Do not look at page 43!)**

   a Australia   **b** USA   **c** UK

4 **What are these objects?**

 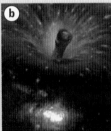   

5 **Where are these cities?**

   a Boston   **b** São Paulo   **c** Cape Town   **d** Seville

6 **In which countries/cities are these buildings?**

Task: Complete a survey about transport
Preparation: reading and writing

1 Work in pairs. Student A: Look at the survey on this page.
Student B: Look at the survey on page 141.
Check any unknown words with your teacher or in your dictionary.

2 **a** Write the questions in the survey in full.

you / drive a car?   *Can you drive a car?*
How far / walk every week?   *How far do you walk every week?*

b Practise reading the questions clearly. Ask your teacher if you need help with pronunciation.

Task: speaking

1 Work in the same pairs: Student A and Student B. Ask and answer your questions.

► Useful language a

2 Work with a group of three or four students. Student As work together. Student Bs work together. Tell the group what you learnt about your partner.

► Useful language b

TRANSPORT SURVEY

1 How far / walk every week?

_____
* 0 to 5 kilometres ○
* 6 to 10 kilometres ○
* 11 to 20 kilometres ○
* more than 20 kilometres ○

2 How often / travel by car?

_____
* several hours every day ○
* every day or nearly every day ○
* several times every week ○
* not very often ○

3 What / think of the roads in your town?

_____
* excellent ○
* good ○
* okay ○
* poor ○
* I don't know ○

4 ever take / taxis?

_____
* often ○
* sometimes ○
* not very often ○
* never ○

5 ride a scooter? ○

_____

6 ride a motorbike? ○

_____

7 How / usually travel when you go on holiday?

_____
* by plane ○
* by train ○
* by bus ○
* by car ○

8 Which of these types of transport / like best?

_____
* plane ○
* boat ○
* motorbike ○
* bicycle ○

Waterloo International *eurostar*

Real life
Buying a ticket

1 Florence is in London. She wants to travel to Paris. Put the conversation in a ticket office in the correct order.

- ☐ Here you are.
- ☐ Platform eighteen.
- ☐ Single.
- ☐ Single or return?
- ☐ Thanks. Which platform is it?
- ☐ 1 That's £94.50.
- ☐ A ticket to Paris, please ... the six o'clock train.
- ☐ Thank you. Sign there, please.

2 **T5.9** Listen and check. Practise the conversation in pairs.

3 **T5.10** Listen to two conversations and answer the questions below for each one.

a Where does the person want to go?
b Does he/she want a single or a return ticket?
c What time is the train?
d Which platform is it?
e What time does it arrive?

4 Work in pairs. Student A: Read the information below. Student B: You are the ticket clerk. Read the information on page 144.

> It is 11.30 in the morning and you are in London. You want to buy a return ticket to Glasgow in Scotland. You want to come back on Sunday. You would like to know the cost, the time of the train, the platform number and the arrival time. Write your questions and then speak to the ticket clerk.

5 Change roles. Student B: Read the information below. Student A: You are the ticket clerk. Read the information on page 138.

> It is 9.30 in the morning and you are in Brighton, in the south of England. You want to go to London for the day and come back this evening. You would like to know the cost, the time of the train, the platform number and the arrival time. Write your questions and then speak to the ticket clerk.

Useful language

a Answering questions

Yes, often / sometimes / every day.

No, never.

About (five) kilometres/minutes/hours.

I walk to (the city centre).

I think it's (good).

I like (travelling by car / walking) best.

b Talking about your partner

Giulio likes travelling (by train).

Marina doesn't/can't (ride a bicycle).

Yumiko thinks taxis are (expensive).

Follow up: writing

Write about how you use public transport.

I travel to school by ...
The journey is about ...
I ... use public transport.
I think public transport in my town is ...

CONSOLIDATION

Ⓐ Listening and speaking: Personal information

1 Write one word in each gap.

Elspeth (a) __is__ a really good friend of mine. She' (b) _____ about twenty-five years old and she (c) _____ in Edinburgh, in (d) _____ big flat near (e) _____ city centre. She (f) _____ at the Scottish Museum and her job (g) _____ very important to her. She isn't (h) _____ but she's (i) _____ a boyfriend, Nick. They (j) _____ got a car because they (k) _____ like driving, but they (l) _____ their bicycles all round the city. Elspeth (m) _____ going to restaurants, (n) _____ to the cinema, and meeting people and she' (o) _____ very friendly.

2 `C1` Listen and check.

3 Take two minutes to think about one of your friends. Think about:

- his/her age
- his/her work
- his/her family
- travel
- where he/she lives
- married or not?
- his/her likes and dislikes
- possessions

4 Work with a partner. Speak about your friend for one minute!

Ⓑ Question words

1 Complete each question in the quiz opposite with one of the question words from the box. Then choose the correct answer.

Who	When	Where	How old	What

2 In groups, make some more questions about people and places in your country. (Use the verb *be*.)

3 Ask your questions to the other groups. Then check your answers at the bottom of the page.

QUIZ

How much do you know about the English-speaking world?

1 _____ is Ontario?
a in Canada
b in the USA
c in Britain

2 _____ colour are the buses in London?
a black
b red
c yellow

3 _____ is the Sydney Opera House?
a about thirty years old
b about forty years old
c about fifty years old

4 _____ is Christmas Day?
a December 25th
b December 31st
c January 6th

5 _____ is the singer George Michael from?
a Britain
b the United States
c Greece

6 _____ is the White House in Washington?
a about 100 years old
b about 200 years old
c about 500 years old

7 _____ is not an actress?
a Liv Tyler
b Kiera Knightley
c Serena Williams

8 _____ is the capital city of New Zealand?
a Christchurch
b Auckland
c Wellington

Answers
1a 2b 3b 4a 5a 6a 7c 8c

50

C Listening: Information about times and prices

1 a **C2** Listen to the three conversations. What are the people talking about? Listen and tick (✔) the topics.

> travelling by plane   the zoo   the cinema
> travelling by train   television programmes   a jazz concert

b Put the words in order to make questions.

Conversation 1

1   the first train / Belfast / What time / leave / does?
     <u>What time does the first train leave Belfast?</u>

2   does / arrive / When / it / in Dublin?
     _____

3   it / How / is / much?
     _____

Conversation 2

4   open / What time / the zoo / does?
     _____

5   it / What time / does / close?
     _____

6   How much / it / does / for a ten-year-old child / cost?
     _____

7   you / can / there / travel / How?
     _____

Conversation 3

8   the football / When / does / start?
     _____

9   finish / does / When / it?
     _____

10   is / What time / the film?
     _____

c Listen again and answer questions 1–10.

D *can* and *can't*

Use *can* and *can't* to make sentences about your school.

a   buy drinks and snacks
     You can buy drinks, but you can't buy snacks.
b   study other languages (not only English)
c   park your car
d   come to evening classes
e   study on computers
f   use the library at the weekend

E Vocabulary: Alphabet quiz

Work in pairs. Complete the sentences with words from Modules 1–5. The first letter of each word is given.

a   My father's sister is my a<u>unt</u> .

b   My mother's son is my b_____ .

c   What time does the shop c_____ ?

d   Every night I write in my d_____ .

e   Her brother's an e_____ , he works for a big building company.

f   My f_____ colour is red.

g   Their new house has got a beautiful g_____ with a swimming pool.

h   When does Alan h_____ lunch?

i   Can I see your i_____ card, Madam?

j   Sony is a J_____ company.

k   I'm sorry, I don't k_____ your name.

l   Ludmila studies l_____ at university.

m   My sister's a m_____ – she plays the piano.

n   Underground trains stop at n_____ .

o   Banks o_____ at 9.30 in Britain.

p   My son's a p_____ officer.

q   In Britain people wait in a q_____ to buy tickets for the cinema.

r   A lot of people r_____ bicycles in the Netherlands.

s   Jennifer's not married. She's s_____ .

t   Many people t_____ to work by train.

u   My cousin's father is my u_____ .

v   Kieron v_____ his grandfather every week.

w   I often w_____ for a bus for one hour!

y   Liam is two y_____ old.

z   This z_____ hasn't got many animals.

Eating and drinking

▶ *There is* and *There are*
▶ *some* and *any*
▶ *How much* and *How many*
▶ **Vocabulary:** Food (countable and uncountable nouns)
▶ **Listening:** Breakfasts around the world
▶ **Reading and speaking:** *Food: Facts and myths*
▶ **Task:** Describe the differences between two pictures
▶ **Real life:** Ordering food and drink

Vocabulary
Food (countable and uncountable nouns)

1 Look at the picture from a hotel restaurant. Is it breakfast, lunch or dinner?

2 Find these things in the picture.

milk	eggs	butter	cereal	oranges	jam
an apple	toast	bread rolls	meat	sausages	
grapes	a banana	cheese	yoghurt	orange juice	
coffee	water	tea	fruit	biscuits	

3 a Put the words in exercise 2 into two groups. Practise saying the words.

things you can count (countable nouns)		
• eggs	•	•
•	•	•
•	•	•

things you can't count (uncountable nouns)		
• milk	•	•
•	•	•
•	•	•
•	•	•

b Can uncountable nouns be plural?

▶ Read Language summary A on page 153.

Language focus 1
There is and *There are*

T6.1 Listen to eight sentences about the picture. Are they true (✔) or false (✘)?

Grammar

1 **Choose the correct alternatives.**

   Singular: There's / There are a banana.

   Plural: There's / There are eight eggs.

   Uncountable: There's / There are some butter.

2 **We often make negative sentences using *no*.**

   There's **no** apple juice.

   There are **no** strawberries.

▶ Read Language summary B on page 153.

Pronunciation

Look at recording 1 on page 168 and listen again. Notice how the sounds at the end of one word link onto the next word.

There's an apple.

There are a lot of grapes.

Practise saying the sentences.

Practice

1 a Write five true sentences and four false sentences about the picture.

b Work in pairs. Test your partner using your sentences. Your partner closes his/her book.

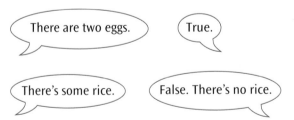

> There are two eggs.

> True.

> There's some rice.

> False. There's no rice.

2 Tick (✔) the sentences that are true about your school. Correct the ones that are false.

a There are twenty students in my class.
   No, there aren't. There are fifteen students.

b There's a video in our classroom.

c There are pictures on the walls.

d There's some paper in the bin.

e There's half an hour left before the end of the lesson.

f There are some plants in the classroom.

g There's a coffee machine on this floor.

Listening
Breakfasts around the world

1 **T6.2** Listen to five people talking about their breakfast. Write down what they have.

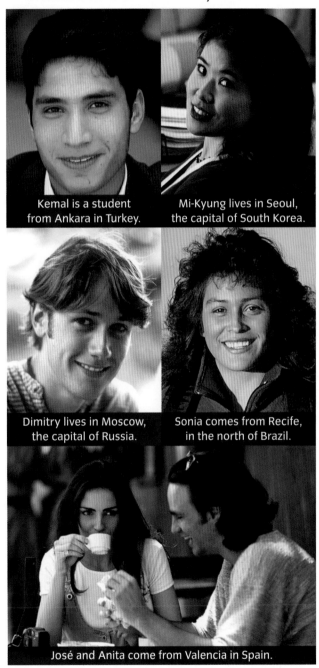

Kemal is a student from Ankara in Turkey.

Mi-Kyung lives in Seoul, the capital of South Korea.

Dimitry lives in Moscow, the capital of Russia.

Sonia comes from Recife, in the north of Brazil.

José and Anita come from Valencia in Spain.

2 Discuss these questions.

a What do you usually have for breakfast?

b Are the breakfasts in the recording the same or different from yours?

c Which ones would you like to try?

3 Write about your normal breakfast, lunch and dinner. What snacks do you have?

Reading and speaking

1 **a** Match these foods to the pictures.

carrots	chocolate	green vegetables
grilled fish	lemons	melon
noodles	nuts	pasta	rice

b **MD** Which of these foods contain …
- vitamins? • protein?
- minerals? • a lot of calories?

2 Work in pairs. Make a list of eight foods that are healthy and eight that are unhealthy.

healthy	unhealthy
green vegetables	chocolate

3 **a** **MD** Read these ideas about healthy eating. Do you think they are true? Compare ideas with other students.

Coffee and tea are bad for you.

There are 'good' foods and 'bad' foods.

Vegetarian food is always healthy.

Fruit juice is good for you.

Carrots help you see in the dark.

It's okay not to eat breakfast.

I think this is true.

I'm not sure about this.

b **MD** Read the text quickly and match the ideas to the paragraphs.

4 Read the text again. Were you right in exercise 3a? Which information is surprising?

5 What are your favourite foods? Which foods don't you like?

Food: Facts and myths

1 <u>Fruit juice is good for you.</u>
True and false. Natural fruit juice is good for you, but it can be bad for your teeth. So yes, have some orange juice with your breakfast or lunch, but don't drink any juice between meals. Try water instead. Up to eight glasses of water a day is good for you, and water hasn't got any calories!

2 _____
False. When you sleep you don't eat for a long time and in the morning it's important to start the day with a good breakfast. Without breakfast you often feel hungry later in the morning and start eating biscuits or chocolate. These sugary snacks are not a good idea. (If you want a healthy snack, try some nuts or melon.)

3 _____
True and false. People drink coffee when they are tired, but it isn't very healthy so don't have more than two cups a day and don't drink any coffee before you go to bed. Tea is generally good for you, but drink it with lemon and don't put any milk or sugar in it! Green tea is especially healthy.

4 _____
False. Vegetarian dishes often contain a lot of cheese and oil and these can be very fattening. It's important to eat some vegetables every day. (Doctors say five portions of vegetables and/or fruit). We need the vitamins and minerals, especially from green vegetables.

5 _____
False. Carrots have a lot of vitamin A and vitamin A is good for your eyes, but nobody can really see in the dark!

6 _____
False. There are good and bad diets. For example, real chocolate contains vitamins and minerals and can help you when you are tired. But it also has a lot of sugar, so don't eat it often. Eat a balanced diet with some rice, pasta, bread or noodles and lots of vegetables and fruit. You also need protein, from meat, grilled fish, cheese or nuts. And you need oil: olive oil and fish oil are particularly good.

Language focus 2
some and *any*

▶ Read Language summary C on page 153.

Practice

1 **a** Complete the sentences with *some* or *any*.

1 It's a good idea to drink _____ fruit juice between meals.
2 Water hasn't got _____ calories.
3 For a healthy snack, you can eat _____ nuts or _____ melon.
4 Don't drink _____ coffee before you go to bed – it's bad for you.
5 It's healthy to put _____ sugar in your tea.
6 Chocolate hasn't got _____ vitamins or minerals in it.
7 It's good to eat _____ pasta, rice or bread every day.
8 Don't eat _____ oil – it's very bad for you.

b Are the sentences true or false, according to the text?

2 **a** Katie wants to eat healthily. Look at her shopping list on page 147 for two minutes, then close your book.

b Work in pairs. Can you remember what Katie wants to buy? There are twelve things.

> She wants to buy some apples and some …

3 **a** When Katie goes shopping she forgets about her list! Look at the things she brings home and answer the questions.

a Which things from her list has she got?
b Which things from her list hasn't she got?

> She's got some grapes but she hasn't got any oranges.

b Is there any unhealthy food in her shopping bag?

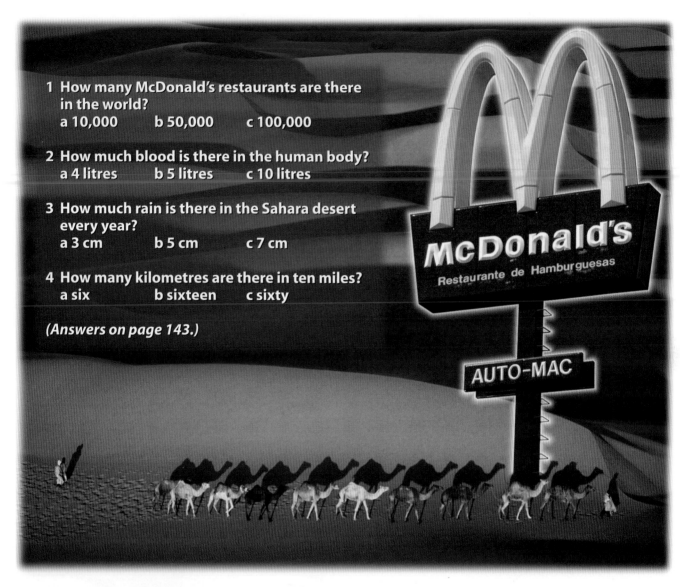

1 **How many McDonald's restaurants are there in the world?**
a 10,000   b 50,000   c 100,000

2 **How much blood is there in the human body?**
a 4 litres   b 5 litres   c 10 litres

3 **How much rain is there in the Sahara desert every year?**
a 3 cm   b 5 cm   c 7 cm

4 **How many kilometres are there in ten miles?**
a six   b sixteen   c sixty

(Answers on page 143.)

Language focus 3
How much and How many

MD Read the questionnaire above and discuss the answers in pairs.

Grammar

Choose the correct alternative.

When we ask questions we use:
• *how many* with countable / uncountable nouns and
• *how much* with countable / uncountable nouns.

▶ Read Language summary D on page 154.

Practice

a Complete the questions with *How much* or *How many*.

1 _____ water do you drink every day?
2 _____ cups of coffee do you drink every day?
3 _____ sugar do you have with your coffee or tea?
4 _____ oil and butter do you eat with your food?
5 _____ red meat do you eat every week?
6 _____ bread/rice/pasta do you have every day?
7 _____ vegetables do you eat every day?
8 _____ fruit do you eat every day?
9 _____ sweets and biscuits do you eat every week?
10 _____ cigarettes do you smoke every day?
11 _____ alcohol do you drink every week?
12 _____ hours' sleep do you have every night?
13 _____ time do you work on a computer every day?
14 _____ times do you go to the gym or play sport every week?
15 _____ kilometres do you walk every day?

b Work in pairs. Ask and answer the questions. Is your partner's lifestyle healthy or unhealthy?

Task: Describe the differences between two pictures

Preparation: listening

1 Look at the picture. Where are the people? Find these things.

soup	prawns	chicken	plates	cups	knives	forks	spoons
sunglasses	a hat	a dress	feathers	balloons	drums		

2 **T6.4** Listen to someone describing the picture. Number the things in the picture she describes.

Task: speaking

1 Work in pairs. Student A: Look at picture A on this page. Student B: Look at picture B on page 148. Do not look at your partner's picture.

2 You have ten minutes to find ten differences between the two pictures. Describe your picture and ask questions.

▶ Useful language a and b

3 How many differences can you find? Compare answers with the class. Did you find all the differences?

▶ Useful language c

Real life
Ordering food and drink

1 Where do you most like to eat and drink? What do you usually order when you eat in a restaurant?

Pronunciation

T6.5 Which food and drink words below are similar in your language? Listen to the pronunciation in English. Is it the same or different? Practise saying the words.

sandwich chocolate salad burger yoghurt
orange juice pizza mayonnaise biscuits fruit
lemonade banana tea spaghetti

2 a Look at the photos. Which restaurant sells pizzas? hamburgers? coffee and cakes?

b **T6.6** Listen to three conversations and answer the questions.

1 Which of the restaurants are they in?
2 What do the people order?
3 How much does it cost?

3 **T6.7** Listen and complete the sentences. Then practise saying them.

a Can I take your ___order___ , please?
b _____ I have two Super King-Size burgers, please?
c _____ to drink with that?
d Eat in or take _____ ?
e Would you like anything _____ ?
f Can we _____ the bill, please?
g _____ the change.
h I'd like to _____ a pizza.
i _____ would you like?
j How _____ is that altogether?

Pronunciation

T6.8 Look at the tapescript on page 168. Listen and notice the polite intonation in these sentences. Practise saying them.

4 Work in pairs. Look at the menu on page 138.

STUDY...

Finding grammar in a dictionary (1)

1 You can use your mini-dictionary to find out if nouns are countable or uncountable.

grape /greɪp/ *noun* (c) a small round juicy fruit that grows in bunches and is used to make wine: *a bunch of black grapes*

ce·re·al /'sɪəriəl/ *noun* (u) 1 a food you eat for breakfast that contains a mixture of wheat, rice, nuts etc, and that you usually mix with milk

2 Find if these words are countable or uncountable.

job money traffic flight
platform economics tennis
music coin game transport
work chewing gum traffic jam

3 For countable nouns you can use your mini-dictionary to find their plural form.

grand·child /'græntʃaɪld/ *noun* [c], *plural* grandchildren /-ˌtʃɪldrən/ the child of your son or daughter: *Rosa is his youngest grandchild*

4 Write the plurals. Check in your mini-dictionary.

CD knife match person
woman tourist glass office
way meal baby wife

Pronunciation spot

International words

a Which words are the same in your language?

restaurant airport hospital
café hotel university
snack bar platform terminal
college information desk

b T6.9 **Listen to the English pronunciation. Is it the same or different?**

c Listen again and mark the stress on the words. Practise saying them.

● restaurant

PRACTISE...

1 Food and drink ☐

Complete the food and drink words.

a c e r e a l   d f r _ _ t   g v _ g _ _ _ _ _ _ s
b b _ t _ _ r   e b _ s c _ _ t s   h y _ g _ _ _ t
c t _ _ s t   f o r _ _ _ _ j _ _ c _   i n _ _ d l _ _

▶ **Need to check? Vocabulary, pages 52 and 54.**

2 *There is* and *There are* ☐

Write true sentences about your town using *There is* or *There are*.

a <u>There are a lot of</u> restaurants.   d _____ trams.
b _____ airport.   e _____ university.
c _____ station.   f _____ cinemas.

▶ **Need to check? Language summary B, page 153.**

3 *some* and *any* ☐

Complete the sentences with *some* or *any*.

a Are there <u>any</u> Mexican students in your class?
b I'd like _____ water, please.
c I haven't got _____ brothers or sisters.
d I've got _____ e-mails from my students.
e I'm sorry but there isn't _____ milk.
f Are there _____ films on TV tonight?

▶ **Need to check? Language summary C, page 153.**

4 *How much* and *How many* ☐

Choose the correct alternatives.

a How (many) / much brothers and sisters have you got?
b How many / much students is / are there in your class?
c How many / much money have you got with you today?
d How many / much languages can you speak?
e How many / much football do you watch on TV every week?
f How many / much homework is / are there tonight?

▶ **Need to check? Language summary D, page 154.**

5 Ordering food and drink ☐

Put the sentences in the correct order.

A: ready / order / you / Are / to ? *Are you ready to order?*
B: soup, / can / Yes / some / have / chicken / please / I ?
A: else / Anything ?
B: sandwich / a / like / Yes / cheese / I'd
A: drink / you / Would / to / like / anything ?
B: please / mineral water, / A

▶ **Need to check? Real life, page 58.**

REMEMBER!

Look back at the areas you have practised.
Tick the ones you feel confident about.
Now try the MINI-CHECK on page 161
to check what you know!

Extraordinary lives

▶ **Past simple:** *was* and *were*, regular and irregular verbs
▶ **Vocabulary:** Years, decades and centuries
▶ **Reading:** *An ordinary life ... an amazing idea*
▶ **Listening:** A true story
▶ **Real life:** Dates and other past time phrases
▶ **Task:** Tell your life story

Language focus 1
Past simple: *was* and *were*

1 **MD** Think of a famous person for each of the following. Compare answers with other students.
• scientist • political leader • artist
• comedian • writer • composer

2 a **MD** Work in pairs. How many questions can you answer about the famous people in the photos?

b **T7.1** Listen and check. What else did you learn?

LEGENDS IN

1 John F Kennedy was President of the United States in:
a the 1950s   b the 1960s   c the 1970s

2 The scientist Marie Curie was born in:
a Paris   b Warsaw   c Geneva

3 Laurel and Hardy were:
a singers   b businessmen   c comedians

4 The Beatles were originally from:
a London   b Manchester   c Liverpool

Grammar

1 Notice the past forms of *be*.
Kennedy **was** president of the USA for three years.
The Beatles **were** school friends.
Beethoven **wasn't** born deaf.
Laurel and Hardy **weren't** singers.

2 Complete the gaps.

➕
I <u>was</u>
he/she/it <u>was</u>
you/we/they _____

➖
I _____
he/she/it _____
you/we/they _____

❓
_____ I?
_____ he/she/it?
_____ you/we/they?

▶ Read Language summary A on page 154.

Practice

1 Write seven sentences about the people in the photos.

Marie Curie wasn't French, she was Polish.

Pronunciation

1 **T7.2** Listen and write down the ten sentences.

2 Notice the weak forms of *was* and *were* and the pronunciation of *wasn't* and *weren't*.

/wəz/   /wə/
He was born in New York.   Where were you born?

/wɒznt/   /wɜːnt/
He wasn't French.   They weren't from London.

3 Listen again and practise the sentences.

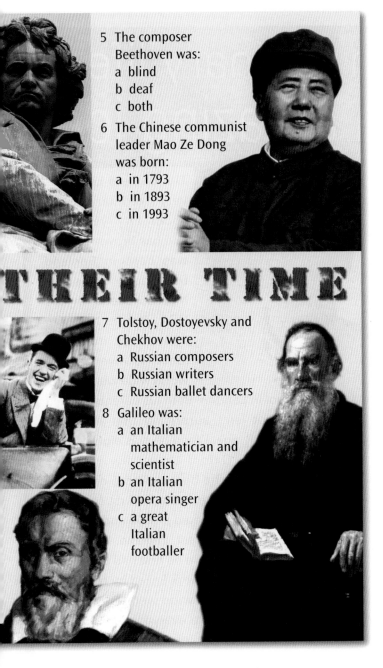

5 The composer Beethoven was:
   a blind
   b deaf
   c both

6 The Chinese communist leader Mao Ze Dong was born:
   a in 1793
   b in 1893
   c in 1993

THEIR TIME

7 Tolstoy, Dostoyevsky and Chekhov were:
   a Russian composers
   b Russian writers
   c Russian ballet dancers

8 Galileo was:
   a an Italian mathematician and scientist
   b an Italian opera singer
   c a great Italian footballer

2 a Complete the questions with *was* or *were*.

1 Where _____ your parents born?
2 How old _____ your parents when you _____ born?
3 Where _____ you born – at home or in hospital?
4 What time of day _____ you born?
5 What day of the week _____ you born on?
6 What _____ your favourite food when you _____ little?
7 Who _____ your best friend when you _____ young?
8 What _____ the name of your first teacher at school?
9 _____ you frightened of anything when you _____ a small child?

b Work in pairs. Ask and answer the questions.

Vocabulary
Years, decades and centuries

1 **T7.3** Listen and circle the year you hear.

a (2006) / 2001   d 1989 / 1999   g 1804 / 1904
b 1984 / 1985   e 1978 / 1878   h 1917 / 1970
c 1919 / 1990   f 1914 / 1940   i 2020 / 2030

Pronunciation

1 Listen again. Notice the stress.

•   •
two thousand and six

•   •
nineteen eighty-five

•   •
nineteen ninety

2 Listen again and practise saying the dates.

---

2 **T7.4** Check the words in bold in a bilingual dictionary. Work in pairs. How many sentences below can you complete? Listen and check.

a The Beatles were first **popular** ... *in the 1960s.*
b Napoleon I was **Emperor** of France ...
c Bill Clinton was President of the USA ...
d William Shakespeare was born ...
e The Russian **Revolution** was ...
f The first **landing** on the **moon** was ...
g The Second World **War** was ...
h Mozart was born ...
i Madonna's first **hit single** was ...
j Leonardo da Vinci was born ...

from 1804 to 1815	in 1917
from 1939 to 1945	in 1969
in the eighteenth century	~~in the 1960s~~
in the fifteenth century	in the 90s
in the sixteenth century	in the 80s

3 Use another phrase to say these.

a 1970–1979   *the nineteen-seventies*
b 1930–1939
c 1960–1969
d 1920–1929
e 1600–1699

4 Work in pairs. Write five sentences like the ones in exercise 2 about famous people in your country.

▶ Read Language summary C on page 155.

Reading

1 Tim Berners-Lee invented something very important. Do you know what it was?

2 **MD** Check the meaning of the words and phrases in the box.

ordinary surprising to become to be interested in to graduate a network to decide to be linked

3 Read the text. Then complete the fact file at the bottom of the text.

Language focus 2
Past simple: regular and irregular verbs

1 Look back at the text about Tim Berners-Lee. Find two sentences about his life now and four sentences about his life in the past.

2 Underline the verbs in the sentences about his life in the past. Are they regular or irregular?

Grammar

1 Regular verbs

a Find the past form of these verbs in the text.
invent   study
work   graduate
love   decide

b How do we form the Past simple of regular verbs?

2 Irregular verbs

Find the past form of these verbs in the text.
have   make
go   get
leave   write
become

▶ Read Language summary B on page 154.

An ordinary life ... an amazing idea

Tim Berners-Lee looks very ordinary. He's about fifty years old and has brown hair. He was born in England but now lives in Massachusetts in the USA. But in 1989 Tim had a very important idea. He invented the world wide web (www).

Tim went to school in London. Both his parents worked with computers so it isn't surprising that he loved computers from an early age. When he was eighteen, he left school and went to Oxford University where he studied physics. At Oxford, he became more and more interested in computers, and he made his first computer from an old television. He graduated in 1976 and got a job with a computer company in Dorset, England. In 1989, he went to work in Switzerland where he first had the idea of an international information network linked by computer. He decided to call it the world wide web, and he also decided to make his ideas free to everyone – that is why today we do not pay to use the Internet.

In 1994 he went to live in the United States where he now works. In 1995 he wrote an article in the New York Times where he said, 'The web is a universe of information and it is for everyone.' Today his idea of a web, where people from all over the world can exchange information, is real.

Tim Berners-Lee: Fact file	
His important idea	
Place of birth	
Place(s) of study	
Place(s) of work	
Personal details	
Now lives in	

Practice

1 Use the prompts to make sentences about Tim Berners-Lee.

a born / England *He was born in England.*

b go to school / London

c when / 18 / go to Oxford University

d at university / become / interested in computers

e make / his first computer from a television

f graduate / 1976

g get a job / computer company / England

h go / Switzerland / 1989

2 Work in pairs. Close your books and tell your partner six things you remember about Tim's life.

3 a **MD** Use your mini-dictionary to find the Past simple forms of these verbs. Which are regular/irregular?

> arrive begin believe can take share
> need die describe steal want win

b **T7.5** Do you know who invented the telephone? the radio? Listen and read to find if you were correct.

c Complete the text with the Past simple forms. Listen again and check.

Pronunciation

1 **T7.6** Look at the tapescript on page 169. Listen and count the number of syllables you hear.
worked 1 studied 2

2 Notice that only verbs that end in the sounds /t/ or /d/ have an 'extra' syllable in the Past simple.
want-ed wait-ed
need-ed decid-ed

3 **T7.7** Listen to eight pairs of sentences. Write *1* if you hear the Past simple first, and *2* if you hear the Past simple second.

4 Look at the tapescript on page 169. Listen again and practise the Past simple sentences.

Who really invented the telephone and the radio?

Many schoolchildren learn that the Scotsman Alexander Graham Bell (1) _____ (invent) the telephone in 1876. But the real inventor (2) _____ (be) Antonio Meucci, a poor Italian American. He (3) _____ (share) a workshop with Bell in the 1860s, and (4) _____ (make) a 'talking telegraph' for his wife who was ill in bed, so that she (5) _____ (can) call him when she (6) _____ (want) something. But Meucci never (7) _____ (take) his idea to the US Patent Office, because he was too poor to pay the $250 that he (8) _____ (need). So on February 14th 1876 Alexander Graham Bell (9) _____ (take) the invention to the Patent Office instead. Just two hours later another inventor, Elisha Gray (10) _____ (arrive) with the same idea – too late!

Alexander Graham Bell   Guglielmo Marconi

At the time, nobody (11) _____ (believe) that the telephone was an important invention. Bell's father-in-law, also a scientist, (12) _____ (describe) the invention as 'a beautiful toy'. And it was 2002 before the US Congress (13) _____ (decide) that Meucci was the true inventor of the telephone!

But everyone knows that the Italian Marconi (14) _____ (invent) the radio, right? Wrong. Actually, Guglielmo Marconi (15) _____ (steal) his great idea from Nikola Tesla. Tesla (16) _____ (write) an article in 1893 and in it he (17) _____ (describe) his important new invention – the radio.

But just two years later, Marconi (18) _____ (take) the idea to the US Patent Office and soon (19) _____ (begin) to sell it. In 1909 he even (20) _____ (win) a Nobel Prize for his invention.

In 1943 Nikola Tesla (21) _____ (die) in New York, a poor man. That year, the US Congress (22) _____ (decide) that Nikola Tesla was 'the true father of the radio'.

Listening
A true story

1 You are going to hear the true story of how David Platonoff's Russian grandmother came to live in London. Look at the photos and discuss these questions.

a   Which country do you think they show and which period?
b   What kind of life do you think David's grandmother had in Russia?

2 a **MD** **T7.8** Read the statements below and check the words in bold. Then listen and mark the statements true or false.

b Listen again and read the tapescript on page 169. What is your reaction to the story?

3 What do you know about the lives of your grandparents? Do you know any other older people who had an interesting life? What happened to them?

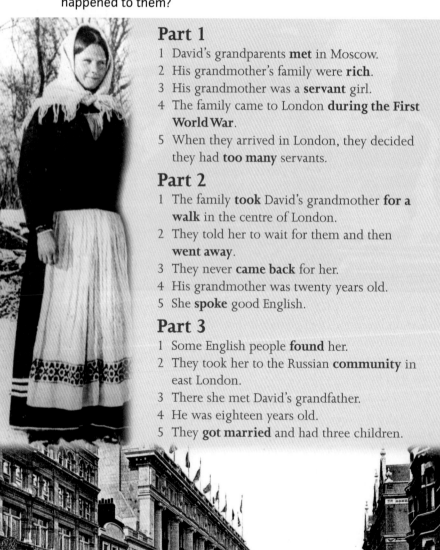

Part 1
1 David's grandparents **met** in Moscow.
2 His grandmother's family were **rich**.
3 His grandmother was a **servant** girl.
4 The family came to London **during the First World War**.
5 When they arrived in London, they decided they had **too many** servants.

Part 2
1 The family **took** David's grandmother **for a walk** in the centre of London.
2 They told her to wait for them and then **went away**.
3 They never **came back** for her.
4 His grandmother was twenty years old.
5 She **spoke** good English.

Part 3
1 Some English people **found** her.
2 They took her to the Russian **community** in east London.
3 There she met David's grandfather.
4 He was eighteen years old.
5 They **got married** and had three children.

Real life
Dates and other past time phrases

1 a Practise saying the months on the calendars below.

1 JANUARY **1**	**2** FEBRUARY **2**
3 MARCH **3**	**4** APRIL **5**
5 MAY **7**	**6** JUNE **10**
7 JULY **12**	**8** AUGUST **15**
9 SEPTEMBER **20**	**10** OCTOBER **21**
11 NOVEMBER **22**	**12** DECEMBER **31**

b Match the dates with the ordinal numbers in the box.

the third	the twenty-first
the second	the first
the twelfth	the fifth
the thirty-first	the tenth
the twenty-second	the seventh
the fifteenth	the twentieth

▶ Read Language summary E on page 155.

Pronunciation

1 Notice the two ways of saying dates in English.

/ð/ • /θ/ •
the seventh of May

• /ð/ • /θ/
May the seventh

2 **T7.9** Listen and say the dates in exercise 1a. Pay attention to the pronunciation of 'th'.

3 **T7.10** What are these dates? Listen and check, then repeat.

a 1/2/1943   d 13/9/2002
b 3/9/1993   e 23/7/1933
c 31/12/1963 f 30/12/2004

2 Work in pairs. Ask your partner about the birthdays in his/her family.

What date is your birthday?

When's your brother's birthday?

3 Put these time phrases in order from now going back into the past. Compare answers with a partner.

when I was twelve	yesterday morning
twenty years ago	~~ten minutes ago~~
last Tuesday	last night
ten years ago	when I was eight
when I was born	two weeks ago
last weekend	your last birthday
~~last month~~	last year
last August	

now

ten minutes ago

last month

past

▶ Read Language summary D on page 155.

4 Work in small groups. Play the board game using a die. Take turns. When you land on a question, choose which member of the group to ask.

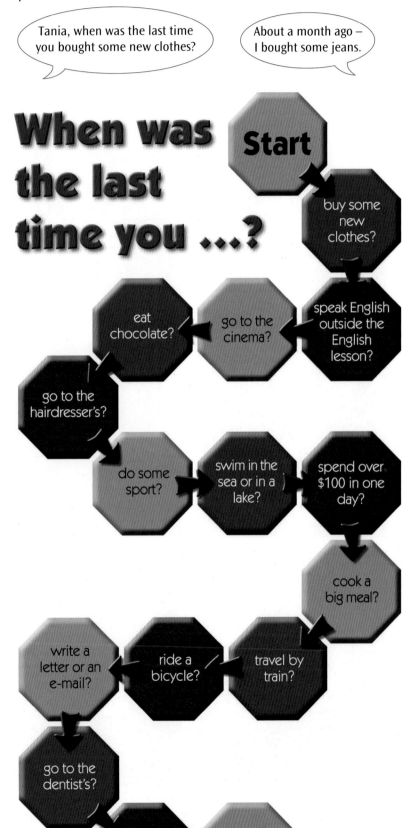

Tania, when was the last time you bought some new clothes?

About a month ago – I bought some jeans.

When was the last time you ...?

Start

buy some new clothes?

speak English outside the English lesson?

go to the cinema?

eat chocolate?

go to the hairdresser's?

do some sport?

swim in the sea or in a lake?

spend over $100 in one day?

cook a big meal?

travel by train?

ride a bicycle?

write a letter or an e-mail?

go to the dentist's?

go on holiday?

Finish

Task: Tell your life story
Preparation: listening

1 Marlene is a singer, from Swansea in Wales. Look at the pictures showing her life story. What can you see?

2 **T7.11** Listen to Marlene talking about her life. Which picture relates to each extract?

Extract A = picture ☐   Extract C = picture ☐   Extract E = picture ☐
Extract B = picture ☐   Extract D = picture ☐   Extract F = picture ☐

Task: speaking

1 *Either* Draw six simple pictures for different times in your life and think about what to say about each picture.

Or Make notes about six important events in your life story.

▶ Useful language

Ask your teacher about any important words or phrases you need.

2 Work in pairs. Tell each other about your life story using your pictures/notes to help you.

3 Choose three things to tell the class about your partner's life story.

Useful language

I was born in (1987).

I went to school in (Warsaw).

As a child I loved (playing tennis).

When I was (thirteen), I became interested in (photography).

I left school when I was (seventeen).

I studied (maths) at university.

I graduated in (2002).

I got a job with (a large company).

I went to work in (Tokyo).

I got married in (1999).

In (1995) I started work (as a receptionist).

Follow up: writing

Write your biography, but do not write your name on it. Put your biographies on the wall or a desk. Read other students' biographies and guess whose they are.

STUDY...

Finding grammar in a dictionary (2)

1 **MD** You can use your mini-dictionary to find the past forms of verbs.

buy /baɪ/ *verb* buys, buying (**bought**)
have bought if you buy something, you give someone money and they give you the thing in return

2 **MD** Find the past form of these verbs.

see open live read stop
study play know

3 Match A and B to make rules for the spellings of regular past forms.

A
a Most verbs (e.g. *open*) ☐
b Verbs that end in *-e* (e.g. *live*) ☐
c Verbs that end in a consonant + vowel + consonant (e.g. *stop*) ☐
d Verbs that end with a vowel + 'y' (e.g. *play*) ☐
e Verbs that end with a consonant + 'y' (e.g. *study*) ☐

B
1 take 'd'.
2 take 'ed'.
3 change the 'y' to 'ied'.
4 double the final consonant and add 'ed'.

4 Write past forms. Then check in your mini-dictionary.

watch try hate cook travel
close finish stay

Pronunciation spot

The sounds /ɔː/ and /ɜː/

a **T7.12** Listen and notice the sounds /ɔː/ and /ɜː/.
/ɔː/ walk, born, August
/ɜː/ first, birthday, work

b **Which sounds are these?**
daughter girl morning learn
third law quarter Turkey

c **T7.13** Listen and check. Then practise the words.

PRACTISE...

1 *was* and *were* ☐

a Do you remember the famous people in the photos on page 60? Complete the questions with *was*, *were*, *wasn't* or *weren't*.

1 There __were__ four English men. Who _____ they?
2 There _____ one woman. She _____ a writer. What _____ her job?
3 How many politicians _____ there?
4 _____ there anyone from Russia?
5 There _____ any Italian composers but there _____ one from Germany. Who _____ he?

b Now write the answers.

▶ **Need to check? Language focus 1, pages 60 and 61.**

2 Dates ☐

Write the dates, years, decades or centuries.

a The Athens Olympic Games were in <u>two thousand and four</u> . (2004)
b Mahatma Gandhi lived from _____ . (1869–1948)
c The film director Steven Spielberg was born _____ . (1946)
d Christmas Day is on _____ . (25/12)
e The American comedy *Friends* was popular in _____ . (1990–2000)
f The economist Karl Marx lived in _____ . (1800–1900)

▶ **Need to check? Vocabulary, page 61 and Real life, page 64.**

3 Past simple ☐

Write the past form of the verbs.

a arrive	*arrived*	e have	_____	i get	_____
b go	_____	f want	_____	j decide	_____
c make	_____	g become	_____	k take	_____
d begin	_____	h leave	_____	l die	_____

▶ **Need to check? Language summary B, page 154.**

4 Past time phrases ☐

Put a word from the box in the correct place in the sentences.

were ago last ~~when~~ yesterday in on

     when
a I went to Sâo Paolo ^I was twenty.
b The concert started half an hour.
c I telephoned Jim morning.
d We were in class together year.
e She came to Spain 2003.
f We took the photograph when we on holiday.
g My birthday is May 16th.

▶ **Need to check? Language summaries C and D, page 155.**

REMEMBER!

Look back at the areas you have practised. Tick the ones you feel confident about. Now try the MINI-CHECK on page 161 to check what you know!

Fact or fiction?

▶ Past simple negative forms and questions
▶ Vocabulary: Describing films
▶ Reading: *Film facts!*
▶ Listening: The author behind the legend
▶ Task: Interview other students about arts and entertainment
▶ Real life: Arranging a night out

Vocabulary
Describing films

1 Look at the photos from films. Which film is ...

• a cartoon?   • a musical?
• a love story?   • a science fiction film?
• a comedy?   • an action film?
• a horror film?   • a historical film?

2 a **MD** Which adjective(s) describes each type of film? Compare answers with other students.

> sad frightening exciting violent interesting
> romantic funny enjoyable boring silly

Pronunciation

T8.1 Listen to the adjectives and put them in the correct column according to the stress. Practise saying the adjectives.

●	● ●	● ● ●
sad		

● ● ●	● ● ● ●	

---

b Work in pairs. Say the name of a film (or TV programme) and your partner says which adjective(s) describes it.

> Shrek.   Funny and romantic.

Film facts!

Important firsts

1895 The Lumière brothers showed the first film in a Paris café

1927 The first talking film *The Jazz Singer* appeared. It was also the first musical film. Other popular musicals include *Singing in the Rain, West Side Story* and *Grease*.

1937 Walt Disney made the first full-length cartoon *Snow White and the Seven Dwarfs*.

1977 The first *Star Wars* film appeared.

1996 *Toy Story* was the first film made by computer.

Reading

1 a **MD** Check the meaning of the words in bold below.

1 Walt Disney made his first long film in 19_____ .
2 Titanic **cost** $_____ million to make.
3 Charlie Chaplin was born in _____ .
4 In _____ they make about 850 films **every** year.
5 *Titanic* **won** _____ Oscars.
6 Cameron Diaz **earned** $_____ for her last film.
7 *Toy Story* appeared in 19_____ .
8 The **average** Lebanese person goes to the cinema _____ **times** every year.
9 There are _____ films of the story of Robin Hood.
10 The Lumière brothers **showed** the first film in _____ in a _____ in Paris.

b Reading race. Work in small groups. Read the text and complete the sentences. Who is first to find the answers?

2 Which films in the text have you seen? Were they good?

The biggest film

The 1997 film *Titanic*, starring Kate Winslet and Leonardo DiCaprio, was the most expensive film ever. It cost $200 million to make. But it was also the most successful. It made $1,750 million and won eleven Oscars!

The top-paid actors

Arnold Schwarzenegger is probably the best-paid actor in the world — he earned $30 million for his last movie. Cameron Diaz and Julia Roberts are the best-paid actresses — both earned $20 million for their last films.

Favourite stories

Some of the most popular stories for films are:

Alice in Wonderland (19 films made)   *Dracula* (15 films made)
Frankenstein (14 films made)   *Robin Hood* (20 films made)
Romeo and Juliet (32 films)

The great star of the silent movies

Charlie Chaplin was the most famous star of the silent movies. He was born in 1889 and acted in 94 films before he died in 1977.

Not Hollywood!

They make many more films in Bollywood (Mumbai, in India) than in Hollywood. Every year the Indians make about 850 new films — the Americans only make about 560. The Lebanese go to the cinema the most. The average person in the Lebanon goes thirty-five times every year. The average American goes just four times every year!

Language focus 1
Past simple negative forms

1 **MD** Use your mini-dictionary to find the Past simple of these verbs. Which are irregular?

sleep	create	follow	give
find	drink	fall in love	

2 **T8.2** There are mistakes in the descriptions of the films in the photos. Can you find them? Then listen and check.

a Dracula was a vampire who lived in a castle in <u>Poland</u>. He always slept during the day, but at night he became a vampire and drank <u>vodka</u>.
(2 mistakes)

b Alice followed a white cat down a hole and had lots of adventures.
(1 mistake)

c Robin Hood lived in a forest in China. He took money from rich people and gave it to his girlfriend, Maid Marion.
(2 mistakes)

d Dr Frankenstein created a monster. The monster was very handsome and people loved it.
(2 mistakes)

e Romeo and Juliet were forty years old. Their families hated each other, but Romeo and Juliet fell in love and got married. Their families were very pleased and Romeo and Juliet lived happily together.
(3 mistakes)

3 Complete the gaps.

Dracula *didn't live* in Poland, he _____ in Transylvania. He _____ vodka, he _____ blood.

Grammar

We make the Past simple negative with *didn't* (= did not) + verb.

He didn't live in Poland. (NOT: ~~He didn't lived.~~)
He didn't drink vodka.

▶ Read Language summary A on page 155.

Practice

1 Write sentences correcting the mistakes about the other films. Use the words and phrases in the box to help you.

rabbit   poor   ugly   to be frightened of   angry   kill themselves

2 **a** The picture shows a scene from Romeo and Juliet 500 years ago, but there are twelve mistakes. Can you find them?

b Make sentences using the verbs in the box.

wear   ride   use   listen to   have   eat   read   drink

People didn't have rollerblades 500 years ago.

c (T8.3) Listen and check your answers.

Pronunciation

(T8.4) Listen and notice the stress in negative sentences.

● ● ●
They didn't have rollerblades.

Listen again and practise the negative sentences.

3 **a** Put these verbs in the correct form to make sentences true for you.

1   I (go) to the cinema last weekend.
2   I (watch) TV last night.
3   I (rent) a video last weekend.
4   I (see) the news yesterday.
5   I (listen to) the radio this morning.
6   I (read) in bed last night.
7   I (play) computer games yesterday.
8   I (buy) a new CD last week.
9   I (buy) a newspaper this morning.
10   I (listen) to music on my way to school.

b Compare your sentences with other students.

I went to the cinema last weekend.

Me too. I didn't watch TV last night.

71

THE LORD OF THE RINGS

- The three Lord of the Rings films appeared in 2001, 2002 and 2003. They are based on the novels of the British writer JRR Tolkien.
- The director Peter Jackson filmed them in New Zealand. They cost more than $300 million to make, and, in all, more than 20,000 actors appeared in the three films!
- After Titanic, they are the three most successful films ever, taking over $3 billion in total!

- The final film The Return of the King won 11 Oscars. In some countries, fans queued for three weeks to buy tickets.
- In New Zealand they had an enormous party for the first night of The Return of the King. They even changed the name of Wellington, their capital city to 'Middle Earth' for the evening!

Listening
The author behind the legend

1 Discuss these questions with other students.

a Did you see any of the *Lord of the Rings* films? If so, did you enjoy them?
b Do you like 'fantasy' stories?

2 **MD** Read the text above about the *Lord of the Rings* films.

3 a **MD** You are going to hear a radio programme about JRR Tolkien, the author of the *Lord of the Rings* books. Read the statements on the right about his life and check the meaning of the words in bold.

b **T8.5** Listen and mark the statements true (✔) or false (✘).

c Listen again and correct the false information.

> He didn't have a happy childhood.

1 Tolkien had a happy **childhood**.
2 His parents died when he was young.
3 He was very interested in **ancient** languages.
4 He was a **professor** at Cambridge University.
5 He invented his own languages.
6 He wrote his first stories to create a fantasy world for his languages.
7 His children didn't like his stories.
8 The *Lord of the Rings* books first appeared in 1974.
9 Only children liked his stories.
10 He saw the films of his books before he died.
11 His family **made a lot of money** from the films.
12 His **great-grandson** acted in one of the films.

Language focus 2
Past simple questions

Put the interviewer's questions in the correct order.
Then look at the tapescript on page 170 and check.

1 have / did / a happy childhood / he?
   Did he have a happy childhood?
2 start writing / did / at a young age / he?
3 a famous writer / how / become / he / did?
4 Tolkien / die / did / when?
5 he / did / the films of his books / see?
6 make / did / a lot of money / his family?

Grammar

1 We form Past simple questions with *did* + verb.

Did Tolkien **have** a happy childhood?
Did he **see** the films of his books?
When *did* he **die**? (NOT When did he died?)

2 Notice the short answers.

Did his family **make** a lot of money?
Yes, they **did**.
No, they **didn't**.

▶ Read Language summary B on page 155.

Practice

1 a MD Put a tick (✔) next to the things you did
when you were ten years old and a cross (✗) next
to the things you didn't do.

1   like sport
2   go abroad for your holidays
3   wear fashionable clothes
4   play out in the street
5   ride a bicycle
6   play a musical instrument
7   work hard at school
8   drink tea and coffee
9   read a lot
10 watch a lot of TV
11 like rock music
12 have a mobile phone

b Work in pairs. Ask your partner about these things.

> When you
> were ten did you
> like sport?

> No, I didn't.
> I hated it.

> I can't
> remember.

c Tell the class about your partner.

---

2 Anna is asking Helena about her weekend.
Write the questions in A. Then match them with
the answers in B.

A
a   Where / go?   *Where did you go?*
b   Who / go with?
c   How / get there?
d   Why / go there?
e   What / think of it?
f   What / do there?
g   When / come back?

B
1   We went to the old town, and to a club in
    the evening.
2   By plane.
3   Because someone told us about it.
4   We went to Prague.
5   Early this morning!
6   It was fantastic.
7   With my friend.

3 Work in pairs. Ask your partner about an
interesting place he/she visited recently.

4 Write sentences about your partner.

Alain went to Madrid last month for a holiday.
He went with his family.
He went there by car.
They went because they like cities.
They visited the old town and went to a concert.
They came back three weeks ago.
They loved Madrid!

73

Task: Interview other students about arts and entertainment

Preparation: listening

1 **T8.6** Listen to six people talking about their favourite films, books, music, etc. Match their answers to the questions below.

a   Who's your favourite actress?
b   When did you last go to a concert?
c   Did you enjoy the film?
d   What kind of music do you like?
e   Do you like ballet?
f   What was the last book you read? 1

2 Work in pairs or small groups. Use the prompts in the circles to write a questionnaire about arts and entertainment.

▶ Useful language a

Task: speaking

1 Choose seven questions from your questionnaire. Interview two students from another group. Make a note of their answers.

▶ Useful language b

2 Tell the class three things you learnt about one student.

Follow up: writing

Write about your answers to the questions.

My favourite book is … . It's by …
The last book I read was … by …
I thought it was …

I like … and … music.
My favourite singer is …
My favourite group is …
The last concert I went to was …
I didn't really enjoy it.

	music	
What kind of	films	
	books	**like?**
	games	
	plays	

	go to the cinema / a concert?
When last	read a book?
	buy a CD / game?

What / see?
Who / by?
Who / in it?
Enjoy it?

Like
- reading?
- rock / classical music?
- going to the cinema?
- ballet / theatre?
- computer games?

Who / What | favourite
- actor / actress
- director / writer?
- singer / group / musical?
- film / book / play / opera / game?

Useful language

a Questions

Who's your favourite (actor)?

What kind of (books) do you like?

When did you last go to (the cinema)?

What did you see?

Who was in it?

Did you enjoy it?

Who was it by?

b Answers

My favourite (actor) is …

It was brilliant.

It was really funny/sad/exciting, etc.

It was okay.

I really enjoyed it.

I didn't really enjoy it.

I hated it.

Real life
Arranging a night out

1 **T8.7** Anna and her friend Tara often go out together. Listen to their conversation and answer the questions.

a What film do they decide to watch?
b What time does the film start?
c Where do they decide to meet and at what time?

2 Put their conversation in order. Then listen again and check.

3 a **T8.8** Listen and complete the sentences.

1 Let's _____ cinema!
2 What _____ ?
3 Why _____ that?
4 _____ the new Johnny Depp film?
5 What _____ on?
6 Why _____ first?
7 That's _____ .
8 _____ at about eight o'clock.

b Practise saying the sentences, copying the recording.

4 a Work in pairs. Write a dialogue arranging to go to the cinema together.

b Act out your dialogue in front of the class.

a ☐ Well, let's go to the cinema! What's on, do you know?

b ☐ 8.00. Yeah, perfect.

c ☐1 Tara, do you want to go out tomorrow night?

d ☐ Yeah, great. I love Johnny Depp! What time is it on? Have you got a newspaper?

e ☐ Okay, that's a good idea. Where do you want to meet for a drink?

f ☐ Well, why don't we have a drink first, then go at 9.30?

g ☐ Yeah here. Erm, let's see. It's on at either 7.30 or 9.30. What do you think?

h ☐2 Okay, but I haven't got much money.

i ☐ Mmm, I don't really like that sort of thing. How about the new Johnny Depp film? My sister saw it last weekend and she thought it was really good.

j ☐ There's an old Star Wars film – why don't we go and see that?

k ☐ How about Macy's? It's near the cinema. Let's meet at about 8.00. Is that okay for you?

Checking and revising

1 Can you make these sentences negative?

a Ehab ~~is~~ a doctor. *isn't*
b Sue and Paul are teachers.
c He was born in 1960.
d They were at university.
e He works in Damascus.
f They come from Ireland.
g He lived in Cairo in 1987.
h They got married last year.
i He's got three children.
j They've got a big house.

2 [T8.9] Listen and tick the sentence you hear.

a She isn't married.
  She wasn't married.
b He doesn't speak English.
  He didn't speak English.
c They aren't at home.
  They weren't at home.
d I've got a pen.
  I haven't got a pen.
e I don't like sport.
  I didn't like sport.
f She's got a car.
  She hasn't got a car.

3 Listen again and repeat.

Pronunciation spot

Stressed syllables

a **MD** You can use your mini-dictionary to find the stress.

in·terest·ing /ˈɪntrəstɪŋ/ *adjective*
unusual or exciting in a way that makes you think, and want to know more: *A good teacher can make any subject interesting.* | *There's a really interesting article about foxes in this month's 'Nature' magazine.*

The ' means that the next syllable is stressed.

b **Find the stress in these words.**

cartoon   comedy   historical
average   successful   popular
create   appear   romantic

c **[T8.10] Listen and repeat.**

1 Describing films ☐

Complete the words to make films and adjectives.
a A c a r t o o n is usually e _ j _ y _ b _ e.
b A h _ r _ o _ film is always f _ i g h _ e _ i _ g.
c A c _ m _ d _ is f _ n _ y.
d A l _ v _ s _ o r _ is always r _ m _ n t _ c.
e A m _ s _ c _ l has often got a s _ l _ y story.
f An a _ t _ o _ film can be very v _ o _ e _ t.
g A s c _ _ n c _ f _ c _ i _ n film is often e _ c _ t _ n g.
h A h _ s t _ r _ c _ l film can be i _ t _ r _ s t _ n g or b _ r _ i _ g.

▶ **Need to check? Vocabulary, page 68.**

2 Past simple forms ☐

Write the Past simple forms.
a appear *appeared*   c fall _____   e give _____   g drink _____
b find _____   d sleep _____   f earn _____   h cost _____

▶ **Need to check? Irregular verbs, page 149.**

3 Past simple negatives ☐

Complete the sentences about your country 100 years ago with a suitable verb in the negative.
a People *didn't play* computer games.   d People _____ hamburgers.
b People _____ pop music.   e People _____ television.
c People _____ cars.   f People _____ jeans.

▶ **Need to check? Language summary A, page 155.**

4 Past simple questions ☐

Write the questions for these answers.
a My last holiday was in August. *When was your last holiday?*
b I went to Paris.
c I went with my sister.
d I got there by plane.
e We climbed the Eiffel Tower.
f I thought it was fantastic.

▶ **Need to check? Language summary B, page 155.**

5 Arranging a night out ☐

Put the words in the correct order.
PARAS: on Saturday / you / go to / want to / the cinema / Do ?
JOE: a good idea / That's ! on / What's ?
PARAS: Bollywood / new / There's / a / musical.
JOE: that sort of thing / I / like / really / don't.
       we / don't / Why / go / film / to the new Will Smith?
PARAS: OK. / cinema / eight / meet / the / Let's / outside / at

▶ **Need to check? Real life, page 76.**

REMEMBER!   Look back at the areas you have practised. Tick the ones you feel confident about. Now try the MINI-CHECK on page 162 to check what you know!

Buying and selling

- ▶ Comparative and superlative adjectives
- ▶ Reading: *The world's most famous markets*
- ▶ Vocabulary: Shops and shopping
- ▶ Real life: Asking in shops
- ▶ Task: Choose souvenirs from your country

Language focus 1
Comparative adjectives

1 a **MD** What do you know about cars? Think of an example for the following.

- a **fast** car   *a Ferrari*
- an **expensive** car
- a **small** car
- a very **comfortable** car
- a very **ugly** car
- an **old** car
- an **easy** car to park

b **MD** Look at the adjectives in bold. Match them with their opposites in the box.

cheap	uncomfortable	difficult	new
slow	attractive	big	

fast — slow

2 Read about Juliana on the right. Answer the questions.
a   What does she want to buy? Why?
b   How much does she want to spend?

3 Look at the advertisements and the pictures. Which of these sentences are true?

a   The Deluxe is older than the Micro. ✔
b   The Micro is bigger than the Deluxe.
c   The Deluxe is more expensive than the Micro.
d   The Micro is easier to park than the Deluxe.
e   The Deluxe is better for Juliana than the Micro.

FOR SALE
Green 1996
Margellen Micro
€650
Phone 543 8799

FOR SALE
1991 Victa Deluxe – red,
very good condition
€1100
Phone 566 4635
evenings only

Juliana is a student. She wants to buy an old car to drive to university with her three friends. She wants to spend about €900, but she doesn't know much about cars. She sees these two advertisements.

Grammar

1 Complete the gaps in the comparative sentences.
   a *The Deluxe is older _____ the Micro.*
   b *The Deluxe is _____ expensive _____ the Micro.*

2 Look at these three types of comparatives.
   a One syllable: *old → older*
   b Two syllables ending in -y: *easy → easier*
   c Three (+) syllables: *expensive → more expensive*

   Write the comparative form of the adjectives in exercise 1.

3 Irregular comparatives:
   good → better, bad → worse

▶ Read Language summary A on page 155.

Practice

1 Compare the cars.

a The Micro is (slow) than the Deluxe.
The Micro is slower than the Deluxe.
b The Micro is (cheap) the Deluxe.
c The Deluxe is (comfortable) the Micro.
d The Micro is (small) the Deluxe.
e The Deluxe is (difficult to park) the Micro.
f The Deluxe is (in good condition) the Micro.
g The Micro is (in bad condition) the Deluxe.

2 a **MD** Look at the photos and check the meaning of the adjectives in the boxes.

b Work in pairs. Use the adjectives to compare the products.

> A Ferrari is faster than a Rolls Royce.

Pronunciation

1 **T9.1** Listen and notice the stressed and weak syllables.

●　　●　/ə/ /ə/　　●
A Ferrari is faster than a Rolls Royce.

　　●　　●　/ə/ /ə/　●
A Swatch is cheaper than a Rolex.

2 **T9.2** Look at the tapescript on page 170 and listen to more sentences about the photos. Practise the sentences paying attention to the stressed and weak syllables.

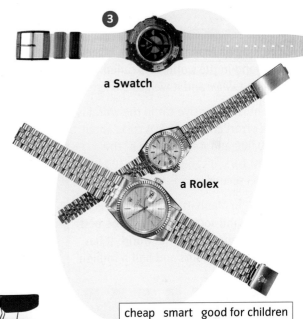

a Swatch

a Rolex

cheap　smart　good for children

a Rolls Royce

a Ferrari

fast　expensive　attractive

cola

mineral water

sweet　healthy　nice

a Vespa

a Harley-Davidson

slow　easy to ride　beautiful

Language focus 2
Superlative adjectives

MD Why are these things famous? Read and check.

The King of Thailand owns the biggest diamond in the world. It is called *The Golden Jubilee* and it weighs 2.6 kg.

The most expensive car in the world is the Ferrari Enzo Coupé. It costs about $650,000 and it is also one of the fastest cars: it can go from 0–100 kmh in 3.65 seconds.

Macy's, in Manhattan, New York, is the busiest (and some people say the best) department store in the world. It has ten shopping floors and half a million items for sale.

Grammar

1 Complete the superlative sentences.

a *The Jubilee Diamond is _____ big _____ diamond in the world.*

b *The Ferrari Enzo is _____ _____ expensive car in the world.*

2 Use the text to complete the table.

adjective	comparative	superlative
fast	faster	the _____
big	bigger	the _____
busy	busier	the _____
expensive	more expensive	the _____
good	better	the _____

▶ Read Language summary B on page 156.

Practice

1 **T9.3** Complete the questions with superlative adjectives. Choose the answers. Listen and check.

1 Where is _____ (tall) hotel in the world?
  a Dubai   b Bangkok   c Hong Kong
2 Who is _____ (rich) person in the world?
  a Bill Gates   b The Sultan of Brunei
  c Ingvar Kamprad, head of IKEA
3 Which is _____ (expensive) city in the world to buy a house or flat?
  a Tokyo   b London   c Vienna
4 Where is _____ (old) university in the world?
  a Bologna   b Karueein   c Oxford
5 What was _____ (successful) European football club in the twentieth century?
  a Bayern Munich b Real Madrid c Manchester United
6 Where is _____ (high) town or city in the world?
  a Cuzco, in Peru b La Paz, in Bolivia c Lhasa, in Tibet
7 What is _____ (common) word in the English language?
  a to   b a   c the
8 Who were _____ (popular) group in the twentieth century?
  a the Rolling Stones   b the Eagles   c the Beatles

2 a Look at page 147. Choose one of the topics.

b Write sentences about five of the questions.

My brother is the most untidy person I know.

Reading

1 Do you like going to street markets? Which is your favourite market? What can you buy there?

2 a **MD** Look at the photos of markets around the world. Which do you think is:
• the oldest?   • the most lively?
• the most colourful?   • the most unusual?
• the most similar to markets in your country?

b **MD** Check the meaning of these words. Can you see any in the photos?

a carpet	a rug	a flower	a toy	a gift
a bird	a herb	a decoration	medicine	

3 Read the text and answer the questions about each market.

a   What is the name?   c   What can you buy there?
b   Where is it?   d   When is it open?

The Grand Bazaar, Istanbul

Sonora Market, Mexico

Do you want to buy a new pair of sunglasses? The latest CD? Or something for your dinner this evening? Nowadays you can shop by telephone, by post or by Internet; but for many people, the most exciting way to shop is also the most traditional – at a street market. You can find markets anywhere in the world. Here are five of them …

The Grand Bazaar in Istanbul, Turkey, is more than 500 years old and it has more than four thousand shops under

in the world. It's the home of a colourful flower, fruit and vegetable market, open from seven o'clock in the morning to midday every day except Sunday. In the evening the piazza becomes a lively place to meet friends and to have a meal.

Every year, thousands of people from all over the world travel to Germany to visit the famous Christmas markets. The old town of Nurnberg has the biggest market, open from the end of November until

The world's most famous markets

one roof! You can buy almost anything, but the most popular items for tourists are the beautiful rugs and carpets.

There are many 'floating markets' in Asia. Perhaps the most famous is in Thailand, at a place called Damnoen Saduak, 100 km from the capital city, Bangkok. From six in the morning to midday, every day, people sell fresh tropical fruit and vegetables from their boats.

Many Italians say that the Campo de' Fiori, in the oldest part of Rome, is the most beautiful square (or 'piazza')

Christmas. Here people can buy toys, hand-made gifts, Christmas decorations, and food and drink, or they can just enjoy the wonderful atmosphere!

One of the world's most unusual markets is in Mexico City: at the Sonora Market. As well as toys and birds, you can buy herbs and natural medicines which (they say) can help with anything – from problems at work to problems with your marriage! It's open every day from early in the morning till late at night.

Floating Market, Thailand

Campo de' Fiori, Italy

Nurnberg Christmas Market, Germany

Vocabulary
Shops and shopping

1 Match the shops in the box to the pictures.

| a clothes shop | a pharmacy | a dry-cleaner's | a butcher's | a hairdresser's |
| a post office | a bakery | a local shop | a gift shop |

2 **MD** Check the meaning of the words in bold and answer the questions.

a Where can you take your **clothes** when they're **dirty**? *a dry-cleaner's*
b Where can you **have a haircut**?
c Where do they **sell** cakes and bread?
d Where can you go for new **jeans**?
e Where can you **get** a **present** for a friend?
f Where do you **post** letters and **parcels**?
g Where can you **buy** sausages?
h Where can you **find everything** (food, drink, newspapers and magazines) in one small shop?
i Where can you buy **toothpaste** and **medicine**?

3 Think of one more thing you can buy or do in each shop.

Real life
Asking in shops

1 **a** **MD** Look at pictures a–e in a department store and the store directory. Which departments are they? Which floors are they on?

Store Directory

Basement
Food hall
Cook and Kitchenware
Luggage
Ground floor
Perfumery
Cosmetics
Handbags
Stationery
First floor
Ladies' clothes
Shoes
Children's clothes
Jewellery
Second floor
DVD/Video/Music
Computers and Gaming
Electrical goods
Men's clothes
Sports
Third floor
Furniture
Restaurant
Books

b **T9.4** Anna visits five different departments. Match the recordings to the pictures.

Recording 1 = picture ☐
Recording 2 = picture ☐
Recording 3 = picture ☐
Recording 4 = picture ☐
Recording 5 = picture ☐

2 a Match the questions in A with the answers in B.

A
1 Do you take credit cards? g
2 Have you got this in a medium?
3 Do you sell diaries?
4 Which floor is that?
5 How much is it?
6 Can I have one of those, please?
7 What time does the store close?
8 Is there a restaurant or café here?

B
a It's on the ground floor.
b It's £25.
c This one?
d At eight o'clock.
e Yes, there's a restaurant on the fourth floor.
f Let me check for you.
g Yes, Visa or Mastercard.
h No, we don't. Try the stationery department.

b Listen again and check.

Pronunciation

1 **T9.5** Listen to the questions in exercise 2a and notice the stress on the important words.

   • • •
   Do you take credit cards?

2 Mark the stresses on the other questions.

3 Practise saying the questions. Copy the polite intonation.

3 a Peter is on holiday. Look at his shopping list.

postcards ✓	sunglasses
T-shirt	toothpaste
stamps	bread
fruit	cake
batteries for camera	

b **T9.6** Listen to his conversations in four different shops and tick the things on the list he buys.

c Work in pairs. Look at the tapescript on page 171 and practise the conversations.

4 Student A: Look at page 142. Student B: Look at page 145. Practise two conversations with a customer and shop assistant in a local shop.

Task: Choose souvenirs from your country
Preparation: listening

1 **a** Match the words and phrases in the box with the photos.

| a leather bag   a CD   a doll   a lamp   a silk scarf   cheese |

b Which country do you think these souvenirs come from?

2 **T9.7** Listen to six people talking about the souvenirs in the photos. Number the souvenirs in the order they are mentioned.

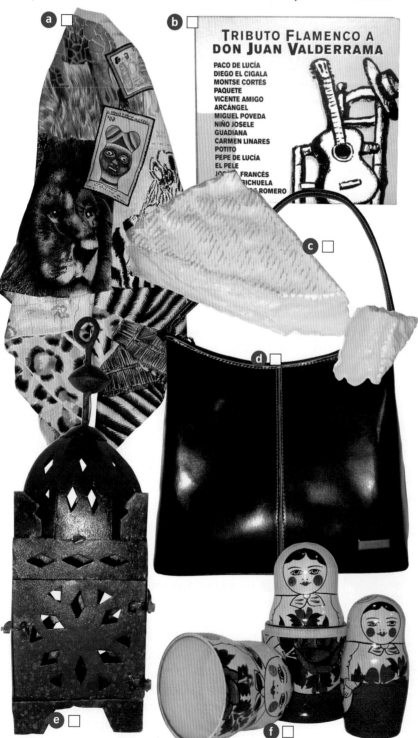

a ☐

b ☐
TRIBUTO FLAMENCO A
DON JUAN VALDERRAMA
PACO DE LUCÍA
DIEGO EL CIGALA
MONTSE CORTÉS
PAQUETE
VICENTE AMIGO
ARCÁNGEL
MIGUEL POVEDA
NIÑO JOSELE
GUADIANA
CARMEN LINARES
POTITO
PEPE DE LUCÍA
EL PELE
JO... FRANCÉS
...BICHUELA
...ROMERO

c ☐

d ☐

e ☐

f ☐

Task: speaking

1 Work individually. Read about the people on page 143. Write down some souvenirs from your country (or from the country where you are now) for the people.

2 Work in small groups. Decide the best souvenir for each person.

▶ Useful language a and b

3 Tell the class what your group decided. Did you choose the same souvenirs?

▶ Useful language c

Useful language

a Giving your ideas

I think (a doll) is a good souvenir for (Anna).

(Thailand) is famous for (silk) so …

You can buy some (really good cheese).

How about (a book)?

b Discussing

What do you think?

I think a (CD) is better because …

I think the best thing to buy is a (book).

Yes, that's a good idea.

Yes, but …

c Saying what you decided

For (Amy) we want to buy a …

The best souvenir for (Tom) is a …

In (Italy) we make/have the best (leather) so we decided to give (Helen) (a leather handbag).

STUDY...

Finding spelling in a dictionary (2)

1 **MD** You can use your mini-dictionary to find comparative and superlative forms.

cheap /tʃiːp/ *adjective* (cheaper) (cheapest)
something that is cheap does not cost very much money, or costs less money than you expect

2 Match A and B to make rules for the spellings of short adjectives.

A
a Most one syllable adjectives (e.g. *rich*) ☐
b Adjectives ending in 'e' (e.g. *nice*) ☐
c Adjectives ending in *one consonant + vowel + consonant* (e.g. *sad*) ☐
d Adjectives ending in 'y' (e.g. *friendly*) ☐

B
1 change to '-ier' or 'the -iest'.
2 take '-er' or 'the -est'.
3 double the final consonant and add '-er' or 'the -est'.
4 take '-r' or 'the -st'.

3 **MD** **Write the comparative and superlative forms. Check in your mini-dictionary.**

silly   great   true   hot   young
thin   old   friendly

Pronunciation spot

The sound /ɪ/

a **T9.8** Listen to the /ɪ/ sound in these superlative adjectives. Listen again and repeat.
oldest   smallest   fastest   newest
easiest   slowest   busiest

b **T9.9** Listen to these words and underline the /ɪ/ sounds. Then listen again and repeat.
this   English   tissues   business
married   places   matches   lived
women   dictionary   minute

PRACTISE...

1 Comparative adjectives ☐

a Complete the questions with a comparative form.
1 Who's ___taller___ (tall), you or your teacher?
2 Who's _____ (young), you or your best friend?
3 Which is _____ (good), watching a DVD or going to the cinema?
4 Which is _____ (easy) for you, speaking or understanding English?
5 Which is _____ (important) for you, having a well-paid job or an interesting job?
6 Which month is _____ (hot) in your country, May or September?

b Now write your answers.

▶ **Need to check? Language summary A, page 155.**

2 Superlative adjectives ☐

Write the superlative form and complete the sentences to make them true for you.
a The ___busiest___ (busy) month of the year is ___December___ .
b The _____ (good) day of the week is _____ .
c The _____ (bad) day of the week is _____ .
d The _____ (violent) film I know is _____ .
e The _____ (sad) film I know is _____ .
f The _____ (exciting) holiday in my life was in _____ .
g The _____ (boring) holiday in my life was in _____ .

▶ **Need to check? Language summary B, page 156.**

3 Shops ☐

Write the shops where you bought these things.

Yesterday I went to the shops and I bought some (a) breakfast cereal and a newspaper. Then I bought some (b) chicken and some (c) cakes and bread. I also bought some new (d) jeans and I left my (e) coat for cleaning. Then I had a (f) haircut.

a local shop
b b_____
c b_____
d c_____ s_____
e d_____ c_____
f h_____

▶ **Need to check? Vocabulary, page 82.**

4 Asking in shops ☐

Put the questions in the correct order.
a take / cards / you / Do / credit? Do you take credit cards?
b I / of / have / one / Can / please / those?
c a large / this / got / Have / in / you?
d this / is / much / How?
e you / time / What / do / close?

▶ **Need to check? Real life, page 82.**

REMEMBER! Look back at the areas you have practised. Tick the ones you feel confident about. Now try the MINI-CHECK on page 162 to check what you know!

Street life

▶ Present continuous
▶ Present simple or continuous?
▶ Vocabulary: Clothes
▶ Listening: People who wear uniforms
▶ Vocabulary and writing: Describing people
▶ Task: Complete and describe a picture
▶ Real life: Street talk

Language focus 1
Present continuous

1 Look at the three people who are talking on their mobiles. Do they look happy or not?

2 **T10.1** Listen to their conversations and answer the questions.

a Who are they talking to?
b What do they <u>say</u> they are doing?
c Are they telling the truth or not?

3 **T10.2** Listen and complete the sentences.

a I _____ for a bus.
b I _____ an important report for my boss.
c I _____ home.

Grammar

1 **We use the Present continuous for actions happening now or around now.**

2 **Complete the gaps in the Present continuous forms.**

➕ I'm
He/She'_____ | working late.
You/We/They'_____

➖ I'm not
He/She _____ | tell_____ the truth.
You/We/They _____

❓ What | am I
_____ he/she/it | doing?
_____ you/we/they

▶ Read Language summary A on page 156.

Pronunciation

1 **T10.3** Listen to ten sentences. Which picture(s) above do they describe?

2 **T10.4** Listen and practise the /ɪŋ/ sound at the end of the -ing forms.

    ● /ɪŋ/   ● /ɪŋ/   ● /ɪŋ/
    laughing chatting raining

3 Look at the tapescript for recording 3 on page 171. Listen again and practise the sentences.

Practice

1

MD Use your mini-dictionary to check the spelling of these *-ing* forms.

a eat   c read   e sit   g drive   i ride

b buy   d play   f drink   h get   j clean

2

Work in pairs. Ask and answer about the photos below.

> What's he doing?

> What are they doing?

> He's cleaning windows.

> They're playing football.

3

Make true sentences for you. Then compare with a partner.

a I (sit) near the door.
I'm not sitting near the door.
I'm sitting near the board.

b I (wear) trainers.

c I (chew) gum.

d I (hold) a pencil.

e We (listen) to music.

f I (wear) a jumper.

g Our teacher (write) on the board.

h We (work) hard today.

Vocabulary
Clothes

1 a Look at the people in the pictures. Where are they going?

b **MD** Tick the things you can see in the pictures? Which things are the people wearing? Which are they carrying?

trousers	a skirt	a dress
jeans	shorts	earrings
sandals	a scarf	shoes
tights	boots	a shirt
a hat	trainers	a suit
a tie	a jumper	a jacket
a coat	socks	a T-shirt
a belt	a handbag	a backpack
a briefcase	gloves	a sports bag

2 Work in pairs. Take turns to describe one of the people in the pictures. Do not say who it is. Your partner guesses.

> This person is wearing a suit, a blue shirt ...

3 Describe a student in your class for your partner to guess.

Pronunciation

1 **T10.5** Look at the pairs of words. Are the vowel sounds underlined the same (S) or different (D)? Listen and check.

a t<u>ie</u> / t<u>igh</u>ts S
b c<u>oa</u>t / sc<u>ar</u>f D
c sh<u>oe</u>s / b<u>oo</u>ts
d b<u>e</u>lt / dr<u>e</u>ss
e s<u>o</u>cks / gl<u>o</u>ves

f sh<u>ir</u>t / sh<u>or</u>ts
g sk<u>ir</u>t / s<u>ui</u>t
h s<u>a</u>ndals / h<u>a</u>ndbag
i j<u>u</u>mper / j<u>a</u>cket
j j<u>ea</u>ns / <u>ea</u>rrings

2 Practise saying the words. Pay attention to the vowel sounds.

Street fashion

We went out onto the streets to see what people are really wearing this summer ...

a Pedro, 26, City banker. Going to: a business appointment.

b Dimitri, 22, tourist. Going to: The National Gallery.

c Helen, 32, accountant. Going to: the gym.

d Camilla, 28. Going to: her best friend's wedding.

e Mel, 20, art student. Going to: college.

Listening
People who wear uniforms

Andy

Michelle

1 a Andy and Michelle wear a uniform in their job. What are their jobs?

b **MD** What clothes do they wear in their job? Are their uniforms smart / ugly / heavy / uncomfortable?

c **T10.6** Who do you think wears the following? Listen and check.

a black and white hat	a hat that is 300 years old
a white shirt leather trousers black trousers	
very big shoes tights	

2 Listen again and answer the questions.

a Why is Andy's uniform uncomfortable?
b Why does he wear women's tights?
c Do you think he likes his uniform?
d Does Michelle like her uniform generally? Why?
e Which part of her uniform doesn't she like? Why?

3 Discuss these questions.

- Do you wear a uniform at school or work? Do you like it? If not, would you like to wear a uniform?
- Who wears a uniform in your country? Which uniforms do you like best?

Language focus 2
Present simple or continuous?

It's Friday night and Michelle is getting ready to go out. At work, Michelle wears dark colours and very little make-up, so when she goes out she wears bright colours. This evening she's wearing a new pink top and a blue skirt, and quite a lot of make-up.

MD Look back at the photo of Michelle in uniform and the photo of her above. In what ways does she look different? Read and answer the questions.

a What's Michelle doing at the moment?
b What's she wearing?
c What kind of colours does she usually wear at work?
d What colours does she wear to go out?
e Does she wear a lot of make-up at work?
f Is she wearing make-up tonight?

Grammar

1 Choose the correct alternative.

Present simple:
*She **wears** dark colours at work.*
This is usually true / happening now.

Present continuous:
*She**'s wearing** a pink top tonight.*
This is usually true / happening now.

2 a Words we use with the Present simple:
usually always often normally every day

b Words we use with the Present continuous:
now today at the moment

▶ Read Language summary B on page 156.

Practice

1 **a** Choose the correct tense for the questions.

What do you wear?

1 Do you usually wear / Are you usually wearing smart or casual clothes at college/work? What kind of clothes do you wear / are you wearing today?

2 Do you wear / Are you wearing boots, trainers, sandals or shoes today? What kind of shoes do you normally wear / are you normally wearing?

3 Do you usually wear / Are you usually wearing a watch?

4 Do you wear / Are you wearing socks when the weather's hot?

5 Do you normally wear / Are you normally wearing perfume or aftershave? Do you wear / Are you wearing any at the moment?

6 Do you ever wear / Are you ever wearing glasses?

7 Do you wear / Are you wearing any jewellery today?

8 Do you wear / Are you wearing shorts a lot in the summer?

9 Do you wear / Are you wearing make-up at the moment? Do you normally wear / Are you normally wearing make-up?

10 Do you ever wear / Are you ever wearing a hat? When?

b Work in pairs. Ask and answer the questions.

2 **a** Which questions are the people below discussing? Put the verbs in the correct tense, Present simple or Present continuous.

1 ❝I usually (a) _____ (wear) make-up when I (b) _____ (go) to work, and when I (c) _____ (go) out in the evening of course, but I (d) _____ (not wear) any at the moment because I (e) _____ (work) at home today.❞

2 ❝I'm quite lucky – in my office everyone's quite casual. People normally (f) _____ (wear) jeans and maybe a shirt or jumper. Even the boss (g) _____ (not wear) a suit. Today it's really hot so I (h) _____ (wear) shorts and sandals, and I (i) _____ (not wear) socks.❞

3 ❝I (j) _____ (wear) shorts today because I (k) _____ (go) to the gym and it's very hot, but I (l) _____ (not normally wear) them because I (m) _____ (hate) my legs!❞

b **T10.7** Listen and check your answers.

3 Work in groups. Tell other students about what you normally wear at work/school, at the weekend and when you go out in the evening.

Vocabulary and writing
Describing people

1 **MD** Look at the pictures. Who:

a has got a moustache? *Mike*
b has got long hair?
c has got blue eyes?
d is in his/her thirties?
e is wearing casual clothes?
f is black?
g is slim?
h has got a beard?
i has got a shaved head?
j has got short hair?
k has got blond(e) hair?
l is well-built?
m is wearing smart clothes?
n has got medium-length hair?
o has got a pony-tail?
p is in his/her twenties?
q is very good-looking?

2 Which other words can replace the blue words?

a He's got **blond** hair.
b She's got **blue** eyes.
c He's got a **moustache**.
d She's in **her thirties**.
e She's **tall and slim**.

3 Work in pairs. Use the sentences in exercises 1 and 2 to describe the six people.

4 Write a description of yourself or of a famous person you all know. Describe your (or their) appearance and how you (or they) dress.

I'm (not very tall).
I've got (short blond hair and green eyes).
I'm in my (thirties).
I wear (glasses).
I usually wear (jeans and jumpers).
Today I'm wearing (a suit and tie).

Paolo

Kamilla

Sheena

Pedro

Martha

Mike

Task: Complete and describe a picture
Preparation: listening

1 Look at picture A and answer the questions on the right.

2 **T10.8** Listen to someone describing picture A and find four mistakes.

a Is it morning or evening?
b What is the dog doing? What colour is it?
c What's the girl doing? What's she wearing? What has she got in her right hand?
d What's the young man wearing?
e Describe the two people in the café.

Task: speaking

1 (MD) Look at picture B showing the same street in the evening. Add ten new things from the box below to the picture. Do not show anybody your picture.

> food and drinks
> short/long hair
> happy/unhappy faces
> beards or moustaches
> extra clothes (hats, ties, belts)
> people at the windows
> accessories (sunglasses, mobiles)

2 Work in pairs. Take turns to describe your picture and your partner draws it on the extra copy of Picture B on page 146. Don't look at your partner's picture. Ask questions to complete the picture.

▶ Useful language a and b

3 When you have both finished, compare your picture with your partner's original. Are they the same or not? What are the differences?

Useful language

a Asking questions

What's the woman (on the right) doing?

What's the man (in the middle) holding?

What's he/she wearing?

What's happening in the rooms (above) the café?

What kind of hair has he/she got?

Is he/she smiling?

b Describing your picture

It's raining.

He's got long hair.

She's eating (an ice cream).

Real life
Street talk

1 **a** (T10.9) (MD) Tick (✔) the correct thing to say in each situation. Listen and check.

You are in the street and ...

1 You don't know the time. How do you ask?
  a Excuse me, have you got the time, please?
  b Please what time is it, sir?
  c Tell me the time, please.

2 You are looking for a seat in a café. What do you say?
  a I'd like to sit here.
  b Is anyone sitting here?
  c Can you move, please?

3 A bus is coming. You want to know if it is going to the city centre.
  a Would you like to go to the city centre?
  b How much is it to the city centre?
  c Is this bus going to the city centre?

4 You want to park your car but you do not understand the sign on the road. What do you ask?
  a Am I parking here?
  b Is it okay to park here?
  c Do you want to park here?

5 You only have a five-pound note and you need some coins to pay for the car park. What do you say?
  a Excuse me, have you got any change, please?
  b I'd like some change, please.
  c Give me some change, please.

6 You are trying to find the station in a strange town. What do you ask?
  a What's the station?
  b How long is the station?
  c Is this the way to the station?

7 You want to know when the shops close on Saturdays. What do you ask?
  a Are the shops closed on Saturdays?
  b What time do the shops close on Saturdays?
  c What time are the shops closing on Saturdays?

b Listen again and write the answers.

Pronunciation

1 (T10.10) Listen and notice the polite intonation in the questions. Listen again and repeat, copying the voices on the recording.

2 Practise the conversations with a partner.

2 Choose five of the questions. Walk around the class imagining that you are in the street. Ask the questions to other students. They must answer politely.

CONSOLIDATION

A Grammar: Present simple, Present continuous, Past simple

Choose the correct form of the verb.

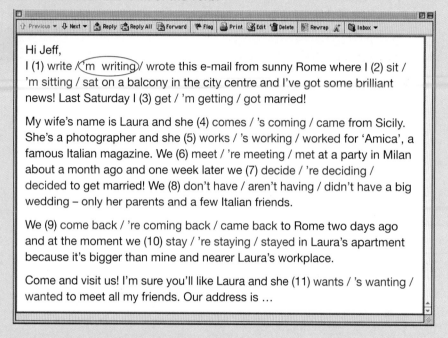

Hi Jeff,

I (1) write / **'m writing** / wrote this e-mail from sunny Rome where I (2) sit / 'm sitting / sat on a balcony in the city centre and I've got some brilliant news! Last Saturday I (3) get / 'm getting / got married!

My wife's name is Laura and she (4) comes / 's coming / came from Sicily. She's a photographer and she (5) works / 's working / worked for 'Amica', a famous Italian magazine. We (6) meet / 're meeting / met at a party in Milan about a month ago and one week later we (7) decide / 're deciding / decided to get married! We (8) don't have / aren't having / didn't have a big wedding – only her parents and a few Italian friends.

We (9) come back / 're coming back / came back to Rome two days ago and at the moment we (10) stay / 're staying / stayed in Laura's apartment because it's bigger than mine and nearer Laura's workplace.

Come and visit us! I'm sure you'll like Laura and she (11) wants / 's wanting / wanted to meet all my friends. Our address is …

B Reading and speaking: Snacks around the world

1 Read about snacks in Germany, Brazil and Japan. Complete the gaps with *a/an*, *some*, *any* or – (no word).

'Well I often have (1)___*a*___ snack at about eleven in the morning. I usually go to a kiosk near here and buy (2)_____ sausage, and then I eat it, standing up at a small table near the kiosk. Then at about four o'clock we usually stop work and have (3)_____ cup of coffee and (4)_____ cakes.'
Suzanne, Germany

'I don't usually have (5)_____ food in the middle of the morning, but in the afternoon, at about five o'clock, I sometimes have a coffee. Yesterday, for example, I had (6)_____ bread roll and (7)_____ cheese. I get very hungry in the afternoons! Oh, yes, and I had (8)_____ iced tea. You can buy it at the beach or on the streets – it's very popular in Brazil.'
Renato, Brazil

'In Japan we eat food from all over the world, and young people like European snacks. Older people like more traditional food. For example, every afternoon my grandfather has (9)_____ Japanese sweets with traditional green tea. At work, on weekdays we usually have a 'three o'clock snack'. Today I had (10)_____ biscuits and tea, but no milk! I find it very strange that English people have milk in their tea!'
Mariko, Japan

2 Work in pairs. Discuss these questions.

a   Do you have snacks between meals?
b   What did you have yesterday?

C Speaking: Real life

1 What do you say in the following situations?

a   You are in a restaurant and you want to pay. What do you say to the waiter?

b   You are in a street market. You want to buy a T-shirt. Ask about the price.

c   You are phoning a pizza restaurant. You want two large pizzas. What do you say?

d   You are buying a ticket in a railway station. The clerk says the price of the ticket but you don't understand him. What do you say?

e   You are in a shop. You want to buy some shampoo but you can't see any. What do you ask the shop assistant?

f   You are in a shop and you want to buy a T-shirt, but it's too small for you. What do you ask the shop assistant?

g   You are in a shop. An assistant asks you 'Can I help you?' but you don't want to buy anything at the moment. What do you say?

2 **C1** Listen and check. Are your questions the same?

3 Practise the situations in pairs.

D Listening: Song: *Return to Sender*

C2 Work in pairs. Student A: Look at page 143. Student B: Look at page 144. Listen to the song and complete the gaps. Then compare your answers with your partner.

E Reading and speaking: Comparatives and superlatives

1 Read about four holidays. Which country is each holiday in? Where can you:

a see a lot of animals?   c go to the beach?
b go skiing?   d visit a historic town?

Skiing holiday

Courchevel, in the French Alps, has the largest ski area in the world with 250 lifts and 600 km of perfect snow. The night life is very active, there are bars and clubs open till late, and fantastic restaurants for all tastes.
The Hotel D'Armor is a modern building with 350 rooms, a swimming pool and sauna, and it's only five minutes from the nearest ski lift.
Prices from €699.00 a week, including ski pass and ski hire.

www.D'Armor.uk

Holiday in Turkey

Situated in beautiful Ölüdeniz, we are only five minutes from the sea. Our very modern Turkish apartment sleeps five and has its own small garden. The town of Fethiye, with its old streets and buildings, is only fifteen km away.
If you want a quiet, peaceful break near the sea, then this is perfect for you!

€650 a week
hotels.wec-net.com.

Holiday in Greece

One and two bedroom traditional apartments near the small but cosmopolitan town of Agios Ioannis on the Pelion peninsula. Enjoy the sun and the wonderful Greek food!
The apartments are self-catering and are only thirty minutes' walk from the beautiful Papa Nero beach.
Only **€450 a week** for a two bedroom apartment.

www.heliostravel.co.uk

African Safari

Kenya – Tanzania – Namibia – Botswana – South Africa – Uganda – Zambia and Malawi.
We are simply the best for safaris. Small groups, friendly guides. Come canoeing, riding and camping! See elephants, lions and other animals in the wild!
Tours are three, five or six weeks.
Prices from €1,350 for three weeks.

Tel 020 7482 142
www.africanadven.co.uk

2 Make eight sentences comparing the holidays using the adjectives in the box.

> expensive cheap long quiet exciting good for families near the sea   good for sport

The skiing holiday is better for sport than the holiday in Greece.
The holiday in Greece is the cheapest.

3 a Which two holidays might be suitable for these people?

1 Adriana (22) and Sueli (23) are from Mexico. They like exciting holidays and want to meet other young people. They like dancing and sport. They want to go on holiday for two or three weeks, but they don't want to spend a lot of money.

2 Tanya and Rod Kilroy are from Canada. They've got two children, Jayne, aged 6, and Tom, aged 8, and they are looking for a quiet family holiday near the sea. They like old places. They haven't got a lot of money.

b Compare the two holidays you chose and decide which is the best.

F Vocabulary

Find three words in the word square for each topic.

```
O R A N G E J U I C E C
B A K E R Y E P B E N L
I C H E A S A T U R P O
B U S Y D W N O S E O T
O P U N U T S Y Z A T H
U B I W A I L O R L G E
G A T F T R O U S E R S
H W I N E X S N E W A H
T R O F E L L G Z I P O
U O Y A R D E C I D E P
N T A B U T C H E R S U
B E L I E V E W B E E R
```

a food	grapes
b drink	
c clothes	
d regular verbs	
e past verbs	
f adjectives	
g shops	

The world around us

- ▶ *can* and *can't* for ability
- ▶ Question words
- ▶ Use of articles (3)
- ▶ Vocabulary: Animals and natural features
- ▶ Reading: *Amazing facts about the natural world*
- ▶ Real life: Saying quantities and big numbers
- ▶ Listening: Man's best friends?
- ▶ Task: Devise a general knowledge quiz

Vocabulary
Animals and natural features

a Which things in the box can you see in the photos? Write the words in the correct column.

a bird	a mountain	a river
an insect	a human being	the earth
a chimpanzee	an elephant	the moon
a volcano	a lake	a kangaroo
a snail	a donkey	a dolphin

animals/ living things	geographical features	planets, etc.
a bird		

b Can you add any more words to each category?

Reading

1 **MD** Read the facts in the text. One is false. Can you guess which? (Check your answer on page 143.)

2 Why are these numbers mentioned in the text? Look back and check, if necessary.

| 3 years | 8 kg | 10% | 240 | 1,500 kph |
| 40,000 km | | 18,000,000 | | 10,000,000,000,000 |

3 Which facts do you find most amazing? Why?

AMAZING FACTS ABOUT

Did you know ...?
- You share your birthday with around eighteen million other people in the world.
- Snails can sleep for up to three years.
- Donkeys kill more people in the world every year than plane crashes.
- The Arctic Tern, a bird which lives in North America and the Arctic, flies to the Antarctic every year – a journey of about forty thousand kilometres.
- There are at least ten thousand billion ants in the world, but only about six and a half billion human beings. That means there are around one thousand five hundred ants for every human being.
- The Earth rotates at around one thousand five hundred kilometres per hour.
- Because of the Earth's rotation, you can throw a ball further if you throw it west.

THE NATURAL WORLD

- Elephants can't jump, pigs can't look up at the sky and kangaroos can't walk backwards.
- Africa is the only continent in the world that doesn't have an active volcano.
- Dogs can't see colours. Guide dogs watch the traffic to see when it is safe to cross – they can't see the difference between red and green traffic lights.
- Chimpanzees can't talk but they can learn sign language. Some chimps learn up to two hundred and forty different signs.
- About ten per cent of people in the world are left-handed. Studies show that dogs and cats also prefer to use either their right or left paws. So check if you have a right or a left-handed pet!
- The average person eats around 8 kilos of dirt during their lifetime. This is because of badly washed fruit and vegetables.

Language focus 1
can and *can't* for ability

Grammar

1 Underline three facts in the text that tell you about animals' abilities.

2 Complete the gaps with *can* or *can't*.
➕ Chimpanzees _____ read sign language.
➖ Elephants _____ jump.
❓ _____ dogs see colours?

▶ Read Language summary A on page 156.

Practice

1 **MD** Make at least six sentences that you know are true using words from each of the boxes and *can* or *can't*.

| chimpanzees | kangaroos | elephants | ants |
| dolphins | dogs | parrots | newborn babies |

| fly | jump (high) | swim | talk | run fast |
| see colours | walk | climb trees | carry heavy things |

Dog's can't see colours.

Pronunciation

T11.1 Look at the tapescript on page 172. Listen and notice the stress and weak forms. Listen again and repeat.

● /kən/ ●   ● /kɑːnt/ ●
Dogs can swim.   Elephants can't jump.

2 Ask and answer with other students. Try to find one student for each activity.

Who in the class can ...

a play the guitar?   e make clothes?
b mend a car?   f play chess?
c write with their other hand?   g read music?
d read really fast?   h sing well?

Can you play chess?   Yes, but not very well.

No, I can't.

Language focus 2
Question words

1 a Work in pairs. How many questions in the Animal quiz can you answer without looking back at the text?

b Look back at the text and check your answers.

2 Circle the question word in each question.

Grammar

1 There are many two-word questions with *how*, *what* and *which*. Match the question words to the answers.

a How far ...?   Los Angeles.
b How tall ...?   Every day.
c How often ...?   Lions.
d How long ...?   Ten metres.
e How fast ...?   Forty kilometres an hour.
f Which city ...?   Ten kilometres.
g Which animals ...? Rock and pop.
h What kinds of music ...? Three hours.

2 **Do you remember? Choose the correct alternative.**
We use:
• *How many* with countable / uncountable nouns.
• *How much* with countable / uncountable nouns.

3 We use *what* when there are a large number of possible answers.
What is the population of China?

We use *which* when there are only a few possible answers.
Which continent has no active volcanoes?

▶ Read Language summary B on page 157.

Practice

1 Choose the correct question word.

a Which / What do kangaroos eat?
b How much / How many water do people need to drink every day?
c What / Which do you like best, dogs or cats?
d How much / How many pets have you got?
e How much / How long do elephants usually live?
f How far / How often do you need to feed a baby?
g How fast / How long does the average person walk?
h How far / How many can you swim?
i How long / How often do you go swimming?
j Which / What is your dog's name?

Animal quiz

1 How much dirt does the average person eat during their life?

2 What kind of animals can't jump?

3 Which continent has no active volcanoes?

4 How fast does the earth rotate?

5 How many ants are there in the world?

6 How long can snails sleep?

7 How do guide dogs know when to cross the road?

8 How far do Arctic Terns fly every year?

9 What is the present population of the world?

2 **a** Make questions to ask your partner. Complete each question in A with words from B, C and, if necessary, D.

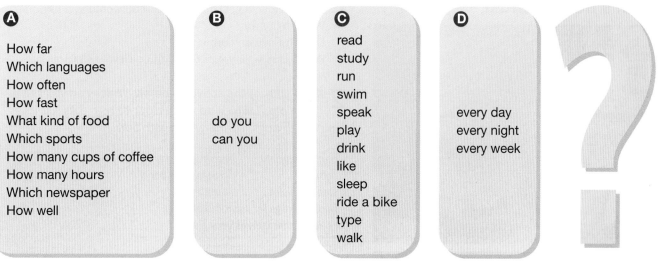

A

How far
Which languages
How often
How fast
What kind of food
Which sports
How many cups of coffee
How many hours
Which newspaper
How well

B

do you
can you

C

read
study
run
swim
speak
play
drink
like
sleep
ride a bike
type
walk

D

every day
every night
every week

b Work in pairs. Ask and answer your questions.

Real life

Saying quantities and big numbers

1 Match the numbers in A with how you say them in B.

A	B
a 50 kph	five thousand
b 500 kg	five billion
c 505	five hundred kilos
d 5,000	five million
e 50,000	five point five
f 500,000	five hundred thousand
g 5,000,000	one metre fifty-five centimetres
h 5,000,000,000	fifty thousand
i 5.5	fifty kilometres per hour
j 1 m 55 cm	five hundred and five

2 **T11.2** Listen and write down the ten numbers you hear. Then listen again and repeat.

a   400

3 **a** Complete the questions with the words in the box.

How far   How fast   How many (x2)
How much (x2)   How old
How tall   What (x2)

1 _____ is the speed limit on motorways in your country?
2 _____ can you drive in town centres?
3 _____ is the population of your country, approximately?
4 _____ people live in your town?
5 _____ is the average woman?
6 _____ does the average man weigh?
7 _____ is your city from the coast?
8 _____ students are there in your school, approximately?
9 _____ , approximately, is your house?
10 _____ does the average person earn in your country?

b Work in pairs. Ask and answer the questions. Don't worry if your answers are not exact.

Listening
Man's best friends?

1 Discuss these questions.

- Do you have a pet cat or dog? If not, would you like one? Why / Why not?
- Do you have any other pets?
- Do you know any pets that can do clever things?

2 **MD** Look at the activities below. Which can you see in the photos? Which do you associate with cats (C), which with dogs (D) and which with both (B)?

being pregnant	having kittens
racing	helping the blind
sleeping a lot	hunting
finding drugs for customs officers	
keeping themselves very clean	

3 **a** How many questions can you answer?

1 How many domestic cats are there in the world today?
2 What do they eat?
3 How many hours a day do they sleep?
4 How long are female cats pregnant?
5 How many kittens do they have at one time?
6 How many breeds (kinds) of cats are there?
7 What is special about sphinx cats?

b **T11.3** Listen to the first part of a radio programme about pets, and check your answers. Did anything surprise you?

4 **T11.4** The second part of the programme is about dogs. Read, then listen and complete the gaps.

People say that (a) *a dog is a man's best friend*. People and dogs first started living together about ten thousand years ago. Now there are (b) _____ dogs just in the USA. The Americans spend over (c) _____ on dog food every year – four times what they spend on baby food!

Altogether there are about (d) _____ breeds of dog. Many dogs work for humans, doing jobs such as helping the blind, helping the police and customs officers to find drugs and even racing! Greyhound racing is popular (e) _____ . The fastest greyhounds can run as fast as (f) _____ .

Perhaps the most famous working dog was Rin Tin Tin, who died in (g) _____ . He earned his money by (h) _____ . He made fifty films and earned about (i) _____ for each one!

Language focus 3
Use of articles (3)

1 Read what three people say about pets. Who do you agree with?

"We all love <u>animals</u> in my family – we've got <u>a cat</u>, a dog and a rabbit. People think that dogs don't like cats, but our dog's really friendly to the cat and the rabbit – it's really sweet."
Jack, 8

"I love dogs, especially big dogs, but I haven't got one because I think it's cruel to keep big dogs in flats. The dog in the flat next door to me is really unhappy – it just walks up and down the balcony all day when the owners are at work. It's really sad."
Alex, 31

"I don't really like animals much, especially cats. I hate cats. I hate the way they rub against your legs – ugh!"
Paula, 23

2 Underline the animals in the text above. Do they have *a*, *the* or no article?

Grammar

Read the rules about the use of the article in English. Tick (✔) the rules if they are the same in your language, and write a cross (✗) if they are different.

1 We use *a/an* to talk about things for the first time or when we don't know which one.
*We've got **a** dog, **a** cat and **a** rabbit.*

2 We use *the* to talk about specific things, or when we know which one.
*Our dog's really friendly to **the** cat and **the** rabbit.*
***The** dog in **the** flat next door is really unhappy.*

3 We use no article to talk about things in general.
***Dogs** don't like **cats**.*

▶ Read Language summary C on page 157.

Practice

1 Which of these things do you like / love / hate / not mind? Write sentences, then compare with a partner.

kittens	big dogs	snakes	spiders	winter
windy weather	snow	really hot weather		
big cities	mountains	long walks in the country		

(I really hate big dogs.) (I don't mind spiders.)

2 **a** Complete the gaps with *a*, *the* or – (no word).

1 I haven't got _____ pet.
2 When I was _____ child I had _____ pet.
3 All _____ people in my family are _____ animal lovers.
4 _____ rabbits are popular pets in my country.
5 I learnt to ride _____ horse when I was young.
6 _____ people in my street/area have a lot of pets.
7 I was frightened of _____ dogs when I was _____ small child.
8 _____ teacher (of this class) loves _____ animals.
9 I'm allergic to _____ cats.

b Which sentences are true for you? Correct the ones that are wrong.

(I wasn't frightened of dogs when I was a small child.)

Pronunciation

1 **T11.5** Listen to the two different pronunciations of *the*.

/ðə/   /ði/
1 the sun   2 the earth

2 **T11.6** Here are some more words often found with *the*. Listen to the pronunciation of *the* and write 1 or 2 next to them.

a the east	the west
b the left	the right
c the beginning	the end
d the morning	the afternoon
e the president	the prime minister
f the king	the queen
g the EU	the USA
h the Arctic	the Antarctic

Look at the examples with pronunciation 2. What kind of sound follows *the*?

3 Listen again and repeat. Pay attention to the pronunciation of *the*.

Task: Devise a general knowledge quiz

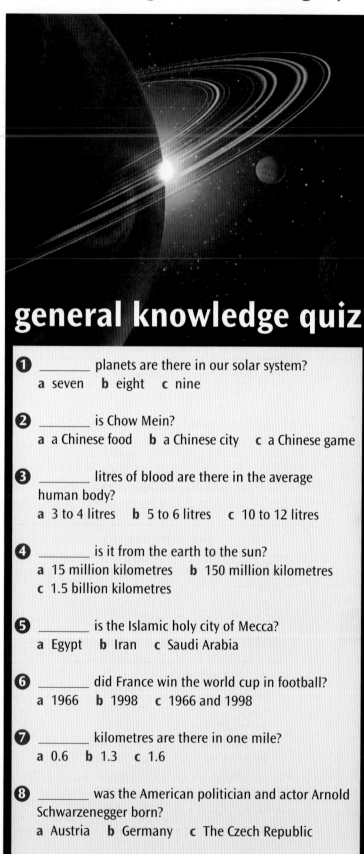

general knowledge quiz

❶ _____ planets are there in our solar system?
a seven **b** eight **c** nine

❷ _____ is Chow Mein?
a a Chinese food **b** a Chinese city **c** a Chinese game

❸ _____ litres of blood are there in the average human body?
a 3 to 4 litres **b** 5 to 6 litres **c** 10 to 12 litres

❹ _____ is it from the earth to the sun?
a 15 million kilometres **b** 150 million kilometres
c 1.5 billion kilometres

❺ _____ is the Islamic holy city of Mecca?
a Egypt **b** Iran **c** Saudi Arabia

❻ _____ did France win the world cup in football?
a 1966 **b** 1998 **c** 1966 and 1998

❼ _____ kilometres are there in one mile?
a 0.6 **b** 1.3 **c** 1.6

❽ _____ was the American politician and actor Arnold Schwarzenegger born?
a Austria **b** Germany **c** The Czech Republic

❾ _____ official languages does Switzerland have?
a two **b** three **c** four

Preparation: listening

1 **MD** Complete the general knowledge quiz with question words.

2 **T11.7** Work in groups. Answer the questions. Then listen and check.

Task: writing and speaking

1 **a** Work in three teams: A, B and C. You are going to invent your own general knowledge quiz, using the categories in the box.

geography	history	nature	science
sport	food and drink	famous people	
music	art	literature	numbers other

b Write at least eight questions, giving three possible answers for each. (You can use the 'fantastic facts' at the back of the book for ideas. Team A: Look at page 144. Team B: Look at page 142. Team C: Look at page 141.)

▶ Useful language a

2 Practise saying your questions clearly, so that the other teams can understand.

3 Play your quiz game in teams. Which team won?

▶ Useful language b

Useful language

a Asking questions
When did (Italy) win the European cup?
Where was (Albert Einstein) born?
What's the capital of (Canada)?
How far is it from (Berlin) to (Warsaw)?
Where does (sushi) come from?
Who wrote (*War and Peace*)?

b Answering questions
It's definitely (a).
I think it's (French).
I'm not sure but I think it was …
I've got no idea.

STUDY...

Recording new vocabulary

1 It's a good idea to have a vocabulary notebook. You can record new vocabulary in different ways:

a   a picture: *a scarf*

b   a translation: *a butcher's = carnicería*

c   a diagram:

a station
a post office
(*places in a town*)—*a cinema*
a library

2 Find three different groups of vocabulary.

potato	eye	walk	fly	nose
jump	run	carrot	climb	head
bean	mouth	mushroom	walk	

3 Use three pages in your notebook and record each group in a different way. Which way do you think is best?

Pronunciation spot

The sounds /w/ and /h/

a   **T11.8** **Listen and notice the sounds /w/ and /h/. Listen again and practise the words.**

/w/ when, where, what, which, why

/h/ how, how often, who, how much

b   **T11.9** **Listen and practise words and phrases with /w/.**

c   **T11.10** **Listen and practise words and phrases with /h/.**

PRACTISE...

1 Animals and natural features ☐

Circle the odd one out.

a   a fish / (a kangaroo) / a dolphin

b   a mountain / a river / a lake

c   an insect / an ant / an elephant

d   the earth / a volcano / the moon

e   a donkey / a cheetah / a snail

f   a parrot / a chimpanzee / a bird

▶ **Need to check? Vocabulary, page 96.**

2 *can* for ability ☐

Put the words in the correct order.

a   speak / you / Japanese? / Can   *Can you speak Japanese?*

b   can't / drive / You

c   very well / can / She / cook

d   you / They / understand / can't

e   but / music / I / can't read / can / sing / I

▶ **Need to check? Language summary A, page 156.**

3 Question words ☐

Write a different question word (or words) in each gap.

a   *Where* were you born?

b   _____ do you like best, coffee or tea?

c   _____ cousins have you got?

d   _____ do you go to the hairdresser's?

e   _____ is the station from here?

f   _____ does it take you to come to school?

g   _____ sugar do you take in your coffee?

▶ **Need to check? Language summary B, page 157.**

4 Saying quantities and big numbers ☐

Write the numbers.

a   250,000   *two hundred and fifty thousand*

b   20,000,000   _____

c   40 kph   _____

d   99.9   _____

e   12m 30cm   _____

▶ **Need to check? Real life, page 99.**

5 Articles ☐

Complete the conversations with *a/an*, *the* or – (no word).

VIC: We had (a) __*a*__ great holiday. We stayed in (b) _____ brilliant hotel.

ROB: Yeah? What kind of things did you do?

VIC: Well, (c) _____ hotel had (d) _____ swimming pool and (e) _____ children loved it so we just relaxed there most days.

ZOE: Jo! There's (f) _____ spider in (g) _____ bath!

JO: I can't help you. I hate (h) _____ spiders!

▶ **Need to check? Language focus C, page 157.**

REMEMBER!

Look back at the areas you have practised. Tick the ones you feel confident about. Now try the MINI-CHECK on page 162 to check what you know!

A weekend away

- ▶ **Future intentions:** *going to, would like to* and *want to*
- ▶ **Suggestions and offers**
- ▶ **Vocabulary and speaking:** Going out and staying in
- ▶ **Task:** Plan a weekend away
- ▶ **Real life:** Talk about the weather

Language focus 1
Future intentions: *going to, would like to* and *want to*

1 **MD** Look at the photos. In which can you see people who are …

- at a wedding?
- at the hairdresser's?
- at a swimming pool?
- dancing in a club?
- relaxing at home?
- having a barbecue?
- going for a walk?
- having a family meal?

2 a **T12.1** Listen to six people talking about their plans for the weekend and complete the table.

Name	plans for Saturday	plans for Sunday
Neela	Saturday night - club with friends	
Phil		
Megan		
Jamie		
Anna		
Sharif		

b **T12.2** Listen and complete the sentences.

1 On Saturday night I'm going out with a _____ _____ of friends.
2 On Sunday I'm going to _____ _____ with my grandparents.
3 The whole family are going to _____ there because it's my grandmother's _____ .
4 I'm not going to _____ _____ this weekend.
5 I want to _____ the _____ I'm reading.
6 It's my boyfriend's birthday and I want to _____ him a digital _____ .
7 I'd like to go away somewhere _____ _____ .
8 On Sunday afternoon I'm going to a _____ _____ .
9 This weekend? Nothing special. On Saturday afternoon I want to _____ the _____ .

Grammar

1 a To talk about future intentions, we often use
be + going to + verb.

➕ *I'm going to have lunch with my grandparents.*

➖ *I'm not going to do much this weekend.*

❓ *Are you going to watch the football tonight?*

b With the verb *go* we usually use *be + going ~~to go~~*.

I'm going out with a group of friends.

2 We can use other verbs to talk about future
intentions, too.

a *want to* + verb
I want to finish my book.

b *would like to* + verb
I'd like to do something with the children.

▶ Read Language summaries A and B on pages 157
and 158.

Practice

1 Write sentences about the people in exercise 2a
using *going to*.

On Saturday Phil's going to stay at home and relax.

2 What are the people in the pictures going to do?

3 **T12.3** Complete the questions with *are*, *do* or
would. Then listen and check.

a ___Are___ you going straight home after this lesson?
If not, where _____ you going?

b _____ you going to do any homework tonight?
What _____ you going to do?

c _____ you want to watch TV this evening?
_____ you want to watch anything special?

d _____ you going to have a busy weekend? What
_____ you like to do?

e _____ you going out anywhere this week? If so,
where _____ you going?

f Are there any films that you _____ like to see at
the moment? Which ones?

g _____ you want to buy anything special in the
next few weeks? What?

h _____ you want to go on holiday this year?
Where _____ you like to go?

Pronunciation

1 **T12.4** Listen and notice that *to* has a weak
pronunciation in the middle of a sentence.

/tə/
Are you going to have a busy weekend?

/tə/
What do you want to do?

2 Listen to recording 3 again and repeat.

4 Work in pairs. Ask and answer the questions in
exercise 3.

Vocabulary and speaking
Going out and staying in

1 What did you do last weekend? Was it busy or quiet? tiring or relaxing? boring or fun?

> My weekend was really boring. I stayed at home and did nothing!

2 **MD** Read the questionnaire about the weekend. Mark the activities 1–4.

1 = I **never** do this
2 = I **occasionally** do this
3 = I **sometimes** / **quite often** do this
4 = I **usually** / **always** do this

3 Compare your answers in small groups. Explain what you do and why.

> I often study at the weekend, because I don't have time in the week. How about you?

4 a Match the words and phrases that go together in A and B. Use the questionnaire to check.

	A	B
1	stay	a walk
2	stay	for the weekend
3	do	at home
4	have a	swimming
5	go	the country
6	go to	the gym
7	go to	with friends
8	go for	in bed
9	go out	the housework
10	go away	party

b Spend a few minutes remembering the phrases. Then test your partner.

> the country   go to the country

5 What's your idea of a perfect weekend? Which of the activities above does it include?

How do you spend weekends?

A Work and rest
At the weekend, do you ever:
- work or study?
- do the housework or the shopping?
- stay in bed until lunchtime?
- stay at home and just relax?

B Sport and exercise
How often do you:
- go to the gym or go swimming?
- go for a long walk?
- play football or another game?
- watch sport on TV?

C Social life
How often do you:
- go out for a meal?
- see relatives?
- have a party or a barbecue at your house?
- go out with a group of friends to a bar or a club?

D Culture
Do you ever:
- go to a concert?
- go to an exhibition or a museum?
- go to the cinema or the theatre?
- read a book?

E Going away for the weekend
Do you ever:
- go away on business for the weekend?
- visit relatives in another part of the country?
- go to the country or to the beach?
- spend the weekend in another city?

Language focus 2
Suggestions and offers

1 **T12.5** It's Lisa's birthday on Saturday. Listen to her conversation with Amy without reading. What do they decide to do?

2 Write the numbers of the missing lines in the gaps. Then listen again and check.

1 How about that new French restaurant
2 I'll speak to Martin and the others
3 Let's book it for eight
4 Where shall we go
5 why don't we all go out for a meal somewhere
6 shall I phone the restaurant and book a table

A: It's your birthday next Saturday, isn't it?

L: Yeah, but I don't really know what I want to do. Maybe I'll stay at home and have a quiet night in.

A: Don't be silly, you can't do that! I know, (a) _5_ ... you, me, Martin, Ben and some of the others maybe?

L: Yeah, okay. That sounds more fun!

A: (b) ____ ?

L: There's Bagatti's but we always go there. (c) ____ ? I can't remember its name …

A: The French Table?

L: Let's go there. I'd really like to try it.

A: Yeah, it sounds good. (d) ____ and check that they can come. Then (e) ____ ?

L: Yes, please, if that's okay.

A: What time? Eight, half eight?

L: (f) ____ , and then we can go somewhere else later.

A: Yes, good idea!

3 Work in pairs. Look at the tapescript on page 173 and practise the dialogue.

Grammar

1 a We make suggestions like this:

Why don't we all go out for a meal?
How about (trying) that new French restaurant?
Shall I phone and book a table?
Let's book it for eight o'clock.

b How does the other person in the conversation answer?

2 a We make offers like this:

I'll speak to Martin and the others.
Shall I phone and book a table?

b How does the other person answer?

▶ Read Language summaries C and D on page 158.

Practice

1 a Put the words in the correct order to make suggestions and offers.

1 coffee / a / about / How?
2 jacket / take / I / your / Shall?
3 the bill / ask / we / Shall / for?
4 home / you / I'll / take
5 go / we / Why / don't / cinema / the / to?
6 another / Let's / drink / have
7 you / tomorrow / call / I / Shall?
8 we / Why / meet / the station / don't / at?
9 the tickets / book / I'll

b **T12.6** Listen and check. How did the other person answer? Did they accept the offer/suggestion?

Pronunciation

Look at Recording 6 on page 173. Listen again and practise. Pay attention to the polite intonation.

2 Which suggestions/offers in exercise 1 might you make in these situations?

a You are arranging a night out at the cinema.
b A friend is spending the evening at your house.
c You meet an old friend in the street.
d You are in a restaurant with a friend.

3 Work with a partner. Write a dialogue for one of the situations in exercise 2. Act it out in front of the class.

module 12 A weekend away

Task: Plan a weekend away

Preparation: reading and listening

1 **MD** Check the meaning of the words in bold. Which of the things in the box can you see in the photos?

a **magnificent cathedral**	a **castle**
beautiful **views**	**sailing**
cliffs and beaches	**B&Bs**
traditional live music	a **golf course**
a **lake** with an **island**	a **lively** bar

2 Read the descriptions of three places and answer the questions.

a   Which photos go with each place?
b   Which of the things in exercise 1 can you find in each place?
c   Which would you most like to visit?

3 **T12.7** Three friends are planning a weekend away. Listen and circle the correct information.

a   They decide to go to …
   (1) the Isle of Wight.
   (2) Canterbury and Leeds Castle.
   (3) Dublin.
b   … because …
   (1) it's not too far.
   (2) it's really beautiful.
   (3) there's something for everyone.
c   They are going to travel by …
   (1) ferry.   (2) train.   (3) plane.
d   All of them like …
   (1) cities.
   (2) walking.
   (3) going out in the evening.
e   On Friday evening they are going to leave at …
   (1) 6.00.   (2) 8.00.   (3) 10.00.
f   They are going to come back on Sunday evening at …
   (1) 6.00.   (2) 8.00.   (3) 10.00
g   They are going to stay in …
   (1) a college.   (2) a B&B.   (3) a hotel.

4 **T12.8** Look at the tapescript on page 173. Listen and practise the sentences.

The Isle of Wight

Just two and a half hours' journey from London, the Isle of Wight is perfect for a weekend break, with its three hundred and eighty square kilometres of farmland, cliffs and beaches. You can stay in a B&B at Freshwater Bay and go for long walks along the cliff paths, and beaches. Or hire a bicycle and ride around the island, stopping at Carisbrooke Castle with its magnificent views over the island. If you want something more exciting, try a one-day paragliding course or go sailing: the Isle of Wight is a paradise for sailors. For children, there is a steam railway which starts from Ryde on the north coast. In the evenings you can relax after a good day's walking in one of the many excellent fish restaurants.

Canterbury and Leeds Castle

With its magnificent cathedral, many museums and old city walls, Canterbury is one of the most historic and beautiful cities in the country. You can stay at a hotel or a B&B and spend your day visiting the nine hundred-year-old cathedral and shopping. Or visit nearby Leeds Castle, which is situated on two islands in the middle of a small lake and is one of the loveliest castles in the country. It was first built in the ninth century and later became the home of King Henry VIII. Today it is a favourite with visitors, with beautiful parks to walk in, as well as gardens, a golf course, a museum, and, in summer, outdoor concerts.

Dublin

Dublin, the capital city of the Republic of Ireland, is situated on the east coast, on the River Liffey, and has an international airport with cheap, frequent flights from London. It's a lively and cosmopolitan city, and if you walk along the famous O'Connell Street you will find exciting shops, bars and restaurants. If you like sightseeing, you can also visit the famous Dublin Castle, Trinity College and Phoenix Park, one of the largest city parks in the world. In the evening you can listen to traditional Irish music in the bars and you can try the most popular drink in Ireland: Guinness, a black beer. Close by the city there are lovely beaches, and just over an hour away are the Wicklow Mountains for walks and beautiful views. And you will have no problems finding good accommodation: Dublin is famous for its excellent B&Bs.

Task: speaking

1 You are going to plan a weekend away with some other students. Make a list of possible places to visit.

2 **a** Work in groups and decide where you would like to go. Think about the following things.

- how to travel
- where to stay
- what to do there
- when to leave / get home

▶ Useful language

b Plan how you will describe your weekend away to other students. Ask your teacher for any words or phrases you need.

3 **a** Work in new groups. Tell the group what you have planned.

> We're going to … because we want to visit …

b Which weekend away sounds the most interesting?

Useful language

Where to go
I'd really like to go to …
It's a long way / not too far.
It takes about two hours to get there.

How to travel
We can fly.
What time shall we leave?
What time do we want to get home?

What to do
What can we do there?
Let's visit the museum.
I'd like to …

Where to stay
Where shall we stay?
I'll book a B&B.

Real life
Talk about the weather

1 How many seasons are there in your country? Which seasons are January, April, July and October in?

2 a Match the phrases and pictures.

It's cloudy.	It's sunny.	It's windy.
It's snowing.	It's raining.	It's cold.
It's foggy.	It's hot.	It's wet.
It's warm.	It's cool.	It's icy.

b **T12.9** Listen and check, then repeat.

 The hottest place in the world is El Azizia in Libya. In 1922 it had the highest temperature ever – 58°C.

 Chicago in the north of the United States is called 'the Windy City'. Florida in the south is known as 'the Sunny State'.

 It never snows in Brazil.

 The wettest place in the world is Mawsynram in India, which has around 1.2 m of rain every year!

 On July 21st 1983 Vostok in Antarctica had a temperature of -89°C, the coldest temperature ever recorded.

 Countries near the Equator, like Malaysia and the Philippines, have only two seasons a year, the wet season and the dry season.

3 **MD** Read the fact file. Why are these places mentioned?

Brazil	Chicago	El Azizia	Malaysia	Mawsynram	Vostok

4 a **T12.10** Listen to Sumalee from Bangkok in Thailand and Cathy from Vancouver in Canada talking about the weather in their countries. Which of these statements are true?

Thailand
1 Thailand has three seasons.
2 The cool season is in April and May.
3 The rainy season is from June to October.
4 When it rains, it usually lasts for about four hours.
5 Bangkok gets very hot in April.
6 The coldest days are in December.

Canada
1 In the north of Canada, there's snow for around eight months of the year.
2 The winters in Vancouver are very bad.
3 It's often cloudy and wet in Vancouver in the winter, but it isn't very cold.
4 The summers in Vancouver aren't very sunny and warm.

b Listen again and correct the statements that are false.

5 *Either* Write a paragraph about the weather in your country.

In … there are … seasons. From … to … it's … . From … to … it's …
The average temperature in my city is about …
It's very … in (winter) and … in (summer).

Or Tell other students about the weather in your country.

STUDY...

Remembering collocations

1 Collocations are words that go together, for example:

stay at home   have breakfast
do my homework

2 It's important to record collocations. You can write them like this and then cover one column and test yourself ...

go out	with friends
see	a film
miss	my family

... or you can make a diagram.

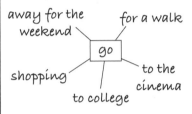

3 Can you remember verbs which go with each of these nouns?

a   _watch_   television
b   _____   economics
c   _____   computer games
d   _____   nothing
e   _____   the radio
f   _____   a new job
g   _____   school
h   _____   by underground
i   _____   a parcel
j   _____   a motorbike
k   _____   to the airport
l   _____   married

Pronunciation spot

Short forms

a (T12.11) **Listen and notice the short forms.**

I'll help you.
I'd like a coffee.
Let's go out somewhere.

b (T12.12) **Listen and write down the number of words you hear. (I'll = 2 words.)**

c Listen again and write the sentences. Then practise them.

PRACTISE...

1 Future intentions ☐

Put the words in the box in the correct place in the sentences.

> to do 'd would 's are 'm

a Lena ^'s^ going to study law.

b What you want to do tonight?

c What you like for your birthday?

d Miko wants visit us next month.

e I like to go for a long walk tomorrow.

f Where you going on holiday?

g I going out for a meal.

▶ **Need to check? Language summary A, page 157.**

2 Going out and staying in ☐

Cross out the noun that doesn't go with each verb.

a play   football / a game / sport
b do   a party / the shopping / the housework
c stay   at home / relatives / in bed
d have   a barbecue / a meal / the gym
e go   school / to an exhibition / swimming

▶ **Need to check? Vocabulary, page 106.**

3 Suggestions and offers ☐

Put the words in the conversation in the correct order.

A: (a) we / for / don't / go / a / Why / walk ?
     Why don't we go for a walk?
B: (b) idea / Good
     (c) we / shall / go / Where?
A: (d) beach / about / How / the ?
B: (e) ring / Steve / shall / OK, / I?
     (f) he / to / Maybe / like / come / 'd
A: (g) and / 's / Yeah / some / take / let / food
B: (h) make / Right, / sandwiches / 'll / some / I

▶ **Need to check? Language summaries C and D, page 158.**

4 The weather ☐

Write the missing letters to make weather words.

a s _ n _ _   c r _ _ n _ _ g   e c _ _ l   g w _ _ m
b f _ g _ y   d s n _ _ _ n _   f c l _ _ _ _   h w _ _ d _

▶ **Need to check? Real life, page 110.**

REMEMBER!

Look back at the areas you have practised.
Tick the ones you feel confident about.
Now try the MINI-CHECK on page 163
to check what you know!

Learning for the future

- ▶ Infinitive of purpose
- ▶ *might* and *will*
- ▶ Vocabulary and speaking: Education and careers
- ▶ Listening: My career
- ▶ Reading: *Easy English?*
- ▶ Task: Find the right course
- ▶ Real life: Applying for a course

Vocabulary and speaking
Education and careers

1 **a** **MD** Which of these subjects do/did you study at school or university? Can you add any other subjects to the list?

politics	management	science
history	literature	business studies
languages	economics	law
design	medicine	information technology
geography	maths	engineering

b Which of the subjects interest you most/least?

> I'm not very interested in history.

Pronunciation

1 **T13.1** Listen and notice the pronunciation of the subjects. Which letters are silent?

2 Listen again and mark the stress. Then practise the words.

---

2 **MD** Put the phrases in the three categories below. (Some can go in more than one column.)

do a (business studies) course	pass/fail an exam
choose a career	get a degree
go to primary/secondary school	take an exam
have an interview	get into university
apply for a job/a course	train to be (a chef)
earn money	be unemployed

school	university	work
take an exam		

3 Work in pairs. Discuss the questions.

a When did you start primary school? When did you go to secondary school? Which did/do you like best? Why?

b What were/are your best subjects at school? Which were/are your worst?

c Are you doing any courses at the moment (apart from this one)?

d Is there anything that you would really like to study?

e Are you taking any exams this year? Do you think you will pass or fail? Why?

f Is it difficult to get into university and get a degree in your country? Which courses are the most difficult to get on?

g What other kinds of training do people do? Where do they do this?

h What are the good/bad things about the education system in your country, do you think?

i Is it important to learn foreign languages in your country? Which languages do most people learn? At what age do they start?

j Is it easy or difficult to get a job at the moment? Are many people unemployed?

k Which careers are most popular with young people? Why are they popular, do you think?

l If you apply for a job in your country, do you normally have an interview? What happens?

m Which careers are most popular with men/women?

n Which professions earn the most money? Is money important to you in choosing a career?

o What else do you look for in a career? Do you have an 'ideal job'?

Listening
My career

1 **T13.2** Listen to four people talking about their careers. Which subjects and jobs did each person mention?

Will, 28   Vicki, 36

Francine, 22   Josh, 15

2 a Work in pairs. Who ...

1 failed all his exams at school?
2 learnt French at primary school?
3 worked for a big finance company?
4 wants to do a career that is very difficult to get into?
5 is going to Lisbon soon?
6 stopped work for a few years?
7 worked as a van driver?
8 owns his own company now?
9 writes for his school magazine?
10 is training to be a teacher?

b Listen again and check.

Language focus 1
Infinitive of purpose

Match the two parts of the sentences. Which people in the photos on page 113 do they describe?

1   He went back to college   to study Portuguese.
2   She stopped work   to get some qualifications.
3   He's writing for his school magazine   to look after her children.
4   She's going to Lisbon   to get some experience.

Grammar

We often use an infinitive (*to* + verb) to say why we do things.
She's going to Lisbon <u>to study</u> Portuguese.

Underline the other examples like this in the exercise above.

▶ Read Language summary A on page 158.

Practice

1 Finish the sentences in as many ways as you can, using the ideas in the box.

check my e-mails	find some information	get a book
pass his exams	study French	train as a nurse
meet some friends	do some studying	check something
look up a word	buy a train ticket	do some shopping

a   I went on the Internet ...   *to check my e-mails.*
                               to find some information.
                               to buy a train ticket.
                               to do some shopping.
b   She went to the library ...
c   I'm going upstairs ...
d   He went to Paris ...
e   Can I borrow your dictionary ...
f   She's going back to college ...
g   I'm going into town ...
h   He worked very hard ...
i   He went to the station ...
j   Can you lend me some money ...
k   I need some time ...
l   I'm phoning the office ...

2 Work in pairs. Can you think of any other ideas?

> You can go on the Internet to get some music.

Reading

1 Discuss these questions.

a   Which foreign languages do most people learn in your country?
b   Do you think English is an easy language to learn or not?
c   Which of these areas of the language are easiest/hardest for foreign students do you think: grammar, pronunciation, spelling or vocabulary? Why?
d   Is your language easy for foreigners to learn? Why / Why not?

2 **MD** Read the text. Which paragraph:

a   is about a man who invented a new form of English with a smaller vocabulary?
b   is about a man who tried to change the spelling of English?
c   introduces the topic?
d   is about how e-mail is changing English?
e   is about a form of English that people use at sea?

3 Work in pairs. Answer the questions.

a   When did Professor Ogden invent Basic English? How many words did it have?
b   Why did Professor Zachrisson invent Anglic? What happened to it?
c   Why is Seaspeak easier than ordinary English?
d   What is 'Internetish', do you think?
e   Is it a good idea to learn Anglic or Seaspeak instead of English?
f   How would you change English to make it easier?

Easy English?

1 English is an important global language, but that doesn't mean it's easy to learn. Many experts have tried to make English easier for students to learn – but they weren't always successful.

2 In 1930, Professor CK Ogden of Cambridge University invented Basic English. It had only 850 words (and just eighteen verbs) and Ogden said most people could learn it in just thirty hours. The problem was that people who learned Basic English could write and say simple messages, but they couldn't understand the answers in 'real' English! It was also impossible to explain a word if it wasn't in the Basic English word list. For example, if you wanted a water melon, you asked for 'a large green fruit with the form of an egg, which has a sweet red inside and a good taste'!

3 RE Zachrisson, a university professor in Sweden, decided that the biggest problem for learners of English was spelling, so he invented a language called Anglic. Anglic was similar to English, but with much simpler spelling. 'Father' became 'faadher, 'new' became 'nue' and 'years' became 'yeerz'. Unfortunately for some students of English, Anglic never became popular.

4 Even easier is the language which ships' captains use: it's called 'Seaspeak'. Seaspeak uses a few simple phrases for every possible situation. In Seaspeak, for example you don't say, 'I'm sorry what did you say?' or 'I didn't understand, can you repeat that?' ... it's just, 'Say again.' No more grammar!

5 In the age of international communication through the Internet who knows? ... a new form of English might appear. A large number of the world's e-mails are in English and include examples of 'NetLingo' like OIC (Oh, I see) and TTYL (Talk to you later). In another fifty years, English as we know it might not exist ... we will probably all speak fluent Internetish!

Language focus 2
might and *will*

Read the statements. Do you agree? Compare answers with a partner.

1 People **won't** learn Latin any more in a few years.
2 In a few years, everyone **will** speak English.
3 English **might not** be the global language in a hundred years' time
   – it **might** be Chinese instead.
4 In the next hundred years many smaller languages **will** disappear.

Grammar

1 **Look at the verbs in bold in the sentences above. Which verb(s)
   means that the speaker:**

   a is sure this will happen?   c that maybe this will not happen?
   b thinks that maybe this will happen? d is sure that this will not happen?

2 **Notice these short forms:**

   They'll (= will) disappear.   They won't (= will not) disappear.

▶ Read Language summary B on page 158.

Practice

1 Complete the sentences with *might (not)* or *will*.

a In a few years time everyone _____ know how to use the Internet.
b In the future people _____ go to school or university. They
   _____ study at home using their computer.
c Tom isn't sure what he wants to do when he leaves school. He
   _____ go to university, or he _____ travel abroad for a year.
d Why not do a course in Japanese? You never know – you _____
   need to speak it one day.
e Denise doesn't like her teacher. She thinks she _____ change her
   class soon.
f Some teachers are worried that computers _____ take their jobs
   one day.

2 Complete the sentences for you using the ideas in the box.

| career and education | holidays and travel | being rich |
| marriage and children | speaking English | other things |

a Next winter I might …   e I might never …
b Next summer I think I'll …   f I'll definitely never …
c Next year I hope I'll …   g One day I hope I'll …
d In ten years' time I might …   h When I'm sixty-five I'll probably …

Pronunciation

1 **T13.3** Listen to ten sentences. Write *P* if they are in the present
   and *F* if they are in the future.

2 Listen again and practise the pronunciation of *I'll* and *won't*.

Task: Find the right course
Preparation: reading and speaking

1 **MD** Read the college brochure and answer the questions.

a Which career(s) does each course train you for?
b Which courses are full-time, which are part-time and which are both? Which courses last for two years?

2 a Three students, Taka, Oliver and Gaby want to choose a course. Work in groups of three.
Student A: Read about Taka on page 141.
Student B: Read about Oliver on page 148.
Student C: Read about Gaby on page 145.

b Tell the group about your student and what they want to study. Listen to your partners and make notes about each student.

Task: speaking

1 a Work individually. Read the brochure again. Decide which courses are suitable for each person.

b Which do you think each person will choose? Why?

2 Work in groups and compare ideas. Try to agree on the best course for each person.

▶ Useful language

3 **T13.4** Listen to the three students talking about the course they chose. Did they choose the same one as you?

4 Which of the courses would you like / not like to do? Why?

CHOOSE YOUR COURSE

■ LEISURE AND TOURISM

For people interesting in a career in tourism. Includes:
- marketing and promotion
- customer service
- information technology

This course is one-year, full-time. You must be at least 16 years old.

■ INFORMATION TECHNOLOGY

For people who need to use computers to work in business or industry. Includes:
- using information technology for business purposes
- programming and software

This is a six-month part-time course (various days) or a one-year full-time course, twenty hours a week.

■ CHILDCARE

For people interested in working with pre-school children in nurseries or in private home. Includes:
- child development
- health and safety
- career options

This is a one-year full-time course, 18 hours a week, or a two-year part-time course (Monday, Tuesday Thursday 6.30–9.30 pm).

■ SPORTS STUDIES

For people who would like to work in sports centres, swimming pools, etc. Includes:
- health and safety
- sports coaching
- fitness and diet

This is a two-year full-time course open to people over 16 years of age, or a four-year part-time evening course (Monday, Tuesday Thursday 6.30–9.30 pm).

■ PERFORMING ARTS

Includes music, dance and drama in the first year. In the second year students can choose special subjects such as:
- singing
- directing
- marketing

Students must be at least 16 at the time of entry. The course is two years, full-time.

■ FASHION DESIGN

A course to help you find work in fashion and the media. Includes:
- clothes design
- using computer software
- photography

This is a one-year full-time course (15 hours a week) open to people over 16 years, or a two-year part-time course (Monday and Wednesday 9.00 am–4.00 pm).

Useful language

Explaining your ideas

I think the best course for (Gaby) is …

(Oliver) will/might choose … because he likes …

(Taka) might enjoy the … course.

Agreeing and disagreeing

Yes, you're right.

I agree with you.

I don't agree because …

Yes, but …

Real life
Applying for a course

Adriana is Italian. She wants to improve her English to get a better job.

1 Read about Adriana. Match her details below with the questions in section A of the application form. (Write n/a 'not applicable' for no information.)

Personal details

farinelli@bellquel.lat.it

n/a

MS

no visa

Farinelli

Adriana Paola

20-11-87

n/a

Via Ezio 60, 04300 Latina, Italy

7-53-58-285

female

Same as daytime number

02426439

Italian

2 Invent details for section B.

APPLICATION FORM

W.E.M.C.O.T.
(West Midland College of Technology)

English as a Foreign Language

Please complete this form using BLOCK LETTERS.

Section A Personal Details

1 Title: (Mr / Mrs / Miss / Ms / Dr, etc.)

2 Surname: ....

3 First Name(s): ....

4 Date of Birth: Day .... Month .... Year ....

5 Sex: Male ☐   Female ☐

6 Nationality: ....

7 Home Address: ....

8 Telephone No: a) Day: .... b) Evening: ....

9 Fax number: ....

10 E-mail address: ....

11 Passport No: ....

12 a) Have you got a student/tourist visa? ....
    b) Date of expiry: ....

Section B Course Details

1 Start Date: ....

2 for .... Terms (Maximum 4)
   Term 1 ☐   Term 2 ☐   Term 3 ☐   Term 4 ☐
   Jan – March   April – June   July – Sep   Oct – Dec

3 Why do you want to study English at WEMCOT?
   ....
   ....

4 What level do you think your English is?
   Elementary ☐   Lower Intermediate ☐   Intermediate ☐
   Higher Intermediate ☐   Advanced ☐   Proficiency ☐

You will have a test on the first day of the course.

Signed: ....
Date: ....

---

3 Adriana goes to register for the course. The college administrator checks all her details with her. Work in pairs and act out the interview.
Student A: You are Adriana. Answer the questions about yourself.
Student B: You are the college administrator. Ask questions to check the information on the form.

4 Act out the same interview with another student. This time give your own details. First complete the application form on page 147.

STUDY...

English outside the classroom

1 To improve your English outside the classroom, it is important that you do things that you find interesting! Read the ideas below. Can you think of any others?

- Find an English penfriend on the Internet or through a magazine.
- Read about the news on the Internet or in the newspaper.
- Read sports reports in English on the Internet or in a newspaper.
- Find a library or bookshop with 'graded readers' of well-known stories in English.
- Find the words of some of your favourite English songs on the Internet.

2 Mark each idea like this:

✔✔   if you would definitely like to try them.

✔   if you think you would enjoy this.

?   if you are not sure.

✘   if you definitely wouldn't enjoy this.

Compare opinions with other students.

3 Choose one idea to try for a few weeks.

4 After a few weeks tell the class how you got on.

Pronunciation spot

The sounds /ɒ/, /əʊ/ and /ɔː/

a `T13.5` Listen. Can you hear the difference between the three 'o' sounds?

1 /ɒ/	2 /əʊ/	3 /ɔː/
job	won't	sport

b `T13.6` Listen and decide if the words are sound 1, 2 or 3.

course	college	office
home	go	show
more	short	shop
both	know	perform

Listen again and repeat.

PRACTISE...

1 Subjects you study ☐

Complete the subjects.

a l <u>aw</u>

b e _ g _ n _ _ r _ n _

c d _ s _ _ n

d e _ o _ _ m _ c s

e s _ i _ _ c _

f h _ _ t _ r _

g m _ d _ c _ _ e

h l _ t _ _ a t _ r e

i g _ _ g _ a _ h _

▶ Need to check? Vocabulary and speaking, page 112.

2 Phrases related to study and jobs ☐

Match A and B to make phrases.

A		B
a	go	an exam
b	go	an exam
c	take	an exam
d	do	a nurse
e	earn	to secondary school
f	apply	a computer course
g	pass	for a job
h	get	to university
i	train as	a degree
j	fail	money

▶ Need to check? Vocabulary and speaking, page 112.

3 Infinitive of purpose ☐

Why do you go to these places? Write two reasons for each.

a the airport   <u>to catch a plane, to meet someone</u>

b a pharmacy   _____

c the beach   _____

d the cinema   _____

e a petrol station   _____

f a library   _____

g a coffee bar   _____

▶ Need to check? Language summary A, page 158.

4 *will* and *might* ☐

Complete the sentences with *will (not)* and *might (not)* to make them true in your opinion.

a In ten years people _____ live on other planets.

b One day people _____ go on holiday on the moon.

c Flying _____ become cheaper in the future.

d People in the future _____ live in cities under the sea.

e There _____ more wars in the future.

f In twenty years' time, there _____ more traffic than now.

g Our children and grandchildren _____ live until they are over a hundred.

▶ Need to check? Language summary B, page 158.

REMEMBER!

Look back at the areas you have practised. Tick the ones you feel confident about. Now try the MINI-CHECK on page 163 to check what you know!

Keeping in touch

- ► Present perfect
- ► Time phrases with the Present perfect and Past simple
- ► Reading: *Getting in touch through the ages*
- ► Vocabulary: Ways of communicating
- ► Real life: Telephoning
- ► Task: Analyse a questionnaire

Reading

1 **MD** Look at pictures a–c and read the information. When did these events happen? How long did it take for people to receive the news?

2 **a** Put these ways of communicating in order from the oldest (1) to the newest (7). Compare answers in pairs but do not read the text.

e-mail	the telephone
the typewriter	the postage stamp
text messages	the fax machine
pen and paper	

b **MD** Read the text and check.

3 Work in pairs. Ask and answer the questions.

a   How did people deliver letters in Ancient Egypt?
b   How much did the first stamp cost?
c   How often did they deliver letters in the 1840s?
d   How are the letters arranged on a modern computer keyboard?
e   When did the first fax machine appear?
f   Why was it difficult to walk with the first walkie-talkies?
g   When was the first text message?
h   How many e-mails do we send every day?

4 What do the pronouns in bold refer to?

a   **it** cost just one penny (paragraph 2)
b   nobody was very interested in **it** (paragraph 4)
c   **it** was so enormous that no one wanted **one** (paragraph 4)
d   after World War Two **they** became popular with police officers (paragraph 5)

5 Work in small groups. Discuss these questions.

- Which information in the text did you find most surprising?
- Do you think people send too many e-mails / text messages?
- Do you ever receive annoying e-mails / phone calls / letters?

500 years ago, it took five months for the news of Christopher Columbus' arrival in America to reach Queen Isabella in Spain.

GETTING IN

1 Nobody knows who wrote the first letter or when, but we know that 4,000 years ago in Ancient Egypt people carried letters by hand over hundreds of kilometres. Very few people could write, so there were special people, called scribes, who wrote letters for everyone else.

2 In those days you didn't need a stamp. The first stamp didn't appear until 1840 and it cost just one penny. Nowadays one of these original stamps costs €375. Letter writing was so popular in the 1840s that they delivered the post several times a day!

b 150 years ago, it took two weeks for news of President Lincoln's assassination in the USA to reach Europe.

c In 1969, when Neil Armstrong first walked on the moon, it took just 1.3 seconds for his words to reach the Earth!

TOUCH THROUGH THE AGES

3 An American company – Remington and Sons – made the first typewriter in 1871. All the letters in the word 'typewriter' were on the top line of the keyboard so that salesmen could demonstrate the machine more easily. Amazingly, the letters are still in the same place on the modern computer keyboard!

4 In 1876, when Alexander Graham Bell demonstrated a fantastic new invention called the telephone, nobody was very interested in it. The first fax machine appeared at around the same time, but it was so enormous that no one wanted one – in fact fax machines didn't become popular for another hundred years.

5 Then there was the walkie-talkie, a small two-way radio first used by the US army in the 1930s. However, since they weighed around 13.5 kilos, the talking was perhaps easier than the walking! After World War Two they became popular with police officers. Before that they had to use whistles to call for help!

6 Nowadays of course we can send messages and pictures around the world in a few seconds using computers and mobile phones. It's hard to believe that e-mail was only invented in 1971, and the first text message was sent in 1992. Today we send over a billion text messages around the world every single day, and an incredible thirty-six billion e-mails!

Vocabulary
Ways of communicating

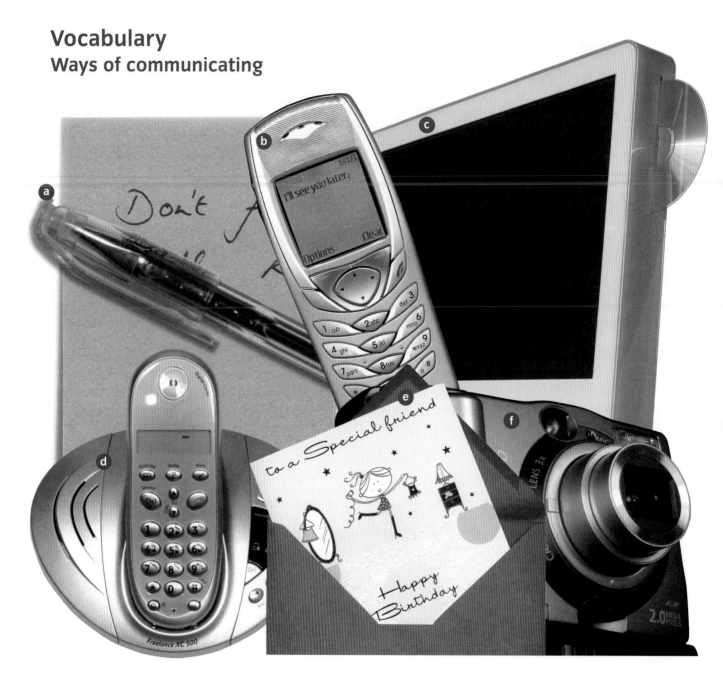

1 What can you see in the photos? Which phrases in the box do you associate with each item?

> take/send a photo
> write a letter
> make a phone call
> write a note
> post a letter/card
> send/receive an e-mail
> go on the Internet
> send a card
> send/get a text message
> leave a message
> check your messages
> call someone

2 **MD** Work in pairs. Complete the sentences in as many ways as you can using the phrases from exercise 1.

a If you need to contact someone urgently, you can … or …
b The cheapest way to keep in touch is to … or …
c If you need to find some information quickly, you can …
d If the person you call doesn't answer, you can …
e 100 years ago if people wanted to communicate with each other, they …
f If you want to wish someone happy birthday, you can …
g If you're on holiday and want to contact your friends, you can …
h If you go out and you want to leave a message for a member of your family, you can …
i If you want to say thank you for a meal or present, you can …
j If you're bored and can't think of anything to do, you can …

Language focus 1
Present perfect

1 **T14.1** Listen to five people talking about different forms of communication. Which question below is each person answering?

> **1 How many phone calls have you made so far today?**
>
> **2 How many e-mails have you received this week?**
>
> **3 How many hours have you spent on the Internet this week?**
>
> **4 How many mobile phones have you owned in your life?**
>
> **5 How many letters have you written this year?**
>
> **6 How much TV have you watched this week?**
>
> **7 How many books have you read this year?**
>
> **8 How many computers have you owned?**

2 **T14.2** Listen and complete the sentences.

a I've spent _____ on the Internet so far this week.
b I haven't watched _____ so far this week.
c I've had _____ in my life so far.
d I haven't written _____ so far this year.
e I've read _____ this week so far.

Grammar

1 We use the Present perfect to describe past actions that are connected to the present. Very often they happen in a time period that is not finished.

*I've sent about ten e-mails (so far **today**).*
*I've owned three computers (**in my life**).*
*I haven't written any letters (**this week**).*

We do not say exactly when these things happened with the Present perfect – it is not important.

2 We form the Present perfect with *have/has* + past participle.

a Regular past participle: verb + *-ed*
I've watched fifteen hours of TV this week.
b Irregular past participles: *made, sent, written, read*
He's read about eight books so far this year.

3 Complete the table.

➕ I/you/we/they	'_____	sent	an e-mail.
he/she	'_____		
➖ I/you/we/they	haven't	got	any text messages.
he/she	_____		
❓ _____	I/you/we/they	written	a note?
_____	he/she		

▶ Read language summary A on page 158.

Practice

1 **a** Write sentences answering the questions in the questionnaire.

I've made two phone calls so far today.

b Compare your sentences in groups.

> I haven't made any phone calls so far today. How about you?

2 **MD** Use your mini-dictionary to find the past participle of the verbs.

a	lose	_____	g	receive	_____
b	forget	_____	h	use	_____
c	phone	_____	i	buy	_____
d	pay	_____	j	take	_____
e	check	_____	k	keep	_____
f	leave	_____	l	have	_____

3 Use the Present perfect to make true sentences for you.

a write a letter in English
b phone the emergency services
c lose your mobile
d forget to post an important letter
e buy a book online
f have a virus on your computer

I've never written a letter in English.
I've written lots of letters in English.

4 Work in pairs. Ask your partner about his/her sentences.

> Have you ever written a letter in English?

> Yes, I have. I've written a few letters in English.

Pronunciation

1 **T14.3** Listen and write down the eight sentences you hear.

2 Listen again and underline the stressed syllables.
I've <u>lost</u> my <u>mo</u>bile.

3 Practise the sentences. Pay attention to the stressed syllables.

123

Hi Mike

Have you spoken to Mum this week? I phoned her yesterday and she sounded really ill, and apparently she was in bed all last weekend. I m away on business until Thursday — could you go round and check that everything s okay? I m a bit worried.

Hope you re okay,

Katie X

Hi Grace

I tried to call you at about three o clock but you weren t at your desk and your voice mail wasn t on. Do you want to come out for a meal tonight? I m celebrating because I ve just passed my driving test. We re going to Chez Max at 8.30. I ve never been there before but everyone says it s fantastic. I really hope you can come — let me know.

Rosie X

PS I ve just heard the news about you and Alex! Congratulations — when did it happen? I want to know all the details!

Language focus 2
Time phrases with the Present perfect and Past simple

1 Read the e-mails above. Answer the questions.

a   What is the relationship between the two people do you think?
b   Why are they sending the e-mail?

2 Underline the Past simple verbs in the e-mails like this _____ and the Present perfect verbs like this ﹏﹏.

Practice

1 Choose the correct tense in the e-mails below.

Hi Mum and Dad!

A quick line to say we (a) ve just arrived / just arrived at Pat and Dave s and we re safe and well, but very tired. The plane (b) has finally landed / finally landed at nine o clock yesterday evening after ten hours delay! We (c) have stayed / stayed in a hotel in London last night, and (d) have caught / caught the train to Cardiff at ten o clock. Dave (e) has just picked / just picked us up from the station.

See you soon.

C and M X

Phil,

Just wanted to say thanks for a great time last weekend — we (f) have really enjoyed / really enjoyed ourselves. The food and company (g) have been / were fantastic, and it (h) has been / was great to see all the family again.

Lucy (i) has started / started her new job this week, and Josh (j) has gone / went back to school, so everyone is very busy.

Take care and thanks again. Speak soon.

All the best,

Simon

> # Grammar
>
> **1 Past simple**
>
> a   **If we say exactly when an action happened in the past, we cannot use the Present perfect. We use the Past simple.**
>
> *I **tried** to call you at **about three o'clock**.*
> *I **phoned** her **yesterday**.*
> *She **was** in bed all **last weekend**.*
>
> **These words show that the action is finished.**
>
> b   **We use the Past simple in questions with When.**
> ***When** did it **happen**?*
>
> **2 Present perfect**
>
> a   **We use the Present perfect with time periods that have not finished.**
> ***Have** you **spoken** to Mum **this week**?*
>
> b   **If we don't say when something happened, we often use the Present perfect, especially with words like just, recently, ever and never.**
> *I've **just passed** my driving test.*
> *Have you **ever been** to Chez Max?*
> *I've **never been** there before.*

▶ Read Language summary B on page 159.

2 a Put the questions into the correct form, Present perfect or Past simple.

1 you pass your driving test? When / you pass?
2 you / take any other exams recently? When / you take them?
3 you / eat in a restaurant this week? When and where / you go?
4 you / be ill at all this year? When / you ill?
5 you / ever / be in hospital?
6 you / ever / go / on a long flight? When and where / you go?
7 you / go to stay with friends recently? Who / you visit?
8 anyone you know / start a new job recently? When / they start?

b Work in pairs. Ask and answer the questions.

Real life
Telephoning

1 a Jane wants to make four telephone calls. Look at her list. Who is she going to call and why?

To phone
- ☐ Julia at Thompson travel about plane tickets
- ☐ Paul about tomorrow night
- ☐ Dad about Mum's birthday present
- ☐ Tania to tell her about the tickets

b **T14.4** Listen and number the calls in the order you hear them.

c Did she speak to everyone on her list? If not, what did she do / is she going to do?

2 Listen again and complete the sentences.

Conversation 1
a Hello, _____ Paul, please?
b Sorry, _____ .
c Do you know when _____ ?
Conversation 2
d Hello, _____ Jane Hancock. _____ the flight tickets.
Conversation 3
e This is Tania Shaw. Sorry _____ .
f Please _____ after the tone.
g Hi, it's Jane here. _____ back?
Conversation 4
h Hello Mum, _____ . Is _____ ?
i Can you _____ ?

Pronunciation

1 **T14.5** Listen and repeat, copying the polite intonation.
Hello, can I speak to Paul, please?
Is that Julia?
Can you call me back?
Is Dad there?
Can you ask him to call me?

2 **T14.6** Listen and repeat.
Speaking.   Sorry, he's not here.   Yes, of course.

---

3 Complete the telephone calls.

a You phone your friend, Joe. His sister, Suzi answers.

SUZI: Hello?
YOU: (1) _____
SUZI: I'm not sure if he's in … just a minute. JOE!!! Sorry he's not here. He's probably still at college. He's usually here after four o'clock.
YOU: (2) _____
SUZI: Okay, what's your number?
YOU: (3) _____
SUZI: Okay, I'll tell him.
YOU: (4) _____
SUZI: Bye.

b You call your friend, Sergio, but you hear an answering machine message.

SERGIO: Hello, this is Sergio speaking. I'm afraid I'm not here at the moment, but if you'd like to leave a message, please speak after the tone. (BEEP)
YOU: _____
_____

4 Work in pairs. Practise both calls. Use your own names.

How do you feel about communication technology?

I How often do you use your mobile?
A I use it all the time – to call people, to take photos, for the Internet. It's an essential part of my life.
B I use it a lot. It's the main way I keep in touch with people.
C I use it for important calls when I'm out, but that's all.
D I don't have one.

2 How do you feel about the phone?
A I really hate calling people. I wait for them to call me.
B My phone calls are short. I just say what I need to say.
C If I'm not busy, I enjoy long phone chats with my friends.
D I love my phone. I spend hours every day chatting – I couldn't live without it!

3 How do you feel about computers?
A I love them. I spend a lot of my free time on the computer. It's my favourite way to relax.
B They're really useful in my job/studies, etc. but I'm not really interested in them.
C I use a computer sometimes but I don't like them.
D I'm a bit frightened of computers. I don't know how to use one.

4 What do you think about e-mail?
A It's a fantastic way of keeping in touch with people you don't see very often.
B It's better than phoning because you don't need to talk to the other person.
C It's okay for some situations, but with friends, I prefer to phone.
D I never use it.

5 How often do you use chat rooms on the Internet?
A All the time. I love them!
B Quite often.
C I go into them sometimes, but I'm not very interested really.
D I've never been in a chat room.

6 A new mobile/computer with lots of new features appears in the shops. How do you feel?
A Excited – I want one ... now!
B I'll wait and see what other people say about them.
C Oh, no! Not something new to learn about!
D I don't pay any attention. I'm not interested.

7 How do you keep in touch with your friends? Put these in order of most to least important.
A texting   **c** e-mail
B phone   **D** letters

Task: Analyse a questionnaire
Preparation: reading

MD Work individually. Complete the questionnaire on the left.

Task: speaking

1 Work in pairs. Ask and answer the questions, explaining why you feel that way. Keep a note of your partner's answers.

▶ Useful language a

2 You are going to summarise the similarities and differences between you and your partner. Plan what you will say.

▶ Useful language b

3 Work in groups, but not with your partner. Summarise your own and your partner's answers.

4 Discuss with the class. Do your friends use communication technology in the same way as you? Is there a big difference between you and your parents/grandparents?

Useful language

a Discussing your answers
I agree.
I'm the same.
I'm completely different because ...
Personally, I (love the phone).

b Comparing
She uses (the Internet) a lot, but I never (use it).
She never (sends e-mails).
He loves/hates (new things).
He thinks (computers are boring), but I (love them).

Revising

1 At the end of a course, it is a good idea to revise what you have studied. Which approach below do you think is best each time, a or b?

a You revise for about half an hour to an hour every day.

b You do all your revision in one evening/weekend.

a You read through your Students' Book and notebook and hope that you can remember what you have read.

b You read through your books and try to do old exercises again to check that you can remember. If you can't, you go back and study that section again.

a You try not to worry if there is something you don't understand.

b You ask your teacher or check in the language summary if there is something you don't understand.

2 Compare opinions with other students. Do you have any other ideas for revising?

Pronunciation spot

The sounds /æ/ and /ʌ/

a Use the irregular verb list on page 149 to complete the gaps with the Past simple and Past participle forms of the verbs.

		Past simple	Past participle
1	run	_ran_	_run_
2	sing	___	___
3	drink	___	___
4	ring	___	___

b T14.7 Listen and check. Notice the difference between sound 1 /æ/ and sound 2 /ʌ/.

1 /æ/	2 /ʌ/
r<u>a</u>n	r<u>u</u>n

c T14.8 Listen to ten words and decide if they are sound 1 /æ/ or sound 2 /ʌ/.

---

1 Ways of communicating ☐

Complete the sentences. (There may be more than one answer.)

a You see a beautiful view so you get out your camera and _take a photo_ .

b You phone a friend, but her brother answers and says that she's out so you _____ .

c You borrow your friend's mobile to _____ .

d When you come home, you play your answering machine to _____ .

e It's your friend's birthday so you _____ .

▶ **Need to check? Vocabulary, page 122.**

2 Present perfect ☐

Complete the sentences with the Present perfect form of the verb.

a I _'ve been_ (go) abroad twice this year.

b I _____ (never break) an arm or leg.

c I _____ (miss) an English lesson this week.

d I _____ (never steal) anything.

e I _____ (go) out a lot in the evening recently.

f I _____ (just have) lunch.

▶ **Need to check? Language summary A, page 158.**

3 Time phrases with the Present perfect and Past simple ☐

Use the time phrases to decide if the verb in brackets should be Present perfect (PP) or Past simple (PS).

a I (see) your cousin yesterday. PS

b My parents (just come back) from Paris.

c My sister (take) her driving test last week, but she (not pass).

d I (never meet) her husband.

e We're too late! The film (start) at 7.15.

f (you ever go) skiing?

▶ **Need to check? Language summary B, page 159.**

4 Telephone language ☐

Complete the phone conversations with the phrases in the box.

ask him to call me   call me back   can I speak to   he's not here   of course

A: Hello, (a) _____ Richard, please?

B: Hi Jan. I'm sorry, (b) _____ at the moment.

A: Can you (c) _____ ?

B: Yes, (d) _____ .

C: ... please leave a message after the tone. (BEEP)

D: Hi Mark. It's Julie. Can you (e) _____ ?

▶ **Need to check? Real life, page 125.**

REMEMBER!

Look back at the areas you have practised. Tick the ones you feel confident about. Now try the MINI-CHECK on page 163 to check what you know!

Going places

▶ Prepositions of movement
▶ *have to*, *don't have to*, *can* and *can't*
▶ Vocabulary: Things in a town
▶ Listening: A tour of Edinburgh
▶ Real life: Following directions
▶ Task: Plan a website about your town

Vocabulary
Things in a town

1 **MD** Look at the photos of five cities. Which of the things in the box can you see?

a palace	a bridge	a canal
a cathedral	a church	a hill
a sports stadium	a mountain	a river
a shopping centre	a square	a mosque
traditional buildings	an art gallery	a temple
beautiful views	modern buildings	a statue

2 a **T15.1** Listen to five people talking about their cities. Which things in the box do they mention?

1 Fabrizio from Venice, Italy
2 Yumi from Kyoto, Japan
3 Murat from Istanbul, Turkey
4 Claudia from Rio de Janeiro, Brazil
5 Marina from St Petersburg, Russia

b Which of these cities would you most like to visit. Why?

┌─────────────────────────────────────┐
│ **Pronunciation** │
│ │
│ **T15.2** Listen and repeat. Then write the words in │
│ the correct column according to the stress. │
│ │
│ | ● • | • ● | ● • • | • ● • | │
│ |-----|-----|-------|-------| │
│ | *river* | | | | │
└─────────────────────────────────────┘

3 Look at some postcards from other cities on page 145. Choose one and describe it to your partner. Your partner says which one it is.

4 Work in pairs. Describe your town/city.

(There are a lot of parks.)　(There isn't a beach.)

128

1 Venice
2 Kyoto
3 Istanbul
4 Rio de Janeiro
5 St Petersburg

Scottish National Gallery

John Knox's House

The Royal Mile

Holyrood Palace

Edinburgh Castle

Listening
A tour of Edinburgh

1 Look at the photos. What do you know about Edinburgh?

2 **T15.3** Rosa and Marcus are taking a bus tour. Listen to the guided tour and match the pictures to the extracts.

Extract 1 ☐
Extract 2 ☐
Extract 3 ☐
Extract 4 ☐
Extract 5 ☐

3 **MD** Listen again and complete the sentences with the correct numbers.

a   St Margaret's Chapel, the oldest part of the building, is nearly _____ years old.
b   The Royal Mile is Edinburgh's longest street. It's _____ kilometres long.
c   John Knox's house is about _____ years old.
d   John Knox was a religious reformer who died in _____ .
e   There are about _____ paintings in the Scottish National Gallery.
f   The Gallery opens at _____ o'clock.
g   Mary Queen of Scots lived in Holyrood Palace from 1561 until _____ .

4 Work in pairs. Ask and answer about the places Rosa and Marcus visit.

How old is St Margaret's Chapel?

5 Discuss these questions.

• Have you ever visited Britain? Where did you go?
• Would you like to visit Edinburgh?
• Which other cities in the world would you really like to visit? Why?

129

Language focus 1
Prepositions of movement

1 Read about Richard. Complete the phrases with the words in the box.

> bridge building road steps taxi
> airport statue ~~stairs~~ park river

2 T15.4 Listen and check your answers.

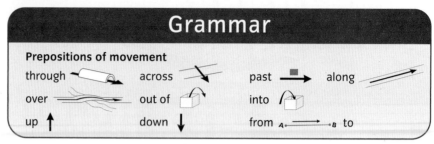

Grammar

Prepositions of movement

through   across   past   along

over   out of   into

up   down   from A——B to

▶ Read Language summary A on page 159.

One day, Richard had a problem at work, so he went for a walk … a very long walk. He walked …

a **down** the _stairs_

b **out** of the _____

c **across** the _____

d **through** the _____

e **over** the _____

f **along** the _____

g **past** a _____

h **up** some _____

i then he got **into** a _____

j which drove him **from** the river to the _____

k and nobody ever saw him again!

Practice

Pronunciation

Listen to recording 4 again and repeat. Pay attention to the stress.

1 Work in pairs. Close your books and describe Richard's walk. Can you remember it exactly?

2 Which prepositions can you use with these things? Think of as many ideas as you can.

> a ladder   a bridge   a field   a square   a shopping centre
> the platform at a station   a road   a car   a hill   a river

> You can go up or down a ladder.

> Or under a ladder.

3 a **MD** Look at the picture. Which of these things can you see?

> a journey   scenery   a track   a tunnel   a ski resort   heights

b Choose the correct alternatives. Use the picture to help you.

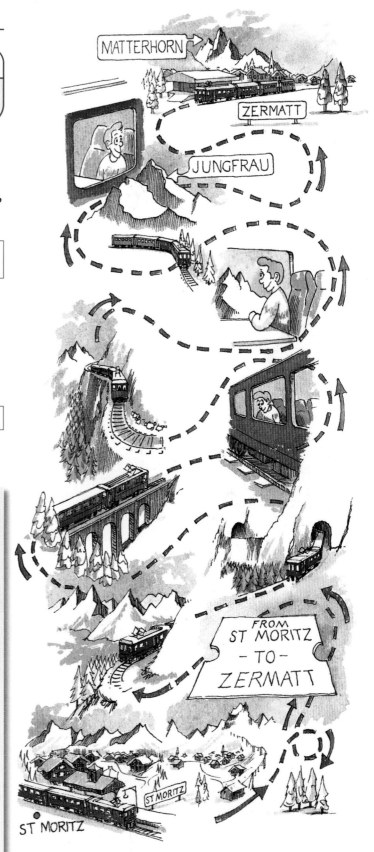

The Glacier Express

As your train moves (1) under / out of the little railway station at St Moritz, get ready for a day to remember! The journey (2) to / from the ski resort of St Moritz (3) to / from the attractive town of Zermatt is only 290 kilometres, but on the way it passes (4) over / through some of the most beautiful scenery in Europe.

During its journey the train goes (5) into / through ninety-one tunnels and travels (6) over / past nearly 300 bridges. If you don't like heights. Don't look (7) up / down when you travel (8) over / under the Oberalp Pass – the track is nearly two thousand metres high!

As you look (9) into / out of the train window you can see some of Switzerland's most amazing mountains – the train goes (10) past / up mountains like the famous Jungfrau. And as your train comes (11) into / out of the station at Zermatt, if you look (12) down / up you will see the Matterhorn, Switzerland's highest mountain.

4 a Cover the text and use the picture to describe the train journey, using the correct prepositions.

b Would you like to travel on this train? Why / Why not?

131

Language focus 2
have to, don't have to, can and can't

Mon–Fri, 8.30am–6.30pm
£1.50 for 2 hours

Mon–Fri, 6.30pm–8.30am
Sunday, all day
FREE

NO BALL
GAMES

SMOKING
AREA

ENTRY FEES

ADULTS: €10
CHILDREN OVER 5: €4
CHILDREN UNDER 5: FREE

MasterCard ✔
VISA ✔
AMERICAN EXPRESS ✘

Passport
control
please show
your passport

OUT OF
ORDER

VACANT

DO NOT
WALK
ON THE
GRASS

1 **MD** Look at all the signs on this page and check any words you don't know. Which signs might you see:
- in the street?
- in a park?
- at an airport?
- in a hospital?
- in a museum?

2 Match the signs a–c with the meanings below.

You **can** ride a bicycle here, but you **can't** drive your car. ☐
You **have to** stop. ☐
You **don't have to** pay in the evening or on Sundays. ☐

Grammar

Look at the verbs in bold in exercise 2. Which means:
- it is necessary to do this?
- it isn't necessary to do this?
- it's okay to do this?
- it isn't okay to do this?

▶ Read Language summaries B and C on page 159.

Practice

1 **a** **MD** Match signs d–m to the sentences below.

1 Dogs _____ go here. ☐
2 You _____ play football here. ☐
3 You _____ take photos. ☐
4 Adults and children over five _____ pay, but children under five _____ pay. ☐
5 You _____ use this toilet. ☐
6 You _____ use Visa or Mastercard but you _____ use American Express. ☐
7 You _____ show your passport. ☐
8 You _____ use a mobile in here. ☐
9 You _____ walk on the paths, not the grass. ☐
10 You _____ smoke in this area. ☐

b Complete the sentences with *have to, don't have to, can* or *can't*.

2 a (MD) Make sentences about school, prison and the army. Use the prompts in the box and *can, can't, have to* and *don't have to*.

You have to wear a uniform in the army.

wear a uniform	study
do a lot of exercise	watch TV
obey instructions	take exams
go out in the evening	smoke
have short hair	work hard
earn your living	get up early

b Compare sentences with a partner.

> You don't have to study in prison.

> Yes, but you can study in prison sometimes.

Pronunciation

1 (T15.5) Listen and write down the sentences. Notice the pronunciation of *have to*.

/hæv tə/
You have to wear a uniform.

/hæv tə/
You don't have to take exams.

2 Listen again and repeat.

Real life
Following directions

1 Have you got a good sense of direction? Do you find it easy to give/follow directions?

2 Check the meaning of these phrases.

1 It's on the right.
2 Go straight on.
3 It's on the left.
4 Take the first street on the left.
5 Take the second street on the right.

3 a (T15.6) Four people ask for directions in the street. Look at the maps below, then listen and write a cross where they want to go.

b (T15.7) Listen and complete the sentences.

1 Excuse me, is the National Gallery _____ ?
2 Yes, it's over there _____ , look.
3 Excuse me, but _____ post office?
4 It's very _____ – go _____ and it's _____ – it's _____ metres.
5 Sorry, but _____ to the river?
6 Yes, take _____ over there, can you see it?
7 Well, _____ for about _____ and you're there.
8 Take the _____ on _____ .

4 Work in pairs. Look at Recording 6 on page 175 and practise the conversations.

5 Imagine you are standing in front of your school. Take turns with your partner to ask for and give directions to places nearby.

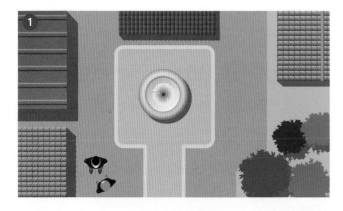

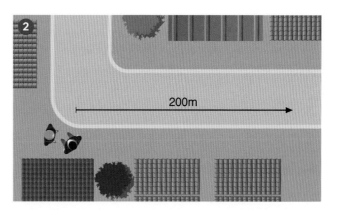

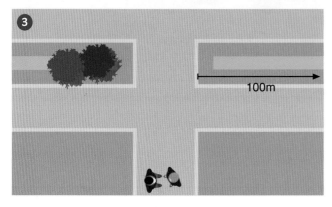

Task: Plan a website about your town

Preparation: vocabulary and reading

1 If you are visiting a new city or area, how do you find out about places of interest?

– on the Internet
– from a guidebook
– from tourist information
– from people you know

2 **MD** Look at the sections on the website. Which adjectives in the box can complete the gaps? (There are many possibilities.)

comfortable	friendly	traditional	difficult
interesting	modern	attractive	lively
fashionable	expensive	peaceful	fun
value for money	delicious	excellent	easy

Task: speaking

1 **a** You are compiling information for a tourist website about a town you know well (either your own or one you have visited) using the ideas above.

b Work individually or in pairs. Make a list of places to include in each section.

2 Think about how you will describe each place. Make notes and ask your teacher for any words or phrases you need.

3 Work in pairs.

Either Explain your web page to your partner, describing the places you want to include and why you recommend them.

▶ Useful language a and b

Or Act out a conversation in the tourist information office. Student A: You are a visitor to the town, with lots of questions about where to go and what to do. Student B: Answer Student A's questions and make recommendations. Then swap roles.

▶ Useful language b and c

Visit our city!

Top places to see
Don't miss the (a) *lively/traditional/attractive* town square.
You will also find many (b) _____ buildings.

Recommended hotels
This small family hotel is (c) _____ and _____ .

Recommended restaurants
… is famous for its (d) _____ food and _____ service.

Shopping
You will find many (e) _____ shops in the town centre. On Saturdays you can visit the marke which is very (f) _____ .

Parking

Parking in the main square is very (g) _____ .

Nightlife

This (h) _____ club has a _____ atmosphere that you will really enjoy.

For families

This fantastic theme park will provide a (i) _____ day for all the family.

Places to visit nearby

This (j) _____ village is just five kilometres from the town centre.

Useful language

a Explaining your web page

I/We chose ... because it's ...

The best (place for shopping/families) is ...

A good (restaurant/hotel/place to visit) is ...

... is/isn't very good.

b Recommending

I recommend ... because ...

Go to ... – you'll really enjoy it.

You can/could try ...

I don't recommend ... because ...

c Asking questions

Can you recommend a good (hotel)?

What are the best places to visit?

What about (restaurants)?

How do I get there?

Is it easy to park?

Follow up: writing

Either Write an introduction to the web page making recommendations to visitors.

If you go to ... , there is lots to see and do. You can go to / visit ... It's really interesting/beautiful/peaceful. I also recommend ... There's a beautiful view / very lively atmosphere.

If you need a hotel, try ... It's very friendly/comfortable, or you can try ...

For eating, I recommend ... It's very ... and the service is ...

In the evening, you could try ... or ...

If you come to visit with your family, I recommend ... and ...

Or Make a poster showing all the information you will put on the website. (You can include photos and illustrations if you want.)

CONSOLIDATION

A Verb practice

Write the correct form of the verb in brackets. You can use the Present simple, the Past simple or the Present perfect.

Matt Groening is the man who (1) _invented_ (invent) the world's most popular cartoon. People in almost 100 countries (2) _____ (watch) *The Simpsons* every week. Groening (3) _____ (be born) in Portland, Oregon in 1954. When he (4) _____ (be) twenty-six he (5) _____ (start) drawing cartoons for *The Los Angeles Reader*, a weekly newspaper. In 1986 Matt (6) _____ (invent) the Simpson family for the popular *Tracey Ullman Show*. He (7) _____ (give) them the names of his family: Matt's father's name is Homer, his mother is Margaret, and he (8) _____ (have got) two sisters, Lisa and Maggie.

The short *Simpsons* cartoons (9) _____ (be) very popular, and in 1989 Fox studios (10) _____ (pay) twenty million dollars for Groening to produce thirteen thirty-minute programmes. After the first show at Christmas 1989, *The Simpsons* (11) _____ (make) two billion dollars just for Simpson tee-shirts, toys and other merchandise!

Groening and his artists, musicians and actors (12) _____ (make) fifteen series of programmes so far, and in spring 2005 the show (13) _____ (become) the longest-running comedy in the history of American TV. Many famous people (14) _____ (appear) on the show, including the actress Elizabeth Taylor, Bono from the rock band U2, British Prime Minister Tony Blair and three US Presidents: Presidents Carter, Clinton and Bush!

B Articles

Complete the gaps in the joke with *a*, *an*, *the* or – (no article).

It was (1) _a_ fine summer day in Sherwood Forest in (2) _____ England, and the year was 1194. Early in (3) _____ morning (4) _____ poor man went into (5) _____ forest to try and find some wood for his fire. Suddenly (6) _____ man wearing (7) _____ green shirt and (8) _____ green trousers rode up and dropped (9) _____ bag of money into (10) _____ poor man's hands. 'Who are you?' asked (11) _____ poor man. 'I'm Robin Hood,' said (12) _____ man in green. 'I take (13) _____ money from rich people and I give it to poor people.' 'Hurrah! hurrah!' said (14) _____ poor man. 'I'm rich! I'm rich!' Robin Hood thought for (15) _____ minute. Then he took out his sword. He pointed (16) _____ sword at (17) _____ man and said, 'Rich, are you? Well, then, give me (18) _____ money!'

C Writing and speaking

1 Work in pairs. Choose one of the following situations and write a short conversation (7–10 lines). Use the page numbers to help you.

a   This is the end of your English course. Talk to another student about your plans or interview a famous person on television about his or her plans.
   Module 12 page 104 and Module 13 page 116

b   An English-speaking tourist is lost in your town and asks you for directions (first decide where you are in town). Give her/him directions.
   Module 15 page 133

c   Telephone a school in Britain. Ask for some information about courses for learning English. You also want to find out about accommodation.
   Module 13 pages 116–117 and Module 14 page 125

d   You are sitting in a café with an Australian friend. It is in the afternoon and you want to go somewhere together in the evening. Try to decide where to go.
   Module 12 page 107

2 Now practise your conversation. Where are the stressed words? Do you need to use polite intonation?

3 Act out your conversation in front of the class.

D Listening: Song: *Trains and Boats and Planes*

1 The words in the box are all in the song. Work in pairs. Check the meaning of any words you don't know. What do you think the story of the song is?

Paris	in love	wait	promised	a trip
had to go back	wish	Rome	a star	

Trains and Boats and Planes

Trains and boats and planes are (going) by
They mean a journey to Paris or Rome
To someone else but not for me.
The trains and boats and planes
Carried you away, away from me.
We are so in love, and high above
We had a ring to wish upon. Wish
And dreams come true, but not for me
The trains and boats and planes
Carried you away, away from me.
You are from another part of the country,
You had to go back a while and then
You said you soon would come back again.
I wait here like I promised to.
I wait here but where are you?
Trains and boats and planes took you away,
But every time I watch them I pray
And if my prayers can cross the land
The trains and the boats and planes
Will bring you back, back here to me.

(Burt Bacharach)

2 `C1` Look at the lines printed in red in the song above. Find one word that is different from the song. Listen and circle the word that is different.

3 Listen to the song again and write in the correct words.

~~going~~ → passing

4 Which is the correct story of the song, a or b?

a He travelled to Paris and Rome on holiday by train and boat and plane. He met her and they fell in love and had dreams about their future, but she had to return to her country. He promised to visit her but he didn't, so she feels very unhappy.

b She met a man in her country and they fell in love. He returned to his country and he promised to come back to her, but he didn't. Usually when she sees trains and boats and planes she thinks about holidays and feels happy, but now when she sees them she thinks of him and is unhappy.

5 Work in pairs. Discuss these questions.

a Have you got any friends from different countries? Where and when did you meet them?

b Have you ever met someone nice or interesting on holiday? Where and when?

E Vocabulary: Word groups

Find three words in the word square for each topic.

S	P	O	R	T	S	S	T	A	D	I	U	M
D	O	N	K	E	Y	X	C	F	O	G	G	Y
A	B	Y	A	W	W	G	E	I	C	L	W	S
R	M	O	N	D	I	P	L	A	V	A	M	N
T	E	N	G	I	N	E	E	R	I	N	G	O
G	M	U	A	T	D	R	P	E	Q	G	X	W
A	A	K	R	F	Y	S	H	S	Z	U	T	I
L	I	W	O	T	I	K	A	J	H	A	D	N
L	L	D	O	B	W	J	N	O	H	G	P	G
E	Z	Q	E	R	M	A	T	H	S	E	T	Y
R	G	S	Q	U	A	R	E	G	H	S	L	P
Y	L	E	T	T	E	R	R	P	H	O	N	E

animals	*donkey*
weather	
school subjects	
ways of communicating	
things in a town	

Module 6: Real life, exercise 4, page 58

Student A: Choose something to eat and drink from the menu. Order your food.
Student B: Take Student A's order. Tell him/her how much it costs.
Then swap roles.

Menu

Breakfast

croissant and jam	1.50
fried eggs, tomatoes and toast	2.00
sausages and eggs	2.25

Burgers

king size	3.00
classic	2.75
with cheese	3.25

Cakes – *homemade*

chocolate	1.50
coffee	1.50
apple	1.75

Drinks

tea	1.00	hot chocolate	1.00
coffee	1.50	lemonade	1.00
mineral water	1.75	fruit juice	1.00

Sandwiches

tuna mayonnaise	2.50
egg mayonnaise	2.50
cheese and tomato	2.50

Extras

French fries	2.00
salad	2.50
bread	1.50

Module 5: Real life, exercise 5, page 49

Student A

> It is 9.30 in the morning and you are in Brighton, in the south of England. You have information about trains to London: The next train is at 9.49. It arrives in London at 10.40. It costs £10.40 for a single ticket and £16.50 for a day return ticket. It leaves from platform 3.

Module 1: Practice, exercise 3, page 12

Student A

Antonio Banderas – actor – Spain – married – born 1960	Christina Aguilera – singer – the USA – single – born 1980

Module 4: Task, exercise 1, page 39

Student A

Hi, My name's Marina, and I come from Tachov in the Czech Republic. It's a town in the west of the country. I'm eighteen years old and I study engineering at the university here. I am interested in all types of sport, especially hockey and basketball. I also love reading and computers and I love dogs – my family have four!
Please write back!

Marina

Hi! My name's Joao and I come from Bela Horizonte in the south of Brazil. I'm twenty-five years old and I'm at university. I'm studying languages at university. I speak Portuguese (of course) and also English and Spanish. I love rock music, but I don't like classical music. I'm also very interested in sport. I play tennis every day. I want to talk to people from all over the world to learn more about their culture.

Joao

ACTIVITIES

Module 1: Task, exercise 1, page 14

Student B

1 Look at Chrissie's documents and complete the table about Chrissie.

US DRIVER'S LICENCE

Full Name
Christina Elizabeth NAGANO

Date of Birth   10.10.82

Mrs Chrissie Nagano,
4685 Sterling Drive
Boulder
Colorado 80301
United States

Creations

Chrissie Nagano
Marketing Manager

Fax 324 • 471 • 0807
Cellphone 324 • 809 • 6439
E-mail chrissie@creations.com

Digital Creations for a Changing Planet

Useful language

a Questions

What's his first name / surname / full name?

How do you spell it?

What's her work / home / mobile number?

What's his job?

How old is she?

Where's he from?

Is she married?

b Other useful phrases

I don't know.

Sorry, I don't understand.

2 Ask Student A questions about Jamie. Write the information on the table.

▶ Useful language a and b

	Chrissie	Jamie
Full name		
Age		
Address		
Job		
Where from?		
E-mail address		
Telephone number		
Married / Single?		

Communication activities

Module 3: Real life, exercise 4, page 30

Student A

Ask and answer with your partner to complete the gaps.

> What time is *Jennifer Lopez in concert* on?

> It's on Wednesday at twenty to eight.

TV THIS WEEK

Don't miss …

Jennifer Lopez in concert (1 _____ , Channel 5)
Two hours of Jennifer Lopez in concert at Wembley Arena last month
Holiday! (Thurs 7.25, BBC 1)
Holiday reports from Hong Kong, Morocco, Budapest and Rio de Janeiro
Friends (2 _____ , Channel 4)
Ross and Rachel go to the beach (R)
Live Football (Sat 2.45, Sky Sports 2)
Chelsea V Manchester United … the big one!
Romeo and Juliet (3 _____ , BBC 2)
The Kirov Ballet perform the classic ballet at the Royal Opera House

Best films

The Matrix (USA, 1999) (Mon 9.55, Channel 4)
Sci-fi action starring Keanu Reeves
Shrek (USA, 2001) (4 _____ , BBC 1)
Comedy for all the family
Love Actually (UK 2003) (Wed 8.15 and 11.45, Sky Movies plus) For the first time on TV

Module 1: Practice, exercise 3, page 12

Student B

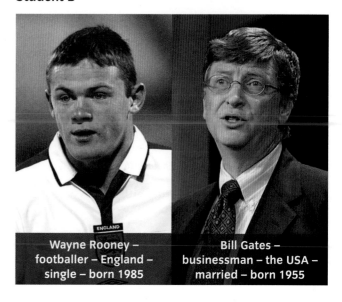

Wayne Rooney – footballer – England – single – born 1985

Bill Gates – businessman – the USA – married – born 1955

Module 4: Task, exercise 1, page 39

Student B

My name's Peter and I come from Singapore. I'm twenty-six years old and I'm a hotel receptionist. I speak two languages English and Mandarin Chinese. My interests are writing and listening to music, playing softball, going to the movies and going out with my friends. I also like cooking and I want to make friends all over the world.

Peter

Hello! My name's Sofia and I come from Santander, a town in the north of Spain. I'm twenty-two years old and I also study music (at the University of Santander) and play the guitar – the Spanish classical guitar. I speak French as well as English (and Spanish, of course) and love football and tennis. I love going to the cinema and going out with my friends. I love all animals, especially cats. We've got five! I hope you write back!

Sofia

Module 13: Task, exercise 2a, page 116

Taka

26 years old, from Japan.
Works as a junior fashion designer in Japan. Staying in England for one year to improve her (very good) English. Wants to do a course where she will meet and talk to people to use her English.

Interests: dance, fashion, photography.

Needs to learn more about computers for her job.

Module 11: Task, exercise 1b, page 102

FANTASTIC FACTS C

GEOGRAPHY
Riyadh is the capital of Saudi Arabia.
Zagreb is the capital of Croatia.
Hanoi is the capital of Vietnam.

NUMBERS
There are 100,000 centimetres in a kilometre.
There are 86,400 seconds in a day.
There are 50 states in the USA.

LANGUAGES
In Jamaica they speak English.
In Brazil they speak Portuguese.
The official languages of Hong Kong are Chinese and English.

SPORT
The 1996 Olympics were in Atlanta in the USA.
There are five players in a basketball team.
The 2002 football world cup was in Japan and Korea.

Module 5: Task, exercise 1, page 48

TRANSPORT SURVEY

1 drive / car? ○
_____

2 ride / bicycle? ○
_____

3 How far / travel every week?
_____
- 0 to 10 kilometres ○
- 11 to 50 kilometres ○
- 51 to 100 kilometres ○
- more than 100 kilometres ○

4 How often / use public transport?
_____
- every day ○
- often, but not every day ○
- sometimes ○
- never ○

5 What / think of public transport in your town?
_____
- excellent ○
- good ○
- okay ○
- poor ○
- I don't know ○

6 How / travel to school or work every day?
_____
- by car ○
- by bus ○
- on foot ○
- other ○

7 How long / your journey?
_____
- 1 to 10 minutes ○
- 10 to 30 minutes ○
- 30 to 60 minutes ○
- more than an hour ○

8 Which of these types of transport / like best?
_____
- train ○
- bus ○
- car ○
- walking ○

Module 3: Real life, exercise 4, page 30

Student B

Ask and answer with your partner to complete the gaps.

> What time is *Holiday!* on?

> It's on Thursday at twenty-five past seven.

TV THIS WEEK

Don't miss ...

Jennifer Lopez in concert (Wed 7.40, Channel 5)
Two hours of Jennifer Lopez in concert at Wembley Arena last month
Holiday! (1 _____ , BBC 1)
Holiday reports from Hong Kong, Morocco, Budapest and Rio de Janeiro
Friends (Fri 9.15, Channel 4)
Ross and Rachel go to the beach (R)
Live Football (2 _____ , Sky Sports 2)
Chelsea V Manchester United ... the big one!
Romeo and Juliet (Sun 8.20, BBC 2)
The Kirov Ballet perform the classic ballet at the Royal Opera House.

Best films

The Matrix (USA, 1999) (3 _____ , Channel 4)
Sci-fi action starring Keanu Reeves
Shrek (USA, 2001) (Sun 3.30, BBC 1)
Comedy for all the family
Love Actually (UK 2003) (4 _____ and 5 _____ , Sky Movies plus)
For the first time on TV

Module 11: Task, exercise 1b, page 102

FANTASTIC FACTS B

GEOGRAPHY

Lake Titicaca is between Bolivia and Peru.
Lake Geneva is between Switzerland and France.
Lake Victoria is between Uganda, Tanzania and Kenya.

FOOD AND DRINK

Sushi is Japanese food (made with rice and fish).
Borscht is Russian soup.
Merlot is a type of red wine.

SPORT

Justine Henin Hardenne won the women's title in the US tennis open in 2003.
Brazil won the world cup in football in 1958, 1962, 1970, 1994 and 2002.
Justin Gatlin won the men's 100m in the Athens Olympic Games in 2004.

FAMOUS PEOPLE

Walt Disney was born in 1901 and died in 1966.
Napoleon was born in Corsica (an island that is part of France) in 1769.
King Henry the eighth of England had six wives.

Module 9: Real life, exercise 4, page 83

Student A

1 Go to the local store and try to buy these things.

some shampoo	*a baseball cap*
a cake	*some postcards*
a film for your camera	

2 You are the shop assistant in a local store. Look at the information and serve the customer.

Prices

bananas	£1.60 a kilo
stamps	(Europe 35 pence, Other 60 pence)
T-shirts	small £9.99 medium £10.99 large £11.99
toothpaste	£1.30

Module 9: Task, exercise 1, page 84

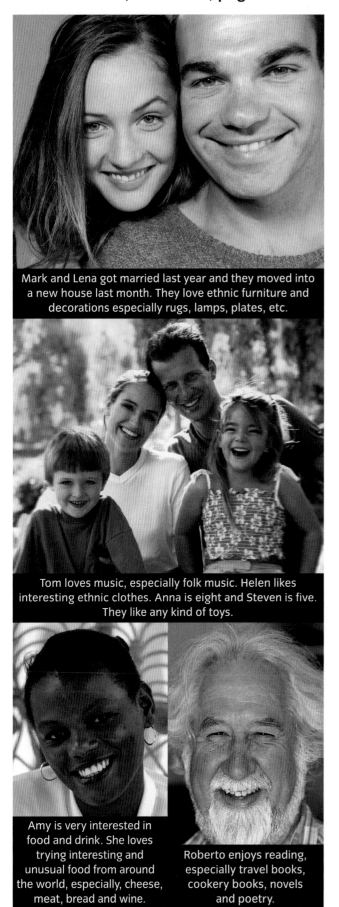

Mark and Lena got married last year and they moved into a new house last month. They love ethnic furniture and decorations especially rugs, lamps, plates, etc.

Tom loves music, especially folk music. Helen likes interesting ethnic clothes. Anna is eight and Steven is five. They like any kind of toys.

Amy is very interested in food and drink. She loves trying interesting and unusual food from around the world, especially, cheese, meat, bread and wine.

Roberto enjoys reading, especially travel books, cookery books, novels and poetry.

Consolidation modules 6–10, Listening, exercise D, page 94

Student A

Return to Sender

1 Listen to the song and complete the gaps.

I (1) _____ a letter to the postman,
He put it in his sack.
Bright and early next (2) _____ .
He brought my letter back.

She (3) _____ upon it:
'Return to sender, address unknown.
No such (4) _____ , no such zone. [1]'
We had a quarrel [2], a lover's spat [2]
I write 'I'm (5) _____ ,' but my letter keeps coming back.

So when I dropped it in the mailbox
I (6) _____ it 'special D [3]'.
Bright and early next morning
It (7) _____ right back to me.

She wrote upon it:
'Return to sender, (8) _____ unknown.
No such number, no such zone.'

This time I'm gonna take it myself
And (9) _____ it right in her hand.
And if it comes back the very next day
Then I'll (10) _____ the writing on it

Return to sender, address unknown.
No such number, no such zone.

[1] a zone = a part of a city or town
[2] a quarrel/a spat = an angry argument (not an important one)
[3] special D = Special delivery

(Otis Blackwell – Winfield Scott)

2 Now check your answers with Student B.

Module 11: Reading, exercise 1, page 96

The false fact is the one about volcanoes. Australia is the only continent with no active volcanoes, not Africa.

Module 6: Language focus 3, page 56

Answers to quiz

1c   2a   3a   4b

Communication activities

Consolidation modules 6–10, Listening, exercise D, page 94

Student B

Return to Sender

1 Listen to the song and complete the gaps.

> I gave a letter to the postman,
> He (1) _____ it in his sack.
> Bright and early next morning,
> He (2) _____ my letter back.
>
> She wrote upon it:
> 'Return to sender, (3) _____ unknown.
> No such number, no such zone. [1] '
> We (4) _____ a quarrel [2], a lover's spat [2]
> I write 'I'm sorry,' but my letter keeps
> coming back.
>
> So when I (5) _____ it in the mailbox
> I sent it 'special D [3].'
> Bright and (6) _____ next morning
> It came right back to me.
>
> She (7) _____ upon it:
> 'Return to sender, address unknown.
> No such (8) _____ , no such zone.'
>
> This time I'm gonna (9) _____ it myself
> And put it right in her hand.
> And if it (10) _____ back the very next day
> Then I'll understand the writing on it
>
> Return to sender, address unknown.
> No such number, no such zone.
>
> [1] a zone = a part of a city or town
> [2] a quarrel/a spat = an angry argument (not an important one)
> [3] special D = Special delivery
>
> *(Otis Blackwell – Winfield Scott)*

2 Now check your answers with Student A.

Module 5: Real life, exercise 4, page 49

Student B

> **It is 11.30 in the morning. You have information about trains to Glasgow in Scotland from London: The next train is at 12.00 It arrives in Glasgow at 5.30. It costs £33 for a single ticket and £55 for a return. It leaves from platform 5.**

Module 11: Task, exercise 1b, page 102

FANTASTIC FACTS A

CAPITAL CITIES
Santiago is the capital of Chile.
Sofia is the capital of Bulgaria.
Kuala Lumpur is the capital of Malaysia.

RIVERS
The River Seine is in Paris.
The River Volga is in Russia.
The River Ganges is in India.

FOOD AND DRINK
Sake is Japanese rice wine.
Tagine is Moroccan food (made with meat and vegetables).
Rigatoni is a type of pasta.

FAMOUS PEOPLE
Marie Curie discovered radium, and won the Nobel Prize in 1903.
Mozart died at the age of 35.
Madonna was born in Bay City in the USA in 1958.

NUMBERS
India has around 1,600 languages.
There are192 countries in the world.
Shakespeare wrote 36 plays.

Module 2, Practice, exercise 3a, page 22

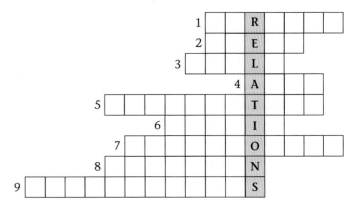

1 Your mother and father are your ...
2 Your brother's daughter is your ...
3 Your mother's brother is your ...
4 Your mother's sister is your ...
5 Your mother's father is your ...
6 Your aunt's son is your ...
7 Your father's mother is your ...
8 Your sons and daughters are your ...
9 Your parents' parents are your ...

Module 9: Real life, exercise 4, page 83

Student B

1 You are the shop assistant in a local store. Look at the information and serve the customer.

Prices

film	24 £4.50	36 £5.50	
postcards	25 pence each		
cakes	small: 60 p		
	large: £1.50		
baseball caps	small £3.00		
	medium £3.50		
	large £4.50		

2 Go to the local store and try to buy these things.

some stamps	*some*
some bananas	*toothpaste*
some batteries for your camera	*a T–shirt*

Module 13: Task, exercise 2a, page 116

Gaby

32 years old

Working in a travel agency at the moment but after ten years wants a change of career. Does not want to work in an office again – would like to do something active, possibly with children.

Needs a part-time evening course, as she will continue to work during the day.

Interests: swimming, basketball, travelling and meeting new people.

Module 15, Vocabulary, exercise 3, page 128

Module 2: Task, exercise 1b, page 23

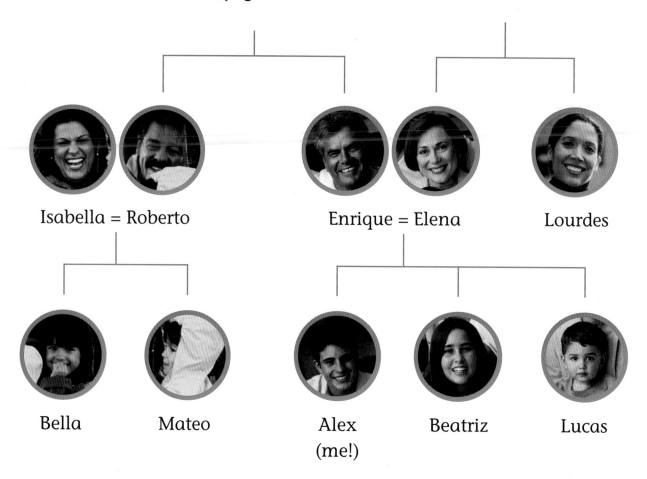

Isabella = Roberto   Enrique = Elena   Lourdes

Bella   Mateo   Alex (me!)   Beatriz   Lucas

Module 10: Task, exercise 2, page 93

Module 13: Real life, exercise 4, page 118

APPLICATION FORM

W.E.M.C.O.T.
(West Midland College of Technology)

English as a Foreign Language

Please complete this form using BLOCK LETTERS.

Section A Personal Details

1 Title: (Mr / Mrs / Miss / Ms / Dr, etc.)
2 Surname: ....
3 First Name(s): ....
4 Date of Birth: Day .... Month .... Year ....
5 Sex: Male ☐ Female ☐
6 Nationality: ....
7 Home Address: ....
8 Telephone No: a) Day: .... b) Evening: ....
9 Fax number: ....
10 E-mail address: ....
11 Passport No: ....
12 a) Have you got a student/tourist visa? ....
     b) Date of expiry: ....

Section B Course Details

1 Start Date: ....
2 for .... Terms (Maximum 4)
   Term 1 ☐   Term 2 ☐   Term 3 ☐   Term 4 ☐
   Jan – March   April – June   July – Sep   Oct – Dec
3 Why do you want to study English at WEMCOT?
   ....
   ....
4 What level do you think your English is?
   Elementary ☐   Lower Intermediate ☐   Intermediate ☐
   Higher Intermediate ☐   Advanced ☐   Proficiency ☐

Module 6: Practice, exercise 2a, page 55

Shopping list

nuts	bananas
orange juice	green vegetables
mineral water	fish
oranges	yoghurt
grapes	pasta
apples	bread

Module 5: Language focus 2, exercise 3, page 47

1 Korea: Seoul
   Argentina: Buenos Aires
   Poland: Warsaw
   Canada: Ottawa
2 Vladimir Putin is a president.
   Jackie Chan is an actor.
   JK Rowling is a writer.
3 People drive on the left in Australia and the UK. In the USA they drive on the right.
4 a a camera   d coins
   b an apple   e an aeroplane
   c a mobile phone
5 Boston is in the USA.
   São Paolo is in Brazil.
   Cape Town is in South Africa.
   Seville is in Spain.
6 a Sydney, Australia
   b Bangkok, Thailand
   c Rome, Italy

Module 9: Practice, exercise 2a, page 80

Complete the questions with the correct superlative form. Then compare answers with a partner.

Your town and country

a Which is (good) restaurant in your town?
b Which is (busy) street in your town?
c Which is (pretty) park in your town?
d Which area has (bad) traffic in your town?
e Which part of your country has (beautiful) scenery?
f Which is (big) city in your country?
g Which is (high) mountain in your country?

People you know

a Who is (tall) person in your class?
b Who writes (fast)?
c Who is (old) person in your family?
d Who is (young) person?
e Who is (rich) person you know?
f Who is (untidy) person you know?
g Who has (long) hair?

Module 6: Task, exercise 1, page 57

Useful language

a Describing your own picture

In my picture ...

there's a (small boy)

there's some (soup)

there aren't any (balloons)

On the left / On the right / In the middle, there's ...

b Asking questions

In your picture, is there a (man) / any (rice)?

Has the man got a (cap)?

How many (spoons) are there?

What colour is the (mother's dress)?

c Talking about differences

In Picture A, there's (a balloon, some soup) but in Picture B ...

Module 13: Task, exercise 2a, page 116

Oliver

18 years old

Doesn't know what he wants to do as a career. Spends a lot of his time playing in a rock band with his friends. He does not really want to do a full-time course because of this.

His parents are worried about him – they want him to study something useful for his career.

Interests: music, drama and computers.

Verb	Past simple	Past participle
be	was/were	been
become	became	become
begin	began	begun
bring	brought	brought
build	built	built
buy	bought	bought
catch	caught	caught
choose	chose	chosen
come	came	come
cost	cost	cost
cut	cut	cut
do	did	done
draw	drew	drawn
drink	drank	drunk
drive	drove	driven
eat	ate	eaten
fall	fell	fallen
feed	fed	fed
feel	felt	felt
fight	fought	fought
find	found	found
fly	flew	flown
forget	forgot	forgotten
get	got	got
give	gave	given
go	went	gone/been
have	had	had
hear	heard	heard
keep	kept	kept
know	knew	known
learn	learned/learnt	learned/learnt
leave	left	left

Verb	Past simple	Past participle
let	let	let
lose	lost	lost
make	made	made
mean	meant	meant
meet	met	met
pay	paid	paid
put	put	put
read /riːd/	read /red/	read /red/
ring	rang	rung
run	ran	run
say	said	said
see	saw	seen
sell	sold	sold
send	sent	sent
show	showed	shown
shut	shut	shut
sit	sat	sat
sleep	slept	slept
speak	spoke	spoken
spend	spent	spent
stand	stood	stood
steal	stole	stolen
swim	swam	swum
take	took	taken
teach	taught	taught
tell	told	told
think	thought	thought
understand	understood	understood
wake	woke	woken
wear	wore	worn
win	won	won
write	wrote	written

LANGUAGE

Module 1

Ⓐ *be*: positive form

I'm (= I am)	from Valencia.
You're (= you are)	a student.
He's (= he is)	twenty years old.
She's (= she is)	Chinese.
It's (= it is)	from Poland.
We're (= we are)	teachers.
They're (= they are)	English.

Ⓑ *be*: negative form

I'm not (= I am not)	a student.
You aren't (= you are not)	married.
He isn't (= he is not)	Italian.
She isn't (= she is not)	Saturday.
It isn't (= it is not)	married.
We aren't (= we are not)	on business.
They aren't (= they are not)	on holiday.

> **REMEMBER!**
> We also use these negative forms. They mean the same.
> *You're not from Moscow.*
> *He/She/It's not English.*
> *We/They're not married.*

Ⓒ *be*: questions and short answers

Questions		Short answers	
Am I	here?	Yes, you **are**.	No, you **aren't**.
Are you	married?	Yes, I **am**.	No, I'm **not**.
Is he	Egyptian?	Yes, he **is**.	No, he **isn't**.
Is she	on holiday?	Yes, she **is**.	No, she **isn't**.
Is it	Friday?	Yes, it **is**.	No, it **isn't**.
Are we	friends?	Yes we **are**.	No, we **aren't**.
Are they	in New York?	Yes, they **are**.	No, they **aren't**.

Ⓓ Question words

What	's	your job?
	are	your names?
Where	's	Alain from?
	are	your friends?
How old	's	Richard?
	are	you?
Who	's	your teacher?
	are	they?

Ⓔ Personal pronouns and possessive adjectives

Personal pronoun	Possessive adjective	
I	my	**My** name's James Taylor.
you	your	How old is **your** car?
he	his	**His** address is 6 Leyton Avenue.
she	her	What's **her** telephone number?
it	its	**Its** full name is the British Broadcasting Corporation (BBC).
we	our	**Our** children are six and eight years old.
they	their	What's **their** e-mail address?

> **REMEMBER!**
> 1 **His** *is for a man.* **His** name's **Paul**.
>   **Her** *is for a woman.* **Her** name's **Anna**.
>
> 2 **Your** *is for singular and plural.*
>   A: What's **your** name? B: **Aldona**.
>   A: What are **your** names? B: **Julio** and **Maria**.

Ⓕ *a* and *an*: indefinite articles with jobs

We use *a/an* for jobs.
Use **an** before vowels (a, e, i, o, u) **an** *actor*, **an** *engineer*
Use **a** before consonants (b, c, d, f, g, h, …) **a** *doctor*, **a** *manager*

Ⓖ Capital letters

We use capital letters for:
– names *Lara Croft, Queen Elizabeth*
– countries *China, the United States*
– nationalities *Brazilian, Greek*
– roads *23 Stamford Road, Fifth Avenue*
– towns/cities *New York, Istanbul*

Module 2

Ⓐ *this, that, these* and *those*

	Here		There	
singular	**this**	(book)	**that**	(book)
plural	**these**	(books)	**those**	(books)

Mr Thomson, **this is** *Jane Dunn.*   **These** *apples* **are** *good.*
Are these *your keys?*   *Who* **are those** *people?*

> **REMEMBER!**
> *In the answer we usually use* **it's** *or* **they're**.
> A: What's this/that? B: **It's** a credit card.
> A: What are these/those? B: **They're** videos.

Ⓑ Nouns: singular and plural

Singular	Plural	Spelling
a credit card	credit cards	+ **s**
a watch	watches	+ **es** (after *ch, sh, s, x, z*)
a family	families	+ **ies** (consonant + *y → ies*)

SUMMARY

C have got

1 Positive, negative and question forms

We use *have got* for:
a possession.
I've got a new mobile.   My school**'s got** twenty-five computers.

b relationships.
José**'s got** a new girlfriend.   They **have got** three children.

We can use *have* instead of *have got*.
My school **has** twenty-five computers.
They **have** three children.

Positive form	I/you/we/they**'ve got** (= have got) he/she/it**'s got** (= has got)	a new telephone number. a television.
Negative form	I/you/we/they **haven't got** (= have not got) he/she/it **hasn't got** (= has not got)	a cassette player. a mobile phone.
Question form	**Have** I/you/we/they **got** **Has** he/she/it **got**	an English–Portuguese dictionary? a CD player?
Short answers	Yes, I/you/we/they **have**. Yes, he/she/it **has**.	No, I/you/we/they **haven't** No, he/she/it **hasn't**.

> **REMEMBER!**
> 1 **He's** American. (he's = he **is**)   **He's** got an American car. (he's = he **has**)
>
> 2 We do not use the short form of the verb in short answers.
>
> Yes, I **have**.   NOT: *Yes, I've.*
> Yes, he **has**.   NOT: *Yes, he's.*

2 Question forms with question words

How many What	brothers answer	has Elena got? have you got for question 2?

D Adjectives

Adjectives:
– go **before** nouns *a comfortable car* NOT: *a car comfortable*
– do **not** change *blue eyes* NOT: *blues eyes*
– do **not** use *and* *a fantastic new motorbike* NOT: *a fantastic and new motorbike*

E a/an with singular nouns and adjectives

1 We use *a/an* + singular nouns.
a diary, **a** job, **a** tourist, **a** photo, **an** apple, **an** address, **an** e-mail (but **a** university)

2 We use *a/an* + adjectives and singular nouns.
a new car, **a** white cat, **a** French cigarette, **an** English teacher

F Possessive 's and of

1 We use a person + **'s** for possession.
Jane's brother   NOT: *the brother of Jane*
Patrick's computer
His friend's car
My father's name

2 If the first noun is plural, the apostrophe comes after the 's':
*my parent**s'** house* (= two parents)
*the teacher**s'** room* (= many teachers)

3 We usually use *of* before things or places.
*a picture **of** a car*   NOT: *a car's picture*
*the Queen **of** England*   NOT: *England's Queen*
*the Tower **of** London*   NOT: *London's Tower*

G Apostrophes

1 We use apostrophes:

a with the short forms of *is* and *has*.
*That**'s** my book.*   *She**'s** got four sisters.*
*He**'s** on holiday.*   *What**'s** your name?*

b To show possession:
*Hannah**'s** teacher.*   *My cousins**'** school.*

2 We do not use apostrophes to show that a noun is plural.

These are my keys.   *They've got two babies.*

Module 3

A Present simple: questions and short answers (*I, you, we, they*)

Question form	Do I/you/we/they	**speak** French? **study** at university?
Short answers	Yes, I/you/we/they No, I/you/we/they	**do**. **don't**.

> **REMEMBER!**
> We do not use the full verb in the short answer.
>
> Do you speak German?   Yes, I **do**.   NOT: *Yes, I speak.*
>   No, I **don't**. NOT: *No, I don't speak.*

We use the Present simple:

a for things that are generally/always true.
*Do you **work** for a big company?*   *Do they **live** in the city centre?*
*Do I **know** your brother?*

b for habits and routines.
*Do you **study** at the weekend?*   *Do they **go** out a lot?*

B Present simple: positive and negative forms

Positive form	I/you/we/they	live in a big city. drink coffee.
Negative form	I/you/we/they	don't like coffee. don't live in a flat.

C Telling the time

After the hour we use past and before the hour we use to.

3.05	*five past three*	3.35	*twenty-five to four*
3.10	*ten past three*	3.40	*twenty to four*
3.15	*quarter past three*	3.45	*quarter to four*
3.20	*twenty past three*	3.50	*ten to four*
3.25	*twenty-five past three*	3.55	*five to four*
3.30	*half past three*		

We can also say *three ten* (3.10), *three thirty-five* (3.35), etc.

> **REMEMBER!**
>
> | at | on | in |
> |---|---|---|
> | *at ten o'clock* | *on Sunday* | *in the morning* |
> | *at night* | | *in the afternoon* |
> | *at the weekend* | | *in the evening* |

Module 4

A Present simple: positive and negative (*he, she* and *it*)

1 In the *he/she/it* positive form of the Present simple, we add 's' to the verb.
*He love**s** chocolate.   She hate**s** dogs.   It open**s** at five o'clock.*

The spelling rules for *he*, *she* and *it*:

Verb	Rule	
Most verbs	add **s**	*Beth come**s** from the USA.* *Paul want**s** a new car.*
Ends in a consonant + *y*	change **y** to **ies**	*This airline fl**ies** to Slovenia.*
Ends in: *ch , sh , s, x, z*	add **es**	*Andrew watch**es** a lot of videos.* *Fran finish**es** work at six.*
do and *go*	add **es**	*My manager go**es** home at eleven!* *Pat do**es** all the housework.*
have	*has*	*He **has** breakfast at seven.*

2 We form the negative with *doesn't* (= does not) + verb.
*He **doesn't eat** meat.*   NOT: *He doesn't eats*
*She **doesn't like** coffee.   It **doesn't open** on Sunday.*

Positive form	he/she/it	likes dogs. loves chocolate.
Negative form	he/she/it	doesn't like (= does not like) my brother. doesn't eat (= does not eat) fish.

B Present simple: questions and short answers (*he, she* and *it*)

1 We form *he/she/it* Present simple questions with *does* + verb.
***Does** he **live** with his parents?*   NOT: *Does he lives?*
***Does** she **like** London?   **Does** it **open** late?*

Question form	Does he/she/it	live with you? rain a lot in Brazil?
Short answers	Yes, he/she/it No, he/she/it	does. doesn't.

2 Notice how we form *Wh-* questions with the Present simple.

What	does	he/she/it	think of Japan? like eating?
Where	does	Juan	come from? live? work?
What time	does	the class Anna	start? go to work?

C Adverbs of frequency

We use frequency adverbs and the Present simple to say *how often* we do something.

```
never   not often              often       always
◄─────────────────────────────────────────────►
0%              sometimes            usually   100%
```

a We usually put the adverb *before* the verb.
*My children **sometimes** watch a video on Sunday evening.*
*Nicolas **never** goes to school on Saturday.*
*I **don't often** visit my brother's family.*
*I **don't usually** like pasta.*

b We put the adverb *after* the verb *be*.
*English people are **usually** very friendly.*
*The winters are **sometimes** very cold.*
*The weather isn't **always** good.*
*I'm **not often** home in the evening.*

Module 5

A *most, a lot of, some, not many*

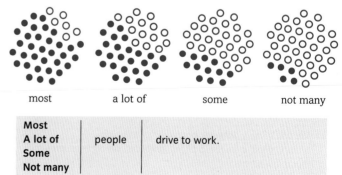

most   a lot of   some   not many

Most A lot of Some Not many	people	drive to work.

B can and can't

1 We use *can* to say that it is possible to do something.
   *You **can** take a train from Paddington Station to Heathrow.*

2 We use *can't* to say it is impossible to do something.
   *We **can't** take a taxi because we've only got £20.*

> **REMEMBER!**
> *a* We always use the base form of the verb after can.
>
>   *You **can eat** Chinese food in the city centre.* NOT: *you ~~can eats~~*
>
> *b* We don't use do or does to make the question form.
>
>   ***Can you find** taxis in the street?* NOT: *~~Do you can find taxis in the street?~~*

Positive form	*I/you/he/she/it/we/they*	**can go** by train. **can take** a long time.
Negative form	*I/you/he/she/it/we/they*	**can't** (= **cannot**) **go** by bus
Question form	**Can** *I/you/he/she/it/we/they*	**travel** by bus?

C Definite, indefinite and zero articles

1 Indefinite article

We use *a* or *an*:
a with jobs.
   *I'm **an** artist.*
b with a singular noun to mean 'one'.
   *We have **a** real problem.*
c with these phrases
   ***a** lot of/**a** long time*

2 Definite article

We use *the*:
a with times of day.
   *in **the** morning/afternoon*
   *(BUT **at night**)*
b with these phrases.
   *in **the** city centre*
   *on **the** right/left*

3 Zero article

We do **not** use *a*, *an* or *the*:
a with towns and cities.
   I'm from Boston.

b with most countries.
   Lyon is in France.
   *(BUT **the** United States, **the** United Kingdom, **the** Czech Republic)*

c with '*by*' + a type of transport.
   by bus/car/train

d with times + days.
   at one o'clock   on Monday

e with these phrases.
   go to work/at home   most people

Module 6

A Countable and uncountable nouns

Countable noun	Uncountable noun
eggs	milk
apples	butter
books	money
CDs	music

1 We can use countable nouns in the singular or plural.
   *Have you got **a** cat? Do you like cats?*

2 Uncountable nouns do **not** have a plural.
   Do you like classical music~~s~~?

Note: A dictionary says if a noun is countable or uncountable.

> **REMEMBER!**
> *a* Bread, toast, cake, milk, fruit juice, water, coffee, tea ... are all uncountable, but we can *talk about:*
>
>   **a piece of** bread/toast/cake
>   **a glass of milk**/fruit juice/water
>   **a cup of** coffee/tea
>
> *b* We can also talk about **a** coffee (= a cup of coffee) and **two** teas ...

B There is and There are

	singular	plural
Positive form	There's a cup.	There are six plates.
Negative form	There isn't a bottle of milk.	There aren't two cups.
Question form	Is there a glass of orange juice?	Are there six glasses?
Short answers	Yes, there is. No, there isn't.	Yes, there are. No, there aren't.

C some and any

1 a We use *some* in the positive when we don't say exactly how many or how much.
      *Have **some** grapes!*
      *There's **some** soup and bread for lunch.*
      *I'd like **some** carrots, please.*

   b *Some* = a small number/a small amount. Notice the difference:
      some onions   a lot of onions
      some money   a lot of money

2 We usually use *any* or *no* in negatives with plural and uncountable nouns.
   *I haven't got **any** money. = I've got **no** money.*
   *There aren't **any** e-mails. = There are **no** e-mails.*
   *There isn't **any** time. = There's **no** time.*

3 We usually use *any* in questions with plurals and uncountables.
   *Have you got **any** brothers or sisters?*
   *Are there **any** buses at night?*
   *Is there **any** meat in this soup?*

	singular countable noun	plural countable noun	uncountable noun
➕	There's **an** apple.	There **are some** grapes.	There's **some** soup.
➖	There **isn't a** bowl.	There **aren't any** glasses. There **are no** glasses.	There **isn't any** water. There's **no** water.
❓	**Is** there **a** cinema?	**Are** there **any** shops?	**Is** there **any** money?

> **REMEMBER!**
> With plural and uncountable nouns:
>
> a We can also use some in these questions:
>   **Would you like some** cheese/coffee/grapes?
>   **Have you got some** grapes/mineral water?
>
> b We usually use some in this question:
>   **Can I have some** wine/cake/oranges?

D Questions with *how much?* and *how many?*

1 We use *how many* with countable plural nouns.
How many brothers/children/oranges have you got?
How many cigarettes does Paul smoke every day?

2 We use *how much* with uncountable nouns.
How much rice/milk/money have we got?
How much coffee does Elena drink in a week?

3 *How much / how many* and *there is / there are*:
We use *there are* with countable plural nouns.
We use *there is* with uncountable nouns.
A: **How many** teachers **are there** in your school?
B: **There are** about twenty, I think.

A: **How much** sugar **is there** in this cake?
B: It's okay. **There's** not much.

> **REMEMBER!**
> We use how much to ask about prices.
>
> **How much** is it/this/that?   **How much** are they/these/those?
> **How much** does it cost?   **How much** do they cost?
> It's £10.   They're £50.

Module 7

A Past Simple: *was* and *were*

Positive form	I/he/she/it you/we/they	**was** at home. **were** at home.
Negative form	I/he/she/it **wasn't** (= **was not**) you/we they **weren't** (= **were not**)	at school. at school.
Question form	**Was** I/he /she/it **Were** you/we/they	friendly?
Short answers	Yes, I/he/she/it **was**. Yes, you/we/they **were**.	No, he/she/it **wasn't**. No, you/we/ they **weren't**.

> **REMEMBER!**
> I was born in 1985.   NOT: ~~I born in 1985~~.   OR: ~~I was borned in 1985~~.

B Past Simple: regular and irregular verbs

1 Regular verbs

Usually we add *-ed* to the verb.
*I/you/he/she/it/we/they work**ed**, want**ed**, finish**ed**, listen**ed**, watch**ed**, play**ed***

Other spelling rules:

Verb	Rule	
Ends in **-e** (*live*)	**+ d**	*She lived in France.*
Ends in a consonant + vowel + consonant (*stop*)	double the final consonant	*He stopped work at 5.30.*
Ends in consonant + y (*study*)	Change **y** to **ied**	*I studied economics.*

2 Irregular verbs

Many common verbs have an irregular past form:
go – went, have – had, meet – met, know – knew.

▶ *Verb list on page 149.*

We use the Past simple to talk about:
a a finished single action in the past.
  *My parents **met** in 1960.*
  *The film **started** at 7.30.*

b a finished state in the past.
  *Kate **had** a happy childhood.*
  *We **lived** in a small city.*

c a repeated action in the past.
  *She always **telephoned** me on Monday.*
  *They **went** swimming every day.*

When we use the Past simple, we often **say** the time of the action: *in 1960, at 7.30, on Monday.*

C Past time phrases

1 *in*

in	+ year	in 1999
	+ decade	in the 1980s
	+ century	in the 20th century
	+ month	in July

2 *from ... to...*

*I worked for the company **from** 1994 **to** 2000.*
*The lesson was **from** half past six **to** eight.*

> **REMEMBER**
> *We do not use a preposition (in, on, from, ...) with:*
>
> *last*   We watched television **last** night.
> *yesterday*   Manuel phoned me **yesterday**.

D Past time phrases with *last, yesterday* and *ago*

These time phrases are very common with the Past simple.

1 *yesterday* and *last*
   *I saw her **yesterday**.* NOT: ~~on yesterday~~
   *We went shopping **yesterday morning/afternoon**.*
   *They went on holiday **last weekend**.* NOT: ~~at last weekend~~
   *He phoned me **last night**.*

2 *ago* (= before now)
   They got married **six months ago**.
   *I phoned you about **three minutes ago**.*

E Ordinal numbers and dates

1st	→	first	11th	→	eleventh
2nd	→	second	12th	→	twelfth
3rd	→	third	13th	→	thirteenth
4th	→	fourth	20th	→	twentieth
5th	→	fifth	21st	→	twenty-first
6th	→	sixth	22nd	→	twenty-second
7th	→	seventh	30th	→	thirtieth
8th	→	eighth	33rd	→	thirty-third
9th	→	ninth	40th	→	fortieth
10th	→	tenth	100th	→	hundredth

We use ordinal numbers:
– for dates: *December 25th:*
                 December the twenty-fifth.
– for floors in a building: *The classroom is on the third floor.*
– as an adjective: *She's Paolo's second wife.*
                 My first car was a Fiat Uno.

Module 8

A Past simple: negative

| I/you/he/she/it/ we/they | **didn't** (= **did not**) | start come | at 10.00. to the park. |

> **REMEMBER!**
> *We use* didn't *+ the base form of the verb.*
> *Regular and irregular verbs are the same.*
>
> She **didn't go** shopping.   NOT: ~~She didn't went shopping~~.

B Past simple questions

Question form

| **Did** | you/he/she | **walk** to work today? |
| **Did** | | **sleep** well? |

Short answers

| Yes, I/you/we/he | **did**. |
| No, I/you/we/he | **didn't** |

> **REMEMBER!**
> *We do not use the full verb in short answers.*
>
> *Did you like Rome?*   Yes, I **did**.   NOT: ~~Yes, I liked~~.
>
>   No, I **didn't**.   NOT: ~~No, I didn't like~~.

What			**think** of South Africa?
Where		you	**live** in Spain?
When		he	**work** there?
What time	**did**	Maria	**go** home?
Who		they	**speak** to?
Why			**leave** early?
How			**travel**?

Module 9

A Comparative forms of adjectives

1 When we compare two things we use *than*.
   *Sarah's older **than** Hannah.*
   *London is more expensive **than** Manchester.*

2 a With all one-syllable adjectives, we use *er + than*.
   This car is **cheaper than** the other one.
   Joe is **taller than** his father.

   b With two-syllable adjectives that end in *y*, we change *y* to *ier + than*.
   busy: *I am **busier** than I was before.*
   pretty: *The old part of the town is **prettier** than the new part.*

   c With other two-syllable adjectives and adjectives of three or more syllables, we use *more* + adjective + *than*.
   Madonna is **more famous than** her husband.
   This shop is **more expensive than** the other one.
   Greek is **more difficult than** Latin.

3 Notice these irregular forms.
   good: *This road is **better** than it was before.*
   bad: *I feel **worse** today than I did yesterday.*

B Superlative forms of adjectives

We form superlatives with *the* + adjective + *est*.
Kate is **the oldest** *in the family.*

or *the* + *most* + adjective.
This is **the most expensive** *restaurant in town.*

The rules are the same as with comparative forms.

Adjective	Comparative	Superlative	Spelling rule
cheap	cheap**er**	the cheap**est**	most one syllable adjectives: **+ er /est**
nice	nic**er**	the nic**est**	adjectives ending in e: **+ r/st**
big	big**ger**	the big**gest**	adjectives ending in consonant + vowel + consonant: **double the final consonant + er/est**
easy	eas**ier**	the eas**iest**	adjectives ending in y: change to **-ier/iest**
famous	**more** famous **more** expensive	the **most** famous the **most** expensive	most two syllable adjectives, and adjectives with three or more syllables: **more/most +** adjective
good bad	**better** **worse**	the **best** the **worst**	irregular adjectives

Module 10

A Present continuous

1   We use the Present continuous to talk about actions happening now.
    I'm using the computer at the moment.
    Ali isn't here; he's working.

    ... or around now.
    We're staying in Montevideo this week.
    I'm reading a really interesting book.

Positive form	I'm he/she/it's you/we/they're	wait**ing**.
Negative form	I'm **not** he/she/it **isn't** you/we/they **aren't**	play**ing**.
Question form	**Am** I **Is** he/she/it **Are** you/we/they	work**ing**?
Short answers	Yes, I am. Yes, he/she/it **is**. Yes, you/we/they **are**.	No, I'm **not**. No, he/she/it **isn't**. No, you/we/they **aren't**.

2   Look at the spelling rules for the *-ing* form.

Verb	Rule	
Most verbs	add *-ing*	*He's flying to South Africa.*
Verbs ending with *-e*	take away the *-e*	*They're living in Beijing.*
Verbs ending with consonant + vowel + consonant	double the final consonant	*She's sitting here.*

3   Notice how we use the Present continuous with question words.

What Where Why Who	am I is she/he are you/we/they	doing? going? waiting? talking to?

B Present continuous and Present simple

1   We use the Present simple to talk about something that is always true.
    Laura comes from Rome.   I don't speak Russian.

    We also use the Present simple to talk about habits and routines, often with words like *normally, usually, sometimes,* etc.
    We often watch a video on Friday night.
    Do you normally wake up early?

2   We use the Present continuous to talk about something that is happening now or around now. Compare these pairs of sentences.
    Jan's phoning his girlfriend. (= now)
    Jan phones his girlfriend about eight times a day. (= habit)

    I'm reading a fantastic book at the moment. (= in the present period)
    I read three or four books a week. (= habit)

Module 11

A can and can't (for ability)

1   We use *can* to say we are able to do something.
    Peter can speak German very well.

2   We use *can't* to say we are not able to do something.
    My dog can't walk at the moment.

> **REMEMBER!**
> a   We do not add an 's' with the he/she/it form.
>
>   *He can speak Turkish.*   NOT: He **cans** speak Turkish.
>
> b   We always use the base form after *can*.
>
>   *She can dance salsa.*   NOT: She **can** dances salsa.
>
> c   We do not use do or does to make the question form.
>
>   ***Can you** play tennis?*   NOT: *Do you can play tennis?*

B Question words

1 One-word questions

What's your name?	Irena.
Where do you come from?	Russia.
When did you come to England?	Two weeks ago.
How did you come here?	By plane.
Which do you prefer, London or Moscow?	Moscow!
Why do you like it better?	Because it's my home city!

a We use *what* if there are many possible answers.
   What's your favourite colour?   Blue.

b We use *which* if there are only a few possible answers.
   Which is easier, Japanese, Chinese or English?   English, I think!

2 Compound (two-word) questions

a We can make compound questions with *what* and *which*.

What kind/sort/type of food do you like?	Italian.
What time does the train leave?	At six thirty.
What colour is your car?	Green.
Which one do you like best?	I really like the yellow one.

b We can make compound questions with *how*.

How far is your home from here?	About six kilometres.
How often do you have English classes?	Three times a week.
How long are your lessons?	One and a half hours.
How fast is your computer?	Very fast!
How much bread have we got?	Not much.
How many cigarettes do you smoke?	About five a day.
How old is your daughter?	She was seven last week.

> **REMEMBER**
> We use **how many** for countable nouns and **how much** for uncountable nouns.
>
> A: How many people are there here?   B: About 200.
>
> A: How much time have we got?   B: Only five minutes.

3 Question words and verb forms

We can use different verb forms with question words.

How was your journey?	Very good, thank you.
Which city **did** you **like** the best?	Madrid.
How many names **can** you remember?	Anne, Susie, Tom and ...
How far do you **travel** every day?	About 100 kilometres.

C Definite, indefinite and zero articles

1 Zero article

We use zero article (no article) with plural nouns or with uncountable nouns.
   Jane loves **children**.
   Meat is good for you.

We use it to speak about things in general.

2 Indefinite article

We use *a/an* before a countable singular noun.
   I'm staying in **a** hotel in Bangkok.

a/an = one, but we don't know which one,
or we use *a/an* when this is the first time we are speaking about something.

3 Definite article

We use *the* before nouns when it is clear that the speaker is talking about something specific or something which we know.

The children are in bed.	= the children in my family/my children;
The meat is fantastic!	= we know which meat, (the meat that I am eating now)
I'm going back to **the hotel** soon.	= we know which hotel because we spoke about it before

Module 12

A Future intentions

1 *Going to* + verb

a We use *going to* + verb when we are talking about our plans or intentions.
   We**'re going to** get married next summer.
   Jane **isn't going to** have a party this year.

b We don't usually say *'going to go'* – we just use the Present continuous.
   I'm going ~~to go~~ out with a big group of friends.
   I'm going ~~to go~~ shopping.

Positive form		
I'm he /she 's you/we/they 're	**going to**	have a party next week.

Negative form		
I'm not he /she isn't you/we/they **aren't**	**going to**	study tonight.

Question form		
Am I **Is** he /she **Are** you/we/they	**going to**	see Karen tomorrow?

	Short answers				Short answers	
Yes,	I he/she you/we/they	am. is. are.	No,	I'm he/she you/we/they		not. isn't. aren't.

2 *Want to* + verb; *would like to* + verb

a We use *want* and *would like* to talk about our wishes.
   Would like is usually more polite.
   I **want to** see the manager!   I**'d like to** book a room, please.

b In the negative we don't often use *wouldn't like to*. We prefer *don't want to*.
   I **don't want to** go out tonight.   NOT: ~~I wouldn't like to go out tonight~~.

1 *Want to* + verb
Positive form

I/you/we/they	**want to**	eat
he/she/it	**wants to**	eat

Question form

Do you	**want to**	eat?
Does he		

Yes, I **do**	Yes, he **does**
No, I **don't**	No, he **doesn't**

Negative form

I/you/we/they	**don't**	**want to**	eat.
he/she /it	**doesn't**		

2 *Would like to* + verb
Positive form

I/you/he/she/it/we/they	**'d like to**	eat.

Negative form

I/you/he/she/it/we/they	**wouldn't like to**	eat.

Question form

Would	I/you/he/she/it/we/they	**like to**	eat?

B Future time expressions

These are some common expressions we use when we are talking about future plans and intentions:

	today, tonight
	this ... morning/afternoon/evening/
	weekend/month/year/summer
I'm going to see Patricia	*tomorrow,*
	tomorrow ... morning/afternoon/
	evening/night
	next ... week/month/year/summer

C Suggestions with *let's, shall we, we could* + verb

Suggestion		Positive response	Negative response
Let's (= let us)		Good idea!	Oh, no! (+ reason)
Shall we	watch a video?	Yes, fine.	Sorry, but (+
We could	go to a club.	Yes, sure.	reason)
Why don't we	go on holiday?	Yes, okay.	

D Offers with *shall I?* and *I'll* + verb

	Offer	Positive response	Negative response
Shall I	order a pizza?	Good idea!	It's OK, thanks. (+ reason)
I'll	make some coffee.	Yes, please, if that's okay. Fine/okay/sure/ thanks. That's very kind of you.	

Module 13

A Infinitive of purpose

We use infinitives to show why we do something.
*I'm studying English **to get** a better job.* (= because I want to get a better job.)
*She went to the bank **to change** some money.* (= because she wanted to change some money.)

B *might* and *will*: modal verbs for possibility

We use *might (not)* and *will (won't)* to say that something is possible or probable in the future.

	'll (= will)	go to university. (you think this will happen)
I/you/he/	**might**	go to university. (you think it's possible)
she/you/they	**might not**	go to university. (you think it's less possible)
	won't (= will not)	go to university. (you think this will not happen)

> **REMEMBER**
> We don't use *to* after might and will.
> It might rain.   NOT ~~It might to rain~~.

Module 14

A Present perfect

1   We form the Present perfect with *has/have* + past participle.

a   **Regular verbs**
Regular past participles are the same as the Past simple form (verb + *ed*)
*I've **finished** the housework.*
Also: *waited, phoned, used, tried*, etc.

b   **Irregular verbs**
Irregular verbs have irregular past participles. (See Irregular verb list on page 149.)
*I've **spoken** to her today.*

Positive form		
I/you/we/they	**'ve** (= *have*)	
he/she/it	**'s** (= *has*)	met Anne before.

Negative form		
I/you/we/they	**haven't**	
he/she/it	**hasn't**	met Anne before.

Question form		
Have	I/you/we/they	
Has	he/she/it	met Anne before?

Short answers					
Yes,	I/you/ we/they	have	No,	I/you/ we/they	haven't.
	he/she/it	has		he /she/it	hasn't.

2   We use the Present perfect to talk about something that happened in the past but is **connected to the present**.

a   It happened in a present time period.
*I'**ve been** very busy **today**.*
*We'**ve had** two holidays **this year**.*

b   It happened 'some time in my life up to now' (my life is not finished).
*She'**s done** lots of different jobs.*
*I'**ve broken** my arm three times.*

We do not say exactly when these actions happened with the Present perfect.

B   **Time phrases with the Present perfect and Past simple**

1   With the Present perfect, we do not say exactly when the action happened.

a   We often use imprecise time words like *just, recently, already, never* or *ever* (= in your life).
*I'**ve just seen** Lucia.*
*They'**ve recently bought** a new car.*
*I'**ve already had** my lunch.*
*I'**ve never met** your brother.*
***Have** you **ever been** to Australia?*

b   We can also use 'present' time words like *today, this week, this year*, etc.
*She'**s started** a new job **this week**.*

c   We also use *always* and *before* with the Present perfect.
*I'**ve always** wanted to go to India.*
*I'**ve heard** about Jim but I haven't met him **before**.*

2   We cannot use the Present perfect with precise past time phrases like *yesterday, last month, at eight o'clock, ten minutes ago*, etc. With past time words like this, we use the Past simple.
*I **went** shopping yesterday.* NOT: ~~I have been shopping yesterday.~~
*I **got** up at seven o'clock.* NOT: ~~I have got up at seven o'clock.~~
*I **spoke** to Alex ten minutes ago.* NOT: ~~I have spoken to Alex ten minutes ago.~~

REMEMBER!
The verb *go* has two past participles: *gone* and *been*.

a   *gone* = gone but not returned.
*Anna's **gone** shopping this morning.* (= she's at the shops now, she hasn't returned)

b   *been* = gone and returned again.
*Anna's **been** shopping this morning.* (= she went to the shops but now she is back)

Module 15

A   **Prepositions of movement**

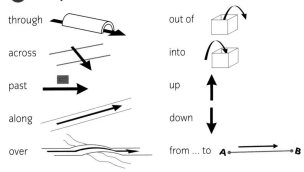

through		out of
across		into
past		up
along		down
over		from ... to

B   *have to* and *don't have to*

1   We use *have to* when it is necessary or obligatory to do something.
*You **have to** drive on the left in Britain.*

2   We use *don't have to* when it is not necessary to do something, but you can if you want.
*You **don't have to** come to the party if you don't want to.*

REMEMBER
When it is **not** okay or it is prohibited to do something we use **can't**.

You can't smoke in the classroom   NOT: ~~You don't have to smoke in the classroom.~~

Positive form		
I/you/we/they he/she /it	have to has to	leave

Negative form			
I/you/we/they he/she/it	don't doesn't	have to	leave

Question form		
Do Does	I/you/we/they he/she /it	have to go?

Short answers		
Yes,	I/you/we/they he/she/it	do. does.
No,	I/you/we/they he/she/it	don't. doesn't

C   *can* and *can't*

We use *can* when it is okay to do something.
*You **can** pay me tomorrow.*
*You **can** go home now.*

We use *can't* when it is not okay or it is prohibited to do something.
*You **can't** eat in here.*
*We **can't** park here.*

Module 1

A Complete the table.

Country	Nationality
Russia	Russian
1 _____	British
Spain	2 _____
3 _____	Italian
4 _____	Japanese

B Complete with the correct form of *be*.

We*'re* Italian.

5 I _____ nineteen years old.

6 They _____ my friends.

7 Claudia _____ on holiday.

8 _____ you from Manchester?

C Make these sentences negative.

I'm married. *I'm not married.*

9 Emily's a student.

_____

10 My parents are from Barcelona.

_____

11 You're in my class.

_____

D Look at the answers. Write the questions.

My name's Tomas. *What's your name?*

12 No, I'm not. I'm single.

_____

13 I'm thirty. _____

14 I'm a nurse. _____

15 It's 07611 993993.

_____

E Write the jobs.

16 m _ s _ c i _ n

17 w _ i _ e _

18 e _ g _ n _ e _

F Which word takes *an*?

19 tourist student address country

G Put in the capital letters.

20 i'm from turkey and ahmed's from dubai.

/20

Module 2

A Put the family words in pairs.

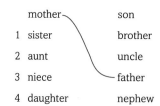

mother — son

1 sister — brother

2 aunt — uncle

3 niece — father

4 daughter — nephew

B Match the pictures to the words.

5 a wallet ☐ and a bottle of water ☐

6 stamps ☐ and coins ☐

7 glasses ☐ and a camera ☐

8 a brush ☐ and a credit card ☐

9 a watch ☐ and a diary ☐

C Complete with the correct form of *have got*.

10 Tania _____ a new mobile.

11 _____ (you) all your things?

12 We _____ (not) a dog now.

13 They _____ five children.

14 _____ your brother _____ a new computer?

15 My sister _____ (not) a job.

D Put in the apostrophe (').

16 These tissues are Jennys.

E Choose the correct word.

17 How/What/Who do you say this in English?

18 Who/Where/What page are we on?

19 How/Who/What do you spell 'beautiful'?

20 How/What/Where does this mean?

/20

Module 3

A Complete the gaps with a verb.

1 Mark and Karina _____ to school on the bus.

2 What time do you _____ dinner?

3 Do your children _____ English?

4 What time do they _____ up in the morning?

5 I don't _____ tea or coffee.

6 The shops _____ at about nine o'clock in the morning.

B Complete the gaps with *do, don't* or – (no word).

7 '_____ you work in an office?' 'No, I _____ . I _____ work in a restaurant.'

8 'Where _____ you live?' 'We _____ live in the city centre.'

9 'I _____ have breakfast at home, I normally _____ a snack at work at about ten o'clock.'

10 '_____ you read the newspaper every day?' 'Yes, I _____ .'

C Write the missing letters to make places.

11 o f _ _ _ _   13 c i _ _ m _

12 b _ _ c h   14 c _ _ y c _ _ t _ _

D Write the times.

15 _____

16 _____

17 _____

E Choose the correct preposition.

18 We have lunch in / at / on about half past twelve.

19 I get up late in / at / on Sundays.

20 They work in / at / on night.

/20

Module 4

A Complete the sentences with a verb in the correct form.

1 Do you _____ a lot of books and magazines?

2 On Saturday Jack _____ to the cinema with his friends.

3 I often _____ to the radio in the evening.

4 My husband never _____ TV.

5 She usually _____ dinner at about seven o'clock in the evening.

6 My sister often _____ shopping at lunchtime.

7 A lot of children _____ football at school.

8 She never _____ her homework.

B Correct the mistakes.

9 My brother live in Berlin.

_____

10 Where are you work?

_____

11 What does study Erica?

_____

12 I go never to bed early.

_____

13 He doesn't speak often English.

_____

14 Is your wife work for a big company?

_____

15 My mother don't like spiders.

_____

C Put the words in order.

16 drink / want a / you / Do ?

_____

17 three / I'd / , please / like / coffees

_____

D Circle the odd one out.

18 running swimming shopping

19 cooking reading doing housework

20 eating driving drinking

/20

Module 6

A Circle the odd one out.

1 melons carrots grapes oranges

2 fish chicken hamburgers rice

3 jam lemons chocolate biscuits

4 coffee milk tea noodles

B Complete with *is* or *are*.

5 _____ there any sugar in this coffee?

6 Oh good! There _____ noodles in the soup!

7 There _____ an apple in my bag.

8 There _____ some fruit in that bowl.

C Choose the correct alternative.

9 I've got a / some / any / no magazine for you.

10 Don't eat a / some / any / no sweets before lunch!

11 I want to listen to a / some / any / no music.

12 I'm sorry, but there are a / some / any / no strawberries today.

D Correct the mistakes.

13 How many son have you got?

_____

14 How much waters do you drink every day?

_____

15 How many money do you want?

_____

16 How much people are there in your office?

_____

E Put the words in the box in the correct place.

'd much can the

17 Hello, I have a coke, please?

18 I like some tea, please.

19 Can I have bill, please?

20 How is that?

/20

Module 7

A Complete the dialogue with the correct form of *was* or *were*.

A: Where (1) _____ you last night? I phoned you three times!

B: Sorry, I (2) _____ at home. I (3) _____ at Keri's birthday party.

A: Oh. (4) _____ it good?

B: Yes, but there (5) _____ many people there. Only four of us!

B Correct the mistakes.

6 My husband worked for ICI for 1998 to 2004.

_____

7 We left Shanghai on 2002.

_____

8 People first used computers in twentieth century.

_____

9 My birthday is on January the twenty two.

_____

10 I watched television the last night.

_____

11 The Berlin Wall came down in 1980s.

_____

12 We went to Chicago I was fifteen.

_____

C Write the past forms of the verbs.

13 make _____

14 write _____

15 become _____

16 buy _____

17 take _____

D Complete the gaps with the correct form of the verbs.

18 I _____ (get) married last year.

19 I _____ (go) to college last year.

20 I _____ (start) a new job last week.

/20

Module 8

A Write the types of film.

1 s_____ f_____
  l_____ s_____

2 c_____y
  c_____n

3 h_____r film
  a_____n film

B Complete the adjectives.

4 f r _ _ _ t _ _ _ ng

5 e x _ _ t _ _ g

6 v _ _ l _ _ t

7 i n t _ _ _ _ t _ _ _

8 e n j _ _ _ b l _

C Make the sentences negative.

9 Meg fell in love with Tom.

_____

10 I slept very well last night.

_____

11 She gave me the parcel.

_____

12 The camera cost $500.

_____

13 He found his keys.

_____

D Write the questions.

14 'Where _____ on holiday?'
   'We went to New Zealand.'

15 'How _____ there?'
   'By plane.'

16 'What _____ there?'
   'We went horse riding and we did lots of shopping.'

17 '_____ a good time?'
   'Yes, we had a great time!'

E Correct the mistakes.

18 Do you want go to see a movie?

_____

19 Let meet at seven o'clock.

_____

20 Why we don't go to that new café?

_____

/20

Module 9

A Complete the sentences comparing two hotels.

1 The Park is _____ (big) The Spa.

2 The Spa is _____ (small) The Park.

3 The Park is _____ (cheap) The Spa.

4 The Spa is _____ (expensive) The Park.

5 The Park is _____ (good) The Spa for children.

6 The Spa is _____ (bad) The Park for children.

B Write the superlative form.

7 hot _____

8 cold _____

9 popular _____

10 friendly _____

11 famous _____

C Complete the shops.

12 b _ _ c h _ _ '_

13 c _ _ t h _ _ s _ _ _

14 h _ _ _ d r _ _ _ _ _ 's

15 l _ c _ l s _ o _

D Correct the mistakes.

16 You take credit cards?

_____

17 Have you this in blue?

_____

18 How much is?

_____

19 Can I have one those, please?

_____

20 What time do close?

_____

/20

Module 11

A Complete the missing letters to make animals or natural features.

1 m _ _ n t _ _ n

2 i _ s _ _ t

3 h _ m _ _ b _ _ _ _ g

4 b _ _ d

5 e _ _ t h

B Correct the mistakes.

6 Do you can play golf?

_____

7 She cans understand Chinese.

_____

8 I can't cooking.

_____

C Choose the correct alternative.

9 How much / How many money have you got?

10 How far / How fast can you translate?

11 Which / Where continent is the biggest?

12 What / Who is your favourite actor?

D Write the numbers.

13 thirty-three point three _____

14 four hundred thousand _____

15 two thousand and eight _____

16 fourteen metres sixty-two centimetres _____

E Put a / an or the in the correct place in the sentences.

17 Sam loves dogs but he doesn't like dog next-door.

_____

18 Money is problem for most people.

_____

19 I can see moon.

_____

20 There's pen in my bag.

_____

/20

Module 12

A Complete the gaps with one word.

A: What are you (1) _____ to do when you finish university?

B: I (2) _____ going to have a long holiday!

A: And after that?

B: I (3) _____ to find a good job with a computer company. I'd (4) _____ to work in Japan or maybe China. How about you? What (5) _____ you want to do?

A: I'd really like (6) _____ travel, maybe to South America.

B Cross out the verb that does not go with the noun.

7 do / make / hate   the housework

8 go to / go / enjoy   shopping

9 see / watch / visit   an exhibition

10 make / have / go to   a party

C Put the words in the correct place in the sentences.

> shall 's about 'll don't

11 I make some coffee for us.

12 **A:** I telephone Pete?

    B: Yes, please, if that's OK.

13 Let have some chocolate.

14 Why we stay at home tonight?

15 How watching that new DVD?

D What's the weather like?

16 _____

17 _____

18 _____

19  _____

20 _____

/20

Module 13

A Write the school subjects.

1 You study computers.

2 You study countries and places.

3 You study things that happened in the past.

4 You study money and finance.

5 You study books by great writers.

B Complete with the words. (You may need to change the tense.)

> apply course degree get
> money pass train

6 Dan's really happy because he _____ all his exams

7 If you want to be a doctor you need to get a _____ in medicine.

8 After Paula finishes college she wants to _____ as a chef.

9 Yasuko _____ for a job in the New York office, but she didn't get it.

10 You need to work harder if you want to _____ good marks.

11 Luciano's doing a really interesting design _____ .

12 Most actors don't earn very much _____ .

C Choose the best alternative.

13 We're not going out because the news says it might / won't rain.

14 When I'm 30, he will / might be 65.

15 Don't wait for Jack. He said he might / might not come.

16 I'm sure the traffic won't / might not be bad on a Sunday morning.

D Make sentences.

17 I / going / the supermarket / buy a few things

_____

18 We / go / the hospital last weekend / visit Rosa

_____

19 I / meet / my boss / talk about my new job

_____

20 Chris / going / the bank / get some money

_____

/20

Module 14

A Correct the mistakes with the Present perfect.

1 Leila haven't been to work this week because she's ill.

2 Are the others gone home?

3 I broken my arm.

4 Anita just has called – can you call her back?

5 It hasn't rain this week.

B Choose the correct alternative.

6 We have been / went away last weekend.

7 I haven't spoken / didn't speak to Mum this week – is she okay?

8 When have you started / did you start your new job?

9 I never sent / have never sent a text message in my life.

10 My grandmother has been / was born in 1935.

C Complete with the verbs.

> leave make post send take

11 Just a minute – I need to _____ a quick phone call.

12 If I'm not at home you can _____ a message with my dad.

13 You look really funny. Just a minute, I'm going to _____ a photo of you.

14 I'm just going out to _____ an important letter.

15 It's Alice's birthday on Sunday don't forget to _____ her a card.

D Put the telephone phrases in the correct order.

16 there / is / Ed?

_____

17 he's / sorry / here / not

_____

18 Sonia / that / is?

_____

19 to / I / Ahmed / please / speak / can / to?

_____

20 to / him / me / call / ask / can / you / please?

_____

/20

163

TAPESCRIPTS

Module 0

Recording 6

a twenty-five
b eighty-eight
c fifty
d nineteen
e ninety
f a hundred
g thirteen
h seventy-five
i thirty
j twenty-three
k seventeen
l ninety-nine

Recording 9

1 Listen and repeat: eight.
2 Open your book at page 36.
3 Put your book on your desk.
4 Look at the picture on page 52.
5 Write your name in your notebook.
6 Put your pen on your desk.

Module 1

Recording 3

Hamburg is in Germany.
Bangkok is the capital of Thailand.
San Diego is in the USA.
Liverpool is in Britain.
Warsaw is the capital of Poland.
St Petersburg is in Russia.
Beijing is the capital of China.
Buenos Aires is the capital of Argentina.
Cairo is the capital of Egypt.
Barcelona is in Spain.
Rome is the capital of Italy.
Monterrey is in Mexico.

Recording 6

a The currency in Australia is the Australian dollar – not the American dollar, of course. In Japan it's the yen, and in France, and other countries like Germany, Italy and Spain it's the euro. In Turkey it's the Turkish lire.
b Stamp number one is from Thailand, number two is from Poland, number three is from Britain and stamp number four is from Egypt.
c Number 1: Mercedes-Benz is a German company, a famous German car company. Number 2: Hyundai is a Korean car company. Number 3: Sony is a famous Japanese electrical company, and number 4: Gucci is a famous Italian fashion company.
d All of these words mean 'hello'. Number one is in Spanish, number two is in Arabic, number three is in Russian, number four is in Chinese and number five is in Italian.
e Nicole Kidman is from Sydney in Australia. Penélope Cruz is from Madrid in Spain, but her home is in Hollywood. Jennifer Lopez is American. She's from New York, but her family are from Puerto Rico.

Recording 7

1 Hello my name's Andrei Vasilev. I'm nineteen years old and I'm from Moscow. I'm a medical student at Moscow University, and I'm not married.
2 Hello, my name's Marisol Martinez, and I'm from Valencia in Spain. Today I'm at Heathrow airport but I'm not here on holiday. I'm here on business. I work for an American company in Spain. I'm thirty-five years old and I'm married with two children.

3 Hi, my name's Toshi Sato and I'm twenty-two years old. I'm on holiday in Europe with my friend Mariko. We're students at Tokyo University. We aren't married.

Recording 8

I'm on holiday. You're here. He's from Italy. She's single. It's here. We're students. They're from Tokyo.
I'm not married. You aren't on holiday. He isn't American. She isn't here. It isn't German. We aren't married.
They aren't here on business.

Recording 11

A: Excuse me, can I ask you a few questions? It's for market research.
B: Yes, of course.
A: Thank you. Okay, question number one, what's your full name?
B: It's William Anthony Barker.
A: Okay, Mr Barker, and where are you from?
B: I'm from Wellington in New Zealand.
A: Lovely, are you here on holiday?
B: Yes, I am.
A: Great. Next question. How old are you? Twenty to twenty-four, or twenty-five to thirty?
B: I'm twenty-six.
A: Great, so that's twenty-five to thirty then, and er, what's your job?
B: I'm a musician; a rock musician.
A: Wow, fantastic! Okay, and er, are you married?
B: No, I'm not. I'm single.
A: Okay, single. Great.
A: Okay and the last two questions. What's your address in England?
B: It's 25 Manor Road, London N10.
A: What's your telephone number?
B: It's 020 7535 3555.
A: Okay, well thank you very much Mr Barker, and have a good holiday in London.
B: Thank you. Bye.
A: Bye.

Recording 12

1 A: Are you on <u>holiday</u>?
  B: Yes, I <u>am</u>.
2 A: Are you <u>married</u>?
  B: No, I'm <u>not</u>.
3 A: Are you <u>American</u>?
  B: No, I'm <u>not</u>.
4 A: Are you <u>here</u> on <u>business</u>?
  B: Yes, I <u>am</u>.
5 A: Is your <u>brother</u> a <u>student</u>?
  B: Yes, he <u>is</u>.
6 A: Is he from <u>London</u>?
  B: No, he <u>isn't</u>.
7 A: Is <u>Monica here</u>?
  B: No, she <u>isn't</u>.
8 A: Are your <u>parents</u> from New <u>York, too</u>?
  B: No, they <u>aren't</u>.

Recording 13

Conversation 1

A = HOTEL RECEPTIONIST, B = GUEST

A: Hello, can I help you?
B: Hello, yes. I've got a reservation. My name's Ream.
A: How do you spell that?
B: R-E-A-M.
A: R-E-A-M. Just a minute. Mrs Emma Ream?
B: That's right.
A: Yes, that's fine. Okay, Mrs Ream. Can you sign here?

B: Okay.

A: And what's your passport number, please?

B: Erm, just a minute. Yes, it's erm, 201-758 …

A: 201-758- … yes?

B: 491.

A: 201-758-491. Okay, thank you very much. Here's your key.

B: What's my room number?

A: You're in room 615. The lift's over there.

B: 615. Okay, thank you.

Conversation 2

A = BANK CLERK, B = CUSTOMER

A: Okay, so I need a few details. First, what's your full name?

B: It's Shireen Rahman. Shireen's S-H-I-R …

A: Yes?

B: -double E-N.

A: S-H-I-R double E-N … Shireen, and how do you spell your surname?

B: Rahman. That's R-A-H-M-A-N.

A: Okay, great. And what's your address?

B: 14 Abbot's Road, Colchester, CO2 7CK.

A: Okay, and what's your home phone number?

B: It's 01206 879879.

A: Okay … 01206 879879, and your work number?

B: 01206 765456.

A: Lovely. And what's your e-mail address?

B: It's s.rahman@firstserve.com.

A: And what's your nationality? British?

B: Yes.

A: And are you married?

B: No, I'm not.

A: And what's your occupation?

B: I'm a medical student.

A: Okay great, and last question. How old are you?

B: I'm twenty-three.

A: Fine, that's everything …

Recording 14

1 What's your surname?
2 How do you spell that?
3 What's your first name?
4 How do you spell that?
5 What nationality are you?
6 Where are you from?
7 What's your address?
8 What's your home phone number?
9 What's your work number?
10 What's your mobile number?
11 How old are you?
12 What's your job?

Module 2

Recording 3

a What's this in English?
b Is this your pen?
c Is that your brother?
d This is my friend Ben.
e These are my parents.
f That's my teacher over there.
g Who are those children?
h Are these your books?

Recording 6

a Have you got your keys with you?
b Have you got an English dictionary?
c Have you got a packet of chewing gum in your bag?
d Have you got a credit card?

e Have you got a cheque book with you?
f Have you got a diary in your bag?
g Have you got a bottle of water with you?
h Have you got a mobile phone?
i Have you got a watch?
j Have you got a camera?

Recording 7

Kemal This is my car and I love it! It is a German car and it is my favourite colour, silver. It is really, really fast, really comfortable and it has got a fantastic CD player – it is just great.

Lisa My favourite thing is not really a thing, it is our pet cat, Billy. We have got four cats in our family, but Billy is my favourite. He is black and white and he has got beautiful green eyes. He is not very friendly with other people but he loves me!

Recording 9

1 Steve Tyler, the guitarist from the rock group Aerosmith, is Liv Tyler's father.
2 Lynne is David Beckham's sister. He's got two sisters, but they aren't famous.
3 Goldie Hawn is Kate Hudson's mother. They are both very famous actresses.
4 Prince William is Queen Elizabeth's grandson. He's Princess Diana's son.

Recording 10

My name's Alex, or Alejandro in Spanish. My family are from Mexico, but we live in London. I'm eighteen and I'm an economics student at London university.

This is my family: my mum, Elena. She's forty-one, and my dad, Enrique. He's fifty-three. He's got a computer business here in London. Then this is my sister, Beatriz. She's at school. I've also got a little brother, Lucas, he's only three. He's really great … really, really funny.

This is my mum's sister, Lourdes, I think she's about thirty-six or thirty-seven. She's a really big lawyer in Mexico. She's very clever, I think. She hasn't got any children … she isn't married. And this is my dad's brother, Roberto. He's a businessman. He's got four or five shops in Mexico City. I think he's quite rich. His wife's name's Isabella. She's a Spanish teacher. She's really nice – really funny, and they've got two children. Bella's about six, I think, and Mateo's four.

Recording 12

Excuse me, how do you say this word?
How do you spell that?
What does this word mean?
What's the English word for this?
Excuse me, what page are we on?

Can you say that again, please?
Can you write it on the board, please?
Can you play the recording again, please?

I don't know.
I don't understand.
I don't remember.
Yes, of course.

Recording 14

1 That thing over there.
2 Those three things.
3 Thank you for those things.
4 It's this Thursday.
5 This Thursday's fine.
6 That's the teacher over there.
7 It's three thirty-three.
8 There are thirteen of those things.

Module 3

Recording 2

a Do you live in a big city?
b Do you go to English classes?
c Do you live with your parents?
d Do you work long hours?
e Do you speak Russian?
f Do you eat in restaurants a lot?
g Do you study at university?
h Do you drink tea?

Recording 5

N = NICKY, J = JEFF

N: When do shops open and close in Australia?
J: They open at about nine and close at about five or half past five, except supermarkets … they close about twelve o'clock at night.
N: And what about pubs and restaurants – what time do they close?
J: On Friday and Saturday they close at about one or two o'clock in the morning.
N: So what time do people start work?
J: Most people start work at about nine and they finish at about five.
N: And do they go home for lunch?
J: No, they eat a sandwich in the park or have lunch in a café.
N: What time do children go to school?
J: Um, they start school about half past eight and finish at about half past three.
N: So what do people do at the weekend?
J: In my city, Sydney most people go to the beach.
N: And do most people live in flats or houses?
J: In the city centre, most people live in flats or apartments, we say, but outside people live in houses with gardens and a lot of people have got swimming pools in their gardens.

Recording 6

1 In Los Angeles, it's nine o'clock in the morning.
2 In São Paulo, it's one o'clock in the afternoon.
3 In London, it's four o'clock in the afternoon.
4 In Moscow, it's eight o'clock in the evening.
5 In Tokyo, it's one o'clock in the morning.
6 In Auckland, it's four o'clock in the morning.

Recording 8

1 A: … because, you see, I don't usually have breakfast. I'm never hungry in the morning.
   B: Really? I love breakfast. I have a really big breakfast every day! I love to start with …
2 C: … so anyway because I'm thirty this year I want to …
   D: Are you thirty this year? Really? Me too! It's horrible, isn't it!
3 E: Are you married?
   F: No. How about you?
   E: No, me neither.
4 G: So do you eat meat?
   H: No, I don't. How about you?
   G: Yes, I eat a little bit, but not much.
5 I: Yeah, and I'm really lucky. I've got a lovely flat in the city centre, just near the station … and I live with some friends …
   J: How fantastic. I still live with my parents, in Kingston. Do you know where that is …?
6 K: So where are you from?
   L: I'm from South Africa, Durban. You're from Argentina, aren't you?
   K: Well Chile, actually, Santiago.

7 M: … because I haven't got any brothers and sisters, you see, I'm an only child.
   N: Yeah, me too. Do you like being an …?

Recording 9

address, business, cousin, bottle, office, married, holiday, normally, waitress, camera, wallet, dinner, parents, tissues

Module 4

Recording 1

Actress Cameron Diaz appears in many films, but she never watches them. The actress hates TV and doesn't have one in her home.
Pop singer Britney Spears loves dolls. She's got hundreds of dolls – the most expensive one cost $500!
In his films, actor Harrison Ford is a man of action – but at home he likes ordinary things. For example, he loves doing housework!
We all know that Superman flies everywhere, but the actor in the TV series, Dean Cain, never travels by plane – he's frightened of flying.
Actor Johnny Depp plays heroes in films, but in real life there is one thing that he is very frightened of: clowns. He hates their faces.
As for film director Woody Allen, he says he hates spiders, dogs, children, small rooms, crowds … and lots of other things, too!

Recording 2

1 He likes housework.
2 She loves dolls.
3 She hates TV.
4 She has a lot of dolls.
5 He never goes on planes.
6 He doesn't like flying.
7 She doesn't watch TV.
8 He doesn't like dogs.
9 He doesn't like crowds.

Recording 3

a She **likes** London.
b He never **watches** TV.
c He **loves** football.
d She **hates** spiders.
e It **opens** early.
f It **closes** late.
g It **starts** at two o'clock.
h It **finishes** today.
i She **understands** English.
j He **goes** to bed late.
k He **does** the housework.
l She **studies** economics.

Recording 8

pens, cousins, boxes, flats, misses, hates, enjoys, waits

Module 5

Recording 1

(answers only)
a 59
b 740
c 100,000,000
d 5
e 77,000,000
f 8
g 9,000,000
h 1,000,000
i 3
j 500,000

Recording 2

Well, she can't take a taxi because she's only got $25 and it costs $35, so that's no good, she can't do that. Mmm, can she take the subway to the airport? Mmm. No, she can't, because it takes ninety minutes and she hasn't got ninety minutes, so not that one.

What about this one? She walks through Central Park, that takes twenty minutes. Then she takes the subway, that takes an hour, and then the Airtrain takes twelve minutes. No, she can't do that because she hasn't got enough time, so that one's no good.

And what about this one? The subway takes five minutes, the bus takes an hour and … which one can she catch? Okay, she can take the bus at twenty past three and it takes an hour so that's twenty past four, that's fine. What about money? The subway costs $2 and the bus costs $13 so that's $15. Yes, she can pay for that, okay. So yes, number four's the only one that she can do.

Recording 3

1 You can't take the bus.
2 Can we take a train?
3 Can I park here?
4 We can walk.
5 They can wait over there.
6 You can go by car.
7 We can't drive there.
8 You can take the ferry.
9 You can't ride your bicycle up there.
10 Can you fly there?

Recording 4

G = GINA, C = CARL

G: Can you travel by tram?
C: No, you can't. We haven't got trams in New York.
G: Can you smoke in the subway?
C: No, you can't. You can't smoke in the stations or the trains.
G: Can you eat on a train?
C: Yes, you can. People eat snacks and even hamburgers on the trains.
G: Can you find a taxi easily?
C: It depends on the time of day. For example, it's not easy to find a taxi in midtown Manhattan between five and six o'clock in the evening, but at other times it's usually okay.
G: Can you have five people in a taxi?
C: No, you can't. The maximum number is four.
G: Can you drive at sixty kilometres an hour?
C: No, you can't. The maximum speed in the city is thirty miles an hour, that's about forty-eight kilometres an hour.
G: Can you ride a bicycle safely?
C: It depends. You can ride safely in Central Park and in some other areas but not in midtown Manhattan. The traffic is bad there.
G: Can you eat in a restaurant at midnight?
C: It depends on the restaurant. Not many restaurants are open at midnight.
G: Can you smoke in a restaurant?
C: No, you can't. You can't smoke in a restaurant or a coffee shop or any eating place.

Recording 5

Passengers Amos and Tenson please proceed to gate 34 immediately. Passengers Amos and Tenson to gate 34.
This is the last call for Gate 6. Final call for Gate 6.
Flight number AA100: please check in at desk 4. That's flight AA100 to check in at desk 4.
Flight number 6143 to Bahrain now boarding at gate number 12. That's flight 6143 boarding at gate 12.
Will Eva Goodwin please return to security? That's Eva Goodwin to security.
Flight number AA100 for London has been delayed by approximately one hour. That's flight number AA100 delayed by one hour because of weather conditions in the UK.

This is the final call for passenger Zhang Chen flying to Hong Kong. Will passenger Zhang Chen please proceed immediately to Gate 14?
Flight AA100 to London now boarding at Gate 12. Flight AA100 boarding at Gate 12.

Recording 6

Passengers for Berlin are requested to check in at Desk number 3. Passengers for Berlin, check in at Desk 3.
Transit passengers arriving on flight AA100 and travelling to Cairo or Milan, please go to the transit desk. Passengers for Cairo or Milan, please go to the transit desk.
Flight number AI264 to Mumbai now boarding at Gate 22. Flight AI264 to Mumbai boarding at Gate 22.
This is a final call for passenger Karen Davis. Will passenger Karen Davis please proceed immediately to gate 12 where her flight is boarding? The last call for Karen Davis for Flight BA0572 to Milan. Please go to gate 12.

Recording 10

P = PASSENGER, C = CLERK

Conversation 1
P: Hello, a single to the airport, please.
C: The Heathrow Express?
P: Yes. How much is it?
C: £15.00
P: Here you are.
C: Thank you. It leaves from platform 7 every fifteen minutes.
P: When is the next one?
C: At 5.40.
P: How long does it take?
C: About fifteen minutes. That train arrives at five to six.
P: Thanks.

Conversation 2
P: A return to Oxford, please.
C: When do you want to come back?
P: Tonight.
C: OK … that's £23.50.
P: Thank you. Can I pay by credit card?
C: Yes. Thank you. Sign there, please.
P: Which platform is it?
C: The next one is on platform 12 at 9.36.
P: And what time does it get to Oxford?
C: It arrives at 10.41.
P: Thank you.

Consolidation Modules 1–5

Recording 2

Conversation 1
A: Hello, Irish Rail Enquiries, Anna speaking.
B: Hello. Can you give me information about trains from Belfast to Dublin?
A: When are you travelling?
B: Tomorrow. What time is the first train in the morning?
A: The first train is at six thirty.
B: And what time does it arrive in Dublin?
A: Eight forty.
B: How much is it?
A: Single or return?
B: Single.
A: £21.
B: Thank you.
A: You're welcome.

Conversation 2

This is London Zoo. Our offices are closed at present and no officer is available. General information on the zoo follows. (pause)

The zoo is open every day from ten a.m. to five thirty p.m. Admission for adults is £10, and for children from seven to fourteen it's £8. Children under seven are free. The nearest underground station is Camden Town which is only ten minutes' walk away. If you come by ...

Conversation 3

C: What time is the football on?

D: It starts at seven.

C: And when does it finish?

D: About 9–9.30. It depends.

C: Oh no! I want to watch a film at nine o'clock!

Module 6

Recording 1

a There's an apple.

b There are a lot of grapes.

c There are five sausages.

d There's a lot of toast.

e There's some tea.

f There are six bread rolls.

g There are no bananas.

h There's no yoghurt.

Recording 2

Kemal Well, I usually have breakfast at home before I go to work. I always have tea, black tea, maybe two or three glasses. And I have cheese and eggs and tomatoes, and in Turkey we have fantastic bread so I usually have bread with butter and jam, and sometimes I have yoghurt, too.

Mi-Kyung I always have breakfast with my family. We usually have white rice, and we have Kim-chi. We cannot live without Kim-chi! Kim-chi is a traditional dish of mixed Korean vegetables. It's very hot and spicy.

Dimitry Well, for breakfast, when I have time, I have tea, usually, black tea with lemon and lots of sugar. Never with milk. Then I have bread and cold meat and some cucumber as well. And then I sometimes have a small cake or some biscuits to finish.

Sonia In Brazil, we have very good tropical fruit, guava, mango and things like that, and we always have fruit for our breakfast – also we have coffee, of course, everybody knows in Brazil we have very good coffee, and maybe bread and jam.

José I don't usually have breakfast. I don't have time because I go to work very early about seven o'clock in the morning, so I just have a cup of coffee for breakfast, in a café with my wife Anita. But I usually stop work for a snack at about eleven, half past eleven and go to a café near my office. I have another cup of coffee and a nice big piece of tortilla – Spanish omelette made with potatoes and eggs – it's really delicious.

Recording 3

1 Eat some fruit.

2 Don't eat any biscuits.

3 Try some melon.

4 Have some tea.

5 Don't have any chocolate.

6 Drink some water.

7 Don't drink any coffee.

8 Eat some bread.

9 Try some water.

10 Don't have any sugar.

Recording 4

There are two women in the picture, and a man and a small boy. I think one of the women is the boy's mother. I think it's a Carnival because the little boy has got a fantastic hat with yellow feathers. He looks great! And there's a young man on the right of the picture. He's got some drums ... three drums.

I can see a lot of food on the table on the left of the picture. There's some soup, yes a big pot of soup and there's some rice, a big plate of rice. There's also a plate of prawns. There are some knives, forks and spoons on the table.

Recording 6

Conversation 1

A: Can I take your order, please?

B: Yes, can I have two Super King-Size burgers, please?

A: Two Super King-Size, yeah?

B: With large fries …

A: Anything to drink with that?

B: Yes, two lemonades, please.

A: Eat in or take away?

B: Sorry?

A: Do you want it to eat here or take away?

B: Oh, eat here, please.

A: Right, that's £8.50, please.

Conversation 2

A: Would you like anything else? Some more coffee?

B: No, thanks. Can we have the bill, please?

A: OK, so it's two coffees and a piece of chocolate cake.

B: That's right.

A: So that's £3.70 for the coffees and £2.90 for the cake. That's £6.60 altogether, please.

B: £6.60. Five, six, seven, there you are. Keep the change.

A: Oh, thank you.

B: That's all right. Goodbye.

A: Bye.

Conversation 3

A: Perfect Pizza, good evening.

B: Yes, I'd like to order a pizza, to be delivered please.

A: All right. What would you like?

B: The one with all the different kinds of cheese. I haven't got a menu, what's the name of it?

A: Right, that's the Cheese Supreme.

B: That's it.

A: And is that regular, large or extra large?

B: How much is the extra large?

A: The regular is £7.60, the large is £10.60 and the extra large is £12.60.

B: Oh ... the large Cheese Supreme, please.

A: Anything else?

B: Yeah, a litre bottle of diet lemonade, please.

A: Right.

B: How much is that altogether?

A: That's £10.60 for the pizza, £1.25 for the drink so that's £11.85 altogether.

B: Okay.

A: All right, what's the address?

B: It's 28 Southlands Road.

Recording 8

Can I have two burgers, please?

Can I have a cheese sandwich, please?

Can I have a glass of water, please?

Can I have the bill, please?

I'd like to order a pizza, please.

I'd like a large one, please.

I'd like a diet lemonade, please.

I'd like another coffee, please.

Module 7

Recording 1

1 John F Kennedy was President of the United States in the 1960s – from 1960 until his death in 1963.
2 Marie Curie was Polish. She was born in Warsaw, the capital of Poland, but she lived a lot of her life in Paris.
3 Laurel and Hardy were comedians and film stars. Their first film was in 1926.
4 The Beatles were all from Liverpool. They were school friends there.
5 From the age of about thirty Beethoven was deaf, but he wasn't born deaf.
6 Mao Ze Dong was born in 1893. He was leader of China from 1949 to 1976.
7 Tolstoy, Dostoyevsky and Chekhov were all Russian writers. Tolstoy's most famous books were *Anna Karenina* and *War and Peace*.
8 Galileo Galilei was an Italian mathematician and scientist. He was born in the sixteenth century.

Recording 2

a He was born in New York.
b Where were you born?
c He wasn't French.
d They weren't from London.
e She wasn't happy.
f They were very late.
g You were right.
h He wasn't in.
i They were sorry.
j You weren't ready.

Recording 3

a 2006
b 1985
c 1990
d 1989
e 1878
f 1914
g 1804
h 1917
i 2030

Recording 4

a The Beatles were first popular in the 1960s.
b Napoleon I was Emperor of France from 1804 to 1815.
c Bill Clinton was President of the USA in the 90s.
d William Shakespeare was born in the sixteenth century.
e The Russian Revolution was in 1917.
f The first landing on the moon was in 1969.
g The Second World War was from 1939 to 1945.
h Mozart was born in the eighteenth century.
i Madonna's first hit single was in the 80s.
j Leonardo da Vinci was born in the fifteenth century.

Recording 6

worked, studied, arrived, loved, needed, waited, believed, lived, wanted, liked, decided, invented, travelled, walked, started, died

Recording 7

a We wanted the bill.
b I needed some money.
c They lived in Spain.
d I liked her.
e They arrived at eight o'clock.
f We worked hard.
g I loved chocolate.
h I believed you.

Recording 8

Part 1

My grandparents were both Russian but they met in London. My grandmother's story was the most interesting. She was a servant girl in Russia and she worked for a rich family. During the First World War this rich family decided to move to London, and they took my grandmother and some of their other servants with them.

But when they got to London they decided they didn't need all these servants – they had too many – so they decided not to keep my grandmother, perhaps they didn't have enough money to keep her … I don't know.

Part 2

So anyway, they decided to take my grandmother for a walk in the centre of London – Oxford Street or somewhere like that, and they said to her 'Wait here. We'll come back in a few minutes.' And then they just went away and never came back.

And she waited, and waited and waited. She was only sixteen years old, a poor servant girl from a farm in Russia … she spoke no English at all, and they left her all alone in the centre of London – can you imagine?

Part 3

Anyway, she walked around for hours and hours trying to find someone who spoke Russian, and in the end she actually found some Russian people who took her to the Russian community in London. There was a big Russian community in Shoreditch in east London in those days.

And there she met my grandfather. He was forty-eight years old, and also Russian, and he decided he needed a wife to look after him. So he married my grandmother and they had two children, my father and my uncle. It's an amazing story isn't it?

Recording 11

A I was born in 1978 in a place called Swansea, which is a town in the south of Wales. My mum and dad were very happy, I think. I was their first daughter.
B I became interested in music when I was very, very young. I always loved music. When I was about three or four, I got a piano, not a real one, a toy piano, for Christmas, and I just loved it. I played with it for hours.
C I went to school in Swansea. I was happy at school most of the time. Music was my favourite subject, of course!
D When I was about twelve, I began to have piano lessons. My mum and dad got a teacher for me, and I learned how to play the piano. It was quite difficult, but I enjoyed it.
E I went to university in Wales. I'm sure you know what I studied, it was Music and Drama, and I graduated in 1999.
F Last year I became a professional singer. I made my first CD. I sang on a CD by someone called Hugh Morris. It was really exciting.

Module 8

Recording 2

a Dracula didn't live in a castle in Poland, he lived in Transylvania. And at night he became a vampire, but he didn't drink vodka, he drank blood as everyone knows!
b Alice didn't follow a white cat, she followed a white rabbit, but she certainly had lots of adventures.
c Robin Hood didn't live in China, he lived in England. It's true that he took money from the rich, but he didn't give it to his girlfriend, he gave it to poor people.
d It's true that Dr Frankenstein created a monster, but the monster wasn't handsome, it was very ugly, and people didn't love it. They were very frightened of it, they hated it.
e Romeo and Juliet weren't forty, they were fourteen years old – very young. It's true that their families hated each other and that the two young people fell in love and got married. But, of course, their families weren't pleased. They were very angry, and Romeo and Juliet didn't live happily together, they killed themselves.

Recording 3

A: Okay, well they didn't wear rollerblades five hundred years ago and they didn't ride scooters, so that's two mistakes.

B: And they didn't use mobile phones, or listen to music on their MP3 players.

A: Where?

B: Here, look.

A: Oh yeah, and they didn't read newspapers then.

B: Are you sure?

A: Yes, of course I am, and they didn't have clocks either.

B: No, okay if you say so. Oh look and the man on the wall's got trainers. They didn't wear trainers five hundred years ago!

A: No, you're right! What else?

B: Well they didn't eat burgers did they?

A: Oh no! And they didn't drink fizzy drinks, look that says cola.

B: Oh yes. Okay, so how many have we got? The rollerblades, the scooter, the burger, the fizzy drink, the clock, the newspaper, that's six. The trainers, the mobile, the MP3 player, nine. What else? This is getting hard now.

A: Mmm.

B: Oh, look! The little boy's got a toy aeroplane. They didn't have aeroplanes in Romeo and Juliet's time!

A: Oh, and the man on the scooter has got a baseball cap, look.

B: Oh yes. Well they definitely didn't have baseball caps then, so that's eleven mistakes. What's the other one. I can't see anything else, can you?

A: No, this is really hard.

B: Yeah. Oh, I know. The man on the scooter's got sunglasses look, under his baseball cap.

A: Oh yes, you're right, and they definitely didn't wear sunglasses in those days, so that's twelve mistakes!

Recording 4

1   They didn't have rollerblades.
2   They didn't eat burgers.
3   They didn't ride scooters.
4   They didn't read newspapers.
5   They didn't listen to music on an MP3 player.
6   They didn't use mobiles.
7   They didn't wear sunglasses.
8   They didn't wear trainers.
9   They didn't have aeroplanes.
10 They didn't drink fizzy drinks.
11 They didn't have clocks.
12 They didn't wear baseball caps.

Recording 5

A: JRR Tolkien wrote books that both adults and children love. Did he have a happy childhood himself?

B: No, he didn't actually – his father died when he was four and then his mother died when he was twelve and he went to live with a cousin who was a Catholic priest … the family were very religious. Tolkien was a religious man all his life.

A: And did he start writing at a young age?

B: Well, actually, his first love was languages, especially ancient languages. In fact he became a professor of Anglo-Saxon – of Old English – at Oxford University.

A: Oh, really?

B: Yes, and as a kind of hobby he 'invented' languages.

A: He invented new languages?

B: Yes, and he wanted to create a fantasy world where people spoke his languages … so that's why he wrote his first stories.

A: So how did he become a famous writer?

B: Well, he started to read his stories to his children and his friends' children, and they loved them, so he wrote more and more and more!

A: So when did the three *Lord of the Rings* books first appear?

B: In about 1954.

A: But, it's not only children who love Tolkien's books.

B: No, of course. In the 1960s the books were very popular with hippies. And they just continued to become more and more successful.

A: So when did Tolkien die?

B: He died in 1973, aged 81.

A: Did he see the films of his books?

B: No, no, no. They appeared a long time after his death!

A: The films made billions of dollars. Did his family make a lot of money from the films?

B: No, unfortunately! Tolkien sold the film rights for his books in 1969 for just £12,000.

A: Oh no! So were his family unhappy about the films?

B: No, not really. In fact his great-grandson Royd Tolkien acted in the last film. He had a small part.

A: Wow! Well, thank you for telling us about JRR Tolkien and now …

Recording 6

1   The last book I read was *His Dark Materials* by Philip Pullman – it was absolutely brilliant.
2   I last went to a concert about three weeks ago – some friends were in a concert at my college.
3   I like different kinds of music but especially rock music – my favourite group are the Red Hot Chili Peppers.
4   I really like Cameron Diaz – she's really pretty and really funny and I think she's a very good actress.
5   It was okay … not fantastic.
6   Yes actually, I love ballet, my favourite is *Swan Lake*.

Recording 9

a   She wasn't married.
b   He doesn't speak English.
c   They weren't at home.
d   I haven't got a pen.
e   I don't like sport.
f   She hasn't got a car.

Module 9

Recording 2

a   A Vespa's slower than a Harley-Davidson.
b   A Vespa's easier to ride than a Harley-Davidson.
c   A Swatch is better for children than a Rolex.
d   A Rolex is smarter than a Swatch.
e   Cola's sweeter than mineral water.
f   Mineral water's healthier than cola.

Recording 3

1   The tallest hotel in the world is the Burj al-Arab hotel in Dubai. It's 321 metres high.
2   The richest person in the world is Ingvar Kamprad from Sweden, head of the IKEA furniture shops. He has a personal fortune of fifty-three billion dollars. Bill Gates, head of Microsoft, has forty-seven billion dollars.
3   The most expensive city to buy a house or flat is Tokyo in Japan because the land is very expensive and there are so many people living there.
4   The oldest university in Europe is Bologna, in Italy but the oldest university in the world is in Karueein, in Morocco. It started in 859 AD – that's more than a thousand years ago.
5   The most successful European football club in the twentieth century was Real Madrid. They won a total of eighty-eight Cups and were European Champions eight times.
6   The highest town in the world is La Paz, the capital of Bolivia. It is 3,600 metres above sea level.
7   The most common word in the English language is 'the'.
8   The most popular group in the twentieth century were the Beatles. They sold 107 million albums in the USA alone.

Recording 4

A = ANNA, B–F = ASSISTANT

1 A: I'd like these, please. And have you got the new Coldplay CD?
  B: Yes, over there. On that stand.
  A: Do you take credit cards?
  B: Yes, Visa or Mastercard. That's £50.20 altogether. Sign there. Thank you.
2 A: Excuse me. Have you got this in a medium?
  C: Let me check for you. Yes, over here.
  A: Oh, it's the wrong colour. Have you got it in blue?
  C: I'm sorry. This is all we've got.
  A: Thanks, anyway.
3 D: Can I help you?
  A: Yes, I want a book about Greece.
  D: You need the travel section over there.
  A: Thank you. And do you sell diaries here?
  D: No, we don't. Try the stationery department.
  A: Which floor is that?
  D: It's on the ground floor.
4 A: Can I try this pen, please?
  E: Sure. Here's some paper.
  A: Mmm. How much is it?
  E: It's £25.00.
  A: Okay, I'll take it. And have you got any diaries?
  E: I'm sorry, we haven't. We only sell them in November and December.
5 A: Can I have one of those please?
  F: This one?
  A: No, the chocolate one.
  F: That's £1.98.
  A: Thank you. What time does the store close?
  F: At eight o'clock.
  A: And is there a restaurant or café here?
  F: Yes, there's a restaurant on the fourth floor. You can take the lift over there.

Recording 6

A = PETER, B–E = ASSISTANT

1 A: How much are these postcards?
  B: Twenty-five pence each. How many have you got?
  A: Eight.
  B: That's two pounds.
  A: And I'd like eight stamps for Canada.
  B: That's £4.80 altogether.
2 A: Do you sell batteries?
  C: Yes, what size?
  A: It's for this camera.
  C: Let me see … Okay. How many do you want?
  A: Two, please.
  C: That's £2.10.
3 A: How much is this T-shirt?
  D: It's £19.99.
  A: Have you got it in a smaller size?
  D: Let me check for you. Yes, I've got one here.
  A: Okay. I'll have it. Do you take credit cards?
  D: Visa or Mastercard. Can you sign here? Thank you.
4 A: Can I have one of those cakes, please?
  E: This one?
  A: No, that one over there.
  E: Anything else?
  A: Yes, some bread.
  E: Large, medium or small?
  A: Small, please.
  E: That's £1.30.

Recording 7

1 A good souvenir from Russia is a Matryoshka doll, you know, with all the smaller dolls inside the bigger ones. You can buy a lot of different kinds. For example, with pictures of the president or of famous people, but I like the traditional ones best. So yes, a doll is the best idea.
2 Last year we were on holiday in Morocco and we loved all the furniture, the tables and lamps, so we bought a traditional Moroccan lamp for our house. It looks great in our living room.
3 I think the best thing to buy is something leather, maybe a leather bag, because here in Italy we make the best bags in the world. So, why don't you buy your friend a leather bag?
4 Spain is famous for music, especially guitar music. I think a CD of Spanish guitar music is a good idea.
5 A souvenir? Well, you can buy some very good cheese in France. So how about a selection of cheese?
6 I went to Kenya on business last month and I wanted to buy something for my wife. She loves clothes so I decided to buy her a silk scarf. She really likes it!

Module 10

Recording 1

1
A: Hello?
B: Hi, it's me.
A: Oh hi, where are you?
B: I'm still in town. I'm waiting for a bus but there's some kind of problem. All the buses are delayed. I'll be a bit late I'm afraid.
A: Again?
B: Look I'm really sorry. I'll see you soon, yeah?
A: Okay.
B: Bye darling.

2
C: Hi darling, how are you?
D: I'm fine, but … where are you? It's eight o'clock!
C: I'm still at work, I'm afraid.
D: Why, what are you doing?
C: We've got a bit of a crisis. I'm finishing an important report for my boss.
D: It sounds very noisy!
C: Sorry darling, I can't hear you. The reception's not very good. I'll call you later, okay?
D: Okay. Speak to you later.

3
E: Hello?
F: Hi Mum, it's me.
E: Hi, where are you?
F: I'm in town. I didn't catch the bus. I'm walking home because I need some books from the library for my homework.
E: Oh right … who's that with you?
F: Oh, I'm chatting to some people I know from school.
E: Well, don't be long, dinner's at seven.
F: Yeah, no problem, Mum. See you soon.
E: Okay, see you, love.

Recording 3

a She's sitting in a café.
b He's waiting for a bus.
c She's standing with her friends.
d She isn't going home.
e They're laughing and chatting.
f It isn't raining.
g They're having a drink.
h She's carrying some books.
i The traffic isn't moving.
j She's wearing school uniform.

Recording 4

laughing, chatting, raining, sitting, waiting, standing, going, having, carrying, moving, wearing

Recording 6

Andy

Our uniforms are interesting because they're very, very old. Imagine … the hats we wear are more than 300 years old. People were smaller then, so the uniforms are really uncomfortable now, and very heavy. You want to move your head all the time, but you can't, of course. The trousers are also old, and they are made of a special kind of leather – also very uncomfortable, so we wear women's tights under them. We don't usually tell people about that, though!

Michelle

Generally, I really like my uniform. It's smart. I wear a white shirt, a black jacket, black trousers or skirt, a kind of black and white tie, and this lovely black and white hat! There's only one thing that I hate … the shoes! Police shoes are really big and ugly. Yuk!

Recording 8

This is a picture of a street. It's a lovely morning and the sun is shining. On the left of the picture there's a girl walking along the street. She's wearing a white skirt and she's listening to some music on her headphones.

In the middle of the picture there's a man with a big black and white dog: the dog is running after a cat. The dog's owner is wearing a pair of sunglasses.

On the right of the picture, there are two women sitting at a table and drinking coffee. One of the women has got short dark hair. She's tall, slim and beautiful.

Recording 9

1 A: Excuse me, have you got the time, please?
   B: Yes, it's ten o'clock.
2 A: Is anyone sitting here?
   B: No, take it.
3 A: Is this bus going to the city centre?
   B: Yes, I think so.
4 A: Is it okay to park here?
   B: Yes, it's fine.
5 A: Excuse me, have you got any change, please?
   B: No, sorry, I haven't.
6 A: Is this the way to the station?
   B: Yes, it's over there.
7 A: What time do the shops close on Saturdays?
   B: At about five thirty.

Consolidation Modules 6–10

Recording 1

a Can I have the bill, please?
b How much is this T-shirt?
c I'd like to order two large pizzas, please.
d I'm sorry, I don't understand. Can you say that again, please?
e Do you sell shampoo?
f Have you got this in a bigger size?
g No, thanks, I'm just looking.

Module 11

Recording 1

1 Dogs can swim.
2 Elephants can't jump.
3 Newborn babies can't see colours.
4 Ants can carry heavy things.
5 Kangaroos can't swim.
6 Some parrots can talk.
7 Chimpanzees can climb trees.
8 Dolphins can jump high.
9 Newborn babies can't walk.

Recording 2

a 400	f 300,000
b 820	g 12,000,000
c 9,000	h 670,000,000
d 4.8	i 7,865
e 20,000	j 12.7

Recording 3

Cats started living with people as pets thousands of years ago, and now there are about 500 million domestic cats around the world. Cats are usually very good hunters and can catch mice and small birds – although they don't often eat them, if they can get normal cat food! In fact, they are very lazy animals: on average, they sleep for about sixteen hours a day. They also spend a lot of time keeping themselves clean by washing their fur with their tongues.

Male cats are called toms and female cats are called queens. Female cats are pregnant for about nine weeks, and usually have between two and five kittens. There are over one hundred breeds of cat, and even a hairless cat called the sphinx cat!

Recording 4

People say that a dog is a man's best friend. People and dogs first started living together about ten thousand years ago. Now there are fifty-three million dogs just in the USA. The Americans spend over two billion dollars on dog food every year – four times what they spend on baby food! Altogether there are about a hundred and fifty breeds of dog. Many dogs work for humans, doing jobs such as helping the blind, helping the police and customs officers to find drugs, and even racing! Greyhound racing is popular in many countries. The fastest greyhounds can run as fast as sixty-five kilometres per hour. Perhaps the most famous working dog was Rin Tin Tin, who died in 1932. He earned his money by making films. He made fifty films and earned about forty-four thousand dollars for each one!

Recording 7

1 There are officially nine planets in our solar system. Mercury is the nearest to the sun and Pluto is the furthest away. But in 2004 scientists discovered Sedna, a possible tenth planet in our solar system.
2 Chow Mein is a type of Chinese food made with noodles and meat.
3 Blood makes up about 8% of the human body, that means that the average adult has about five to six litres of blood.
4 The sun is approximately 150 million kilometres from the earth.
5 The Islamic holy city of Mecca is in Saudi Arabia. It is in the west part of the country.
6 France won the world cup in football in 1998. England won in 1966.
7 There are approximately 1.6 kilometres in a mile – or 0.6 miles in a kilometre.

8 The Terminator actor and governor of California, Arnold Schwarzenegger has lived in the USA for many years but he was actually born in Graz in Austria in 1947.
9 Switzerland has four official languages: German, French, Italian and Romanish.

Recording 9

Do you want some water?
Where were you last night?
What did you do at the weekend?

Recording 10

a big hotel
Is there a hairdresser's near here?
He's got long hair.
Have you got the time?

Module 12

Recording 1

Neela On Saturday night I'm going out with a big group of friends, probably to a club in the city centre. Then on Sunday I'm going to have lunch with my grandparents … the whole family is going to be there because it's my grandmother's birthday.
Phil I'm feeling very tired so I'm not going to do much this weekend, just stay at home and relax. I want to finish the book I'm reading and sleep a lot!
Megan I'm going shopping on Saturday. It's my boyfriend's birthday and I want to get him a digital camera. And then on Sunday we're going to have a barbecue and invite lots of friends.
Jamie I'd like to go away somewhere this weekend, to the country, and maybe go for a long walk. But it depends on the weather.
Anna I'm a hairdresser and I've got to work on Saturday, but on Saturday evening I'd like to see that new film with Keanu Reeves, and then on Sunday afternoon I'm going to a friend's wedding.
Sharif This weekend? Nothing special. On Saturday afternoon I want to watch the football and on Sunday I'd like to do something with the children, maybe take them swimming.

Recording 5

A = AMY, L = LISA

A: It's your birthday next Saturday, isn't it?
L: Yeah, but I don't really know what I want to do. Maybe I'll stay at home and have a quiet night in.
A: Don't be silly, you can't do that! I know, why don't we all go out for a meal somewhere – you, me, Martin, Ben and some of the others maybe?
L: Yeah, okay – that sounds more fun!
A: Where shall we go?
L: There's Bagatti's but we always go there. How about that new French restaurant? I can't remember its name …
A: The French Table?
L: Let's go there. I'd really like to try it.
A: Yeah, it sounds good. I'll speak to Martin and the others and check that they can come. Then shall I phone the restaurant and book a table?
L: Yes, please, if that's okay.
A: What time? Eight, half eight?
L: Let's book it for eight, and then we can go somewhere else later.
A: Yes, good idea!

Recording 6

1 A: How about a coffee?
   B: That sounds nice.
2 A: Shall I take your jacket?
   B: Oh, thanks.
3 A: Shall we ask for the bill?
   B: Yes, good idea.

4 A: I'll take you home.
   B: No, it's okay. I'll call a taxi.
5 A: Why don't we go to the cinema?
   B: Yeah, that's a good idea.
6 A: Let's have another drink.
   B: I'm okay, thanks.
7 A: Shall I call you tomorrow?
   B: Yeah, okay.
8 A: Why don't we meet at the station?
   B: That sounds fine.
9 A: I'll book the tickets.
   B: Great.

Recording 7

J = JULIE, R = ROB, S = SARAH

J: Do you two still want to go away for the weekend – you know, on the 22nd?
R: Yeah, definitely.
S: Yeah, I want to …
J: Because we talked about the Isle of Wight, do you remember?
R: Oh, yes. I'd love to go there. People say it's a really good place for walking, really good cliff walks.
S: Mmm, it's just that I went there last summer and the summer before. I'd like to try somewhere different … a city maybe.
R: Yeah, I can understand that.
J: How about Canterbury? The city's lovely and it's not too far … and we can visit Leeds Castle, too. I'd really like to see Leeds Castle, it looks so beautiful in photos.
S: Yeah, but we can do all that in one day from London – we don't need a weekend.
R: Yeah, you're right, and it's not a great place for walking, if we want to walk …
J: I've got a much better idea! Why don't we go to Dublin for the weekend? I read something about it in the newspaper the other day. You can get really cheap flights, and there's something for all of us …
S: Yeah?
J: Yeah, there are lots of things to see; the castle, the river, Trinity College and things. And it's got really good shops and bars, so there's plenty to do in the evening.
S: It sounds great to me. I love shopping and we all like going out!
J: And you're near the Wicklow Mountains so you can go walking for the day on Sunday, Rob, if you want to.
R: Perfect, well let's go to Dublin then.
S: So … we fly there on the Friday evening after work about what? Six o'clock?
J: Yeah, and then we can come back on Sunday evening about the same time, six o'clock?
R: Yeah, six is good for me. Where are we going to stay – in a hotel?
J: The newspaper article said that B&Bs are really good in Dublin, and they're cheaper than a hotel.
S: Fine. Well, shall we find a B&B then? I'll do that if you like.
J: Okay, and shall I check the times of the flights?
R: Great … perfect!

Recording 8

a How about Canterbury?
b I'd really like to see Leeds Castle.
c I'd like to try somewhere different.
d There are lots of things to see.
e It sounds great to me.
f Let's go to Dublin then.
g Where are we going to stay?
h I'll find a B&B if you like.
i Shall I check the times?

173

Recording 10

Thailand

I = INTERVIEWER, S = SUMALEE

I: So what's the weather like in Thailand, exactly?

S: Well basically, Thailand has three seasons every year. The cool season isn't really cold, just cooler. It's from November to February. Then the hot season is in April and May and the rainy season is from June to October.

I: And does it rain all day in the rainy season?

S: No, no. It rains really heavily, but usually it only lasts for about two hours!

I: So what kind of temperatures do you have?

S: Well in my city, Bangkok, the hottest days in April are about thirty-five degrees, so it's really hot in April, and the coldest in December are about seventeen degrees.

I: So it's never very cold?

S: No, it's never cold.

Canada

I = INTERVIEWER, C = CATHY

I: So is it true that it's always cold in Canada?

C: That's what everyone thinks, but it's not really true. In the Yukon Territory in the north, it's really cold. There's snow there for maybe eight months of the year but in my city Vancouver, on the west coast, it's completely different.

I: So what are the winters like in Vancouver?

C: Most days it's cloudy, I guess, and it can be quite wet, but it isn't really cold.

I: And do you have nice summers?

C: Yeah, the summers are good, it's usually sunny and warm. I guess the average temperature is about 18 degrees, so that's fine!

Recording 12

1 I'd like to drive.
2 I'll post it for you.
3 We're going to stay at home.
4 It's raining and I'm really wet!
5 Let's take a taxi.

Module 13

Recording 2

Will I was always very bad at school. I failed all my exams, and I left secondary school at the age of 16. I'm really sorry I didn't work harder at school. I worked as a van driver for a few years. Then I went to college to get some qualifications. I did a course in information technology. I studied in the evenings after work: for the first time I really enjoyed going to class. I took my exams again and this time I passed! It shows that it's never too late to learn. Now I've got my own computer sales company!

Vicki Before I had children I worked for a big financial company – it was a good job and I earned quite a lot of money, but I worked long hours and there was a lot of travelling abroad. So when my two children were born I stopped work for a few years to look after them. Now they're at school and so I'm training to be a maths teacher – maths was my favourite subject at school. It's a really good job for me because I'll have holidays at the same time as my children.

Francine Languages were always my favourite subjects at school. When I was at primary school they taught us French from the age of eight. I found the lessons interesting, and I soon found that I was good at learning languages, so then I started learning Spanish as well. Now I'm at university. Next year I'm going to Lisbon to study Portuguese. When I graduate, I'd like to look for a job where I can use my languages, in an international company maybe.

Josh I'd really like to be a journalist when I leave school, but it's a very difficult career to get into, so everyone tells me. I want to study history and politics when I go to university, because I think they'll help me with my career, and I'm also helping to write the school magazine, to get some experience of journalism.

Recording 3

a I'll see her at work.
b I won't wait for you.
c I want to go home.
d I'll phone him at the weekend.
e She won't arrive early.
f I'll get up early.
g I go to the gym in the morning.
h We won't walk home.
i I want to speak to her.
j I have two children.

Recording 4

Taka I'd really like to do the course in performing arts, because I'm very interested in dance, but I have to think about my career. I work as a fashion designer and will need to use a computer to design clothes, so I'm going to do the Information technology course. I can study dance and photography in my free time.

Oliver I really like the idea of the performing arts course. I'm in a rock band and I love drama and music, but my parents don't like that idea at all, they don't think it's very useful for my career. They want me to do the information technology course, but I already know a lot about computers and I don't want to spend my life working with computers. So I've decided to do the leisure and tourism course because travelling is quite interesting, and it makes Mum and Dad happy because it's a 'real job'!

Gaby I really liked the idea of the Sports studies course – it looks great – working with people and doing something I enjoy, but if I do the part-time course it's just so long! Four years studying three evenings a week – it's too much. I looked at the childcare course too, but it's working with really small children, and I prefer older children. I don't really know much about small children. So in the end I didn't choose any of these courses. I'm going to look for another sports studies course at a different college, because I want to try to find something shorter.

Module 14

Recording 1

a **Matt** I've spent about thirty hours on the Internet so far this week. I'm really into it. I usually go on about 9.00 in the evening after dinner and things, and I probably stay on until about one, two in the morning. The rest of my family are all in bed, but I can't sleep until really late.

b **Josie** I haven't watched any TV so far this week – I don't own a television. I hate television – it's really bad for you.

c **Richard** I've had three computers in my life so far. The first one was really funny – it was a little box with a really small screen. It didn't have e-mail or the Internet or anything – but it was the most expensive of all my computers!

d **Belinda** I haven't written any letters so far this year, I don't think … no, I don't think so. Nobody writes letters these days, do they? I always send e-mails, or cards if it's a birthday or something personal.

e **Jessica** I don't know how many books I've read so far this year … too many to count. I've read five books this week so far. I usually read about seven or eight in a week. I love reading. If I really like a book, I might read it five or six times.

Recording 3

1 I've lost my mobile.
2 He's forgotten to post this letter.
3 She's phoned three times today.
4 We've sent her a card.
5 Have you sent that e-mail?
6 Has she written to you?
7 I haven't spoken to her this week.
8 He hasn't called today.

Recording 4

Conversation 1

J: Hello, can I speak to Paul, please?
A: Sorry, he's not here.
J: Oh, I see … do you know when he'll be back?
A: Not really, no …
J: OK, I'll try again this afternoon.
A: OK, 'bye.

Conversation 2

B: TKO Travel, good morning.
J: Hello, is that Julia Thompson?
B: Speaking.
J: Hello, this is Jane Hancock, I'm calling about the flight tickets.
B: Oh, right, yes.
J: For Copenhagen? Are they ready yet?
B: Yes, well unfortunately there's a bit of a problem …

Conversation 3

AM: Hello, this is Tania Shaw. Sorry, I'm not here at the moment. Please leave a message after the tone: BEEP.
J: Hi, it's Jane here. Can you call me back? It's about the flight tickets. My number is 890921. Talk to you soon. Bye!

Conversation 4

M: Hello?
J: Hello, Mum, it's me. Is Dad there?
M: He's asleep in front of the television. Shall I wake him up?
J: No, it's okay. Can you ask him to call me?
M: Yes, of course. Is everything okay?
J: Oh yes, I'm fine. I've just got to do all these things before Saturday.

Recording 8

1 stamp   3 month   5 carry   7 just   9 love
2 chat   4 worried 6 camera 8 fantastic 10 study

Module 15

Recording 1

1 **Fabrizio from Venice** Of course, there's lots to see in Venice. It's one of the most famous cities in the world. First of all, there are the canals. We don't have cars in Venice so you have to travel everywhere by canal. The most famous place in Venice is the square, St Mark's Square with St Mark's Cathedral. And there are lots of museums and palaces, and beautiful bridges, too.

2 **Yumi from Kyoto** For me, Kyoto is the most beautiful city in Japan. It's also the oldest city. It has many old traditional buildings and beautiful palaces, temples and gardens. The most famous temple is the Golden Pavilion. There are also very good markets, and also really good shops, and some beautiful modern buildings, too.

3 **Murat from Istanbul** I think Istanbul is maybe the most beautiful city in the world, but of course I come from Istanbul! The city is built on hills around the Bosphoros, and so there are beautiful views across the water. From the water you can see mosques – the most famous is called the Blue Mosque – and palaces and bridges. Istanbul also has a very famous market called the Grand Bazaar. But these days we also have many modern shopping centres and modern buildings and hotels. It's really a fantastic city.

4 **Claudia from Rio de Janeiro** Rio is one of the most exciting cities in South America … first of course we have our famous beach, the Copacabana, and there are many mountains round Rio – the most famous is the Sugar Plum Mountain, where you can see a big statue of Christ, and of course we have our famous stadium … the Maracaná stadium, maybe the most famous football stadium in the world … it's really a great place.

5 **Marina from St Petersburg** You will really love St Petersburg there are so many things to see. The most famous is the Winter Palace, where the Tsars lived, and the Hermitage Museum which is a fantastic art gallery, and we have a very beautiful river too, the River Neva, and of course churches and cathedrals. There is so much to see!

Recording 2

river, mountain, cathedral, museum, palace, gallery, castle, stadium, canal, building, market, temple, garden, statue

Recording 3

1 … and if you look up on the right-hand side of the bus you have a very good view of Edinburgh Castle at the top of the hill. The oldest part of the building – St Margaret's Chapel is nearly 900 years old and the castle as a whole has been occupied since …

2 We are now driving along the street known as the Royal Mile. This is one of the oldest streets in Edinburgh and at 1.6 kilometres (or a mile!) it is the longest. As you can see there are many historic houses in the street and many cafés, bars and restaurants here where you can relax over a drink and …

3 The very old house on your left is John Knox's house. Approximately 500 years old it is the oldest house in the Royal Mile and one of the oldest in Scotland. It is where John Knox the religious leader, died in 1572. Knox was well known in his time …

4 This fine neo-classical building is the Scottish National Gallery and it contains about four thousand paintings, not just by Scottish painters, but also by well-known European painters, such as the Italian master Titian. The gallery opens every day from nine o'clock …

5 And here on the left you can see Holyrood Palace. The palace, which was founded in 1128 is the British Queen's official home in Scotland, and many kings and queens have lived here. The most famous Queen of Scotland, Mary Queen of Scots, lived here from 1561 until 1567 when she moved …

Recording 5

a You have to wear a uniform.
b You don't have to take exams.
c You don't have to study.
d You have to get up early.
e You have to do a lot of exercise.
f You have to have short hair.
g You have to obey instructions.
h You don't have to earn your living.

Recording 6

1 A: Excuse me, is the National Gallery near here?
  B: Yes, it's over there on the right look.
  A: Oh, thank you very much.

2 A: Excuse me, but where's the nearest post office?
  B: It's very near here. Go straight on and it's on the left, it's about 200 metres.
  A: Thank you.

3 A: Sorry, but is this the way to the river?
  B: Yes, take the first street on the left over there, can you see it?
  A: Yes.
  B: Well, go straight on for about a hundred metres and you're there.
  A: Oh great, thanks

4 A: Where's the nearest cashpoint please?
  B: Can you see the statue over there?
  A: Yes.
  B: Go past the statue and take the second street on the right and there's a bank on the left with a cash point there.
  A: Fantastic, thank you.
  B: You're welcome.

Pearson Education Limited
Edinburgh Gate
Harlow
Essex CM20 2JE
England
And Associated Companies throughout the world.

www.longman.com/cuttingedge

© Pearson Education Limited 2005

The right of Sarah Cunningham, Peter Moor and Frances Eales to be identified as authors of this work has been asserted by them in accordance with the Copyright, Designs and Patents Act 1988.

First published 2005
Seventeenth impression 2014

ISBN: 978-0-582-82501-7

Set in 9/12.5pt ITS Stone Informal and 10/13pt Congress Sans.

Printed in China GCC/17

Author acknowledgements

We would like to thank the publishing team for their support and encouragement, in particular Jenny Colley (Senior Publisher), Lindsay White (Project Manager), Shona Rodger (Editor), Rob Briggs (Designer) and Alma Gray (Producer).

The publishers and authors are very grateful to the following people and institutions for keeping user diaries:
Kalli Safras, Elite College, London; Niamh McElwaine, International House, Dublin; Patrick Creed, International House, Dublin and Galway Language Centre; Alan Lee/John McCloskey, Language Link, London; Dave Ruchpaul, TTI School of English, London; Leslie Ann Hendra, International House, London; Emma Metcalf, Chester School of English, Madrid; Jose Andrés Martinez Luciano, Universidad Politécnica (Dpto de Idiomas), Valencia; Giles Perry, Academia Lingua Viva, Madrid; Katherine Ackerley, University of Padova; Richard Straub, University of Trento; Sharon Hartle, University of Verona; Andrea Thurgate, Dida Group, Rome; Diane Wheeler, British Centro Multi-Lingue, Italy; Emma Lush/Berth McNally, International Institute Australia, Brisbane; Luz Aydee Murcia, Myriam Guerrero de Munar, Marcela Del Campo, Cecilia Bonilla, Universidad Javeriana; Tulia Porto de Cubillos, Universidad Sergio Arboleda; Clara Ines Díaz, Universidad Sergio Arboleda, Colombia; Maria Andrea Vera, Asociación Rosarina de Cultura Inglesa, Argentina; Alicja Smreczak-Łach, Wyższa Szkoła Bankowa; Monika Komenda-Wnęk, Politechnika Śląska; Agnieszka Tyszkiewicz-Zora, University of Łódź; Iwona Ewa Gałązka, Politechnika Śląska; Iwona Kałużna, SJO Politechnika Lubelska; Malwina Staszak, Archibald (Private Language School), Poland; Szabó Gabriella, Novoschool Nyelviskola, Budapest; Románé Stahorszki Krisztina, Bill Collinge, ILS Nyelviskola Nyíregyháza, Hungary; Tamara Moskalyova; Larisa Kosyakova, Diplomatic Academy Language School; Elana Gustova, Olga Goliguzova, Language School Megapolis; Yelena Volchkova, Linguistic Centre IFL LC, Russia

and the following people for reporting on the manuscript:
Emma Metcalf, Chester School of English, Madrid; Sharon Hartle, Centro Linguistico, University of Verona; Alastair Agnew, International House, Sydney; Pauline Belimova, 'New People', St Petersburg State University; Susan Clark, Kings School, Oxford; Bursa Uludag University, Turkey; Agnieszka Tyszkiewicz-Zora, University of Łódź, Poland.

We are grateful to the following for permission to reproduce copyright song lyrics:
Music Sales Limited for the lyrics 'Return to Sender' words and music by Otis Blackwell & Winfield Scott © 1962 Elvis Presley Music, USA. Carlin Music Corporation. All rights reserved. International Copyright Secured; and International Music Publications Limited for the lyrics 'Trains and Boats and Planes' words by Hal David and music by Burt Bacharach © 1964 New Hidden Valley Music and Casa David Music, USA, Warner/Chappell Music Ltd. All rights reserved.

Illustrations by:

Adrian Barclay (Beehive) pages 25, 82, 98, 103, 110, 160, 163; Barbara Bellingham (début art) pages 31, 48, 74–75, 106, 141; Francis Blake (Three in a box) pages 18–19, 34–35, 73; Emma Brownjohn (New Division) pages 7, 71, 92, 146; Matt Buckley (Chrome Dome Design) pages 30–31, 110, 132–133; Pete Collard pages 12, 16, 40, 57, 88, 148; Yane Christensen (Sylvie Poggio) pages 6–7, 20, 24, 44–45, 55, 78, 86, 107, 125; Roger Goode (Beehive) pages 52, 54; Gary Kaye page 105; Robert Nelmes (The Organisation) page 131; Pulsar (Beehive) pages 66, 83, 130; Gavin Reece (New Division) page 7

Photo acknowledgements

We are grateful to the following for permission to reproduce copyright photographs:
A1 Pix/Britstock-IFA for page 27(6), /Eric Bach for page 58(1), /Walsh for page 129(a), /Superbild for page 47 (6b), 79 (3 top), 81 (bottom right), 91 (bottom left), 97 (snail), 104(b), 128(2 & 4), /Capel/Sunset for page 138 (Joao); Alamy Images/Michael Klinec for page 42(b), /Andy Bishop for page 91 (bottom centre), /Dynamic Graphics Group/IT Stock Free for page 118, /Sunset for page 143 (bottom left); Art Directors & Trip/Helene Rogers for page 10A (currencies), 46 (centre), 53 (top left), /E.James for page 81 (top right), /D. Palais for page 100(d), /Boris Konov for page 128(5); Aspect Photo Library/J. Alex Langley for page 129(d); Associated Press for page 62; /Borsheim's Jewelry Store for page 80 (top left); John Birdsall for page 14 (top), 46 (left); Neill Bruce Photography for page 80 (bottom); Camera Press for page 22 (centre above), 138 (top left), /Theodore

Wood for page 34 (C. Diaz); Bruce Coleman Collection/Pacific Stock for page 96 (dolphin), /Bruce Reinhard for page 100(b), /Collections/Geoff Howard for page 87(f), 104(d), /Oliver Benn for page 108(1), /Paul Bryans for page 112 (bottom), /Chris Honeywell for page 113 (bottom left); Corbis for page 97 (donkey), 121(b), /Michael Prince for page 14 (bottom left), 15, 91 (top centre), 138 (Marina), /Chuck Savage for page 21 (top), /Paul Barton for page 21 (centre right), /Bob Winsett for page 21 (centre left), /Jack Hollingsworth for page 21 (bottom), /Rob & Sas for page 23 (centre), 146 (Lourdes), /Joe Gemignan for page 23 (right), 146 (Isabella, Roberto, Bella, Mateo), /Ronnie Kaufman for page 23 (left), 104(a), 146 (Elena, engrique, Alex, Beatriz, Lucas), /LWA-Dann Tardif for page 26(3), /Paul A. Souders for page 28(2), 96 (elephant), /Tom Stewart for page 38, 112 (centre above), /Jose Luis Pelaez for page 39, /Macduff Everton for page 42(c), /Georgina Bowatter for page 42(e), /Jon Hicks for page 43(f), /Jon Feingersh for page 53 (top right), /Yann Arthus-Berthand for page 56 (desert), /Bettmann for page 60 (top left), 120(a), /Richard Cohen for page 79 (2 left), /Catherine Karnow for page 80 (right), /Ron Watts for page 87(a), /Sygma/Alan Le Bacquer for page 87(b), /Bohemia Nomad Picturemakers for page 87(e), /Gabe Palmer for page 87(g), /Peter Turnley for page 87(i), /Nancy Ney for page 91 (bottom right), /ESA for page 96-97 (Earth), /Jim Sugar for page 96 (volcano), /Jim Craigmyle for page 100(a), /William Gottlieb for page 100(c), /Reuters for page 100(e), 102, 140 (bottom left), 142, /Marco Cristofori for page 104(c), /Nik Wheeler for page 108(2), /Charles Gupton for page 108(3), /Adam Woolfitt for page 108(4), /Tim Thompson for page 108(5), /NASA for page 121(c), /Reed Kaestner for page 140 (Peter); courtesy of DaimlerChrysler UK Limited for Mercedes-Benz logo page 10(c1); Demon Library for page 26(1); Digital Vision for page 37, /Deil Setchfield for page 46 (right); Eye Ubiquitous/G. Daniels for page 28(3), /Michael George for page 44 (right), /Dean Bennett for page 87(c), /David cumming for page 135 (top); Getty Images/Hulton for page 64 (top), / Image Bank/Juan Silva for page 8, /Yellow Dog Productions for page 13, /Ryan McVay for page 14 (bottom right), 139 (left), /T. Anderson for page 49 (top), /Larry Dale Gordon for page 53 (bottom), /GDT for page 76, /L.D. Gordon for page 145 (top), /Stone/Fisher/Thatcher for page 11(2), 141, /Lorne Resnick for page 42(d), /Brian Bailey for page 53 (centre right), /James Darrell for page 58(3), Zeynep Sumen for page 81 (top left), /Walter Hodges for page 117 (bottom left), /Terry Vine for page 117 (bottom right), /Dave Nagel for page 148 (bottom right), /Taxi/Antonio Mo for page 26(4), /Rob Gage for page 27(5), /Nick Dolding for page 32 (bottom), /Gone Loco, Debut Art for page 126, /Telegraph Colour Library/Heimo Aga for page 43(g), /Jochem D. Wijnands for page 81 (bottom left), /Jochem D. Wijnands for page 81 (bottom left); Ronald Grant Archive for page 34 (centre right), 70 (centre above & centre); Robert Harding Picture Library for page 112 (top), /Lee Frost for page 128(1), /Rolf Richardson for page 129(b); Hutchison Library/David Hodge for page 112 (centre below), /Robert Aberman for page 113 (top right), /Nancy Durrell McKenna for page 113 (bottom right); Image State/Pictor International for page 32 (top right), /Images colour Library for page 115 (top left), /Rob Gage for page 140 (Sophia); Impact Photos/Robin Laurance for page 9(5), /Tony Page for page 28(4), /Pamla Toler for page 29. /Anthony Taylor for page 32 (top left), /Simon Shepheard for page 87(d), /Mark Henley for page 87(h); Kobal Collection for page 68 (top left), 60 (bottom right & bottom left), 69 (centre right & bottom), 70 (top); Jeff Moore courtesy Sony UK Ltd for page 10(c2), courtesy Hyundai page 10(c3), 47 (4a), 113 (bottom left), 122(a), (c), (d), (e), (f), 143 (bottom right); Moviestore Collection for page 68 (top right), 69 (centre), 70 (centre below); Network Photographers/Mark Peterson/SABA for page 58(2), /Harriet Logan for page 101, /Gideon Mendel for page 129(c); NHPA/N.A. Callow for page 96 (ant); PA News Photos/DPA for page 9(3);
Pearson Education/Rob Briggs for page 47(4b, c & d), 84 (all), 122(b), /Peter Lake for page 89 (centre & right); Photographers' Library for page 70 (2 right), 79(4 top and bottom), 129(e); Photo Library.com/Ron Kimball for page 79 (1 below); Photos for Books for page 9(6 & 8), 53 (centre left), 68 (bottom), 72 (top & bottom); Photostage/Donald Cooper for page 117 (top); Pictures Colour Library for page 28(1), 42(a), 47 (6a & c), 81 (bottom centre), 128(3); Popperfoto for page 9(1), 79(1 top), /Pierre Virot for page 79(1 above), /Vision for page 89 (left); Powerstock/Daniel Torello for page 11(3), /Superstock for page 43(h), /Lucille Khornak for page 44 (left), /Enrique Algarra for page 91 (top left), /Serge Krouglikoff for page 91 (top right), /Fabio Cardoso for page 115 (top right), /Nils-Johan Norenlind for page 134 (top), /Chmura for page 134 (bottom), /Antonio Real for page 135 (bottom), /Marcos Welsh for page 143 (top), /Orangestock for page 143 (centre); Reuters/Gary Hershorn for page 9(7), /Paulo Whitaker for page 115 (bottom); Rex Features for page 10(c4), /SIPA for page 10E (centre), /A. Rodriguez for page 22 (top), /Erik C. Pendzich for page 22 (centre below), /Vinnie Zuffante for page 34 (top left), /C. Lucas Film/Everett for page 34 (top right), /C.W. Disney/Everett for page 34 (bottom), 47 (top centre), /Kevin Wisniewski for page 34 (W. Allen), /ZZ/MBZ/SXL for page 36 (left), /Marco Marianello for page 47 (top left), /CNP for page 60 (top right), /Trevor Clark for page 60 (bottom), /CSU Archive/Everett for page 63 (left), /20th Century Fox/ Everett for page 69 (top right), /SNAP for page 70 (bottom), /Mike St Maur Shiel for page 72 (centre right), /Jim Smeal for page 138 (top right), /Robin Hume for page 140 (top left), /PGE for page 140 (top right); Stockmarket/David Lawrence for page 47 (4e); Topham/HIP/Science Museum for page 63 (right), /Image Works for page 56 (right), /Mike Greenlar for page 9(4), /Mitch Wojnarowicz for page 11(1), /Elizabeth Crews for page 26(2), /Jeff Greenberg for page 27(7), /National Pictures for page 10E (right), /PA for page 10E (left), 22 (bottom), 36 (right), 47 (top right), /Picturepoint for page 60–61 (centre), 61 (top right, bottom left & bottom right), 64 (bottom), 69 (top left), 79(3 below), /ProSport/Tommy Hindley for page 9(2), /UPPA for page 61 (top left).

Cover photograph: Telegraph Colour Library

Picture Researcher: Liz Moore.

Designer: Roarr Design

This book is dedicated to Joseph, Jessica and Isabel.

NEW

CUTTING
EDGE

MINI-DICTIONARY

ELEMENTARY

Longman

www.longman.com

Pearson Education Limited
Edinburgh Gate
Harlow
Essex CM20 2JE
England
and Associated Companies throughout the world.

www.longman.com/cuttingedge

First published 2005

Set in Nimrod by Letterpart, UK

Printed in Spain by Mateu Cromo, S.A. Pinto (Madrid)

ISBN 0582 825016

The definitions in *New Cutting Edge Elementary
Mini-dictionary* are taken from *Longman WordWise
Dictionary* © Pearson Education Limited 2000

The British National Corpus is a collaborative initiative
carried out by Oxford University Press, Longman, Chambers
Harrap, Oxford University Computing Services, Lancaster
University's Unit for Computer Research in the English
Language, and the British Library. The project received
funding from the UK Department of Trade and Industry and
the Science and Engineering Research Council, and was
supported by additional research grants from the British
Academy and the British Library.

Welcome to the *New Cutting Edge Mini-dictionary!*

This Mini-dictionary is based on the *Longman WordWise Dictionary*. As in the full-size dictionary, there is all the information you need to know about a word.

What information does the Mini-dictionary provide?

- the pronunciation of the word
- a simple definition
- an example sentence with the word in context
- information about grammar, word combinations, usage and opposites
- a space for you to write a translation

Which words are in the Mini-dictionary?

The Mini-dictionary only includes words and phrases that appear in *New Cutting Edge Elementary Students' Book* or on the Class Cassette/Audio CD. It does not include very simple words that you know already or the meanings of words which are not used in the Students' Book.

How does the Mini-dictionary present grammar?

- Every word in the Mini-dictionary is labelled to show its part of speech. The main labels used are:

  adjective
  adverb
  noun
  verb
  modal verb
  preposition
  pronoun

- Most nouns are also labelled C (countable) or U (uncountable).

A, a

abroad /əˈbrɔːd/ *adverb* when you go abroad, you go to another country: *Have you travelled abroad much?*

accident /ˈæksədənt/ *noun* [C] **by accident** if something happens by accident, no one planned it or expected it to happen: *We met by accident in the street.*

activity /ækˈtɪvəti/ *noun* [C] plural **activities** something that you do: *outdoor activities such as hiking and climbing*

addicted /əˈdɪktɪd/ *adjective* comparative **more addicted**, superlative **most addicted** liking something so much that you do not want to stop doing it: *My kids are addicted to surfing the Net.*

address /əˈdres/ *noun* [C] plural **addresses**
1 the number of the house and the name of the street and town where you live: *My address is 37 King Street, London.*
2 the letters or numbers you use to send an e-mail to someone: *Give me your e-mail address.*

adventure /ədˈventʃə/ *noun* [C] plural **adventures** an unusual, exciting, or dangerous thing that happens to someone: *It's a book about Johnson's adventures at sea.*

aftershave /ˈɑːftəʃeɪv/ *noun* [C, U] a liquid with a nice smell that a man puts on his skin: *Are you wearing aftershave?*

allergic /əˈlɜːdʒɪk/ *adjective* comparative **more allergic**, superlative **most allergic** if you are allergic to something, you become ill if you touch, eat, or breathe it: *I am allergic to peanuts.*

altogether /ˌɔːltəˈɡeðə/ *adverb* when you include everyone or everything: *The bill came to £45 altogether.*

ancient /ˈeɪnʃənt/ *adjective* comparative **more ancient**, superlative **most ancient** many hundreds of years old: *an ancient temple*

angry /ˈæŋɡri/ *adjective* comparative **angrier**, superlative **angriest** if you are angry, you want to hurt or criticize someone because they have done something bad to you: *I am very angry with you.*

annoying /əˈnɔɪ-ɪŋ/ *adjective* comparative **more annoying**, superlative **most annoying** making you feel a little angry: *He has an annoying habit of interrupting.*

appear /əˈpɪə/ *verb* third person singular **appears**, present participle **appearing**, past tense **appeared**, past participle **have appeared**
1 if something appears somewhere, you see it for the first time: *The*

calendars will appear in the shops in September.
2 to take part in a film, play, concert, television programme etc: *He is currently appearing in a play at the Lyric Theatre.*

2 · · · · · · · · · · · · ·

apply for /ə'plaɪ fə/ *verb* third person singular **applies for**, present participle **applying for**, past tense **applied for**, past participle **have applied for** to ask for something in writing, such as a job, a place at a college etc: *I applied for a place on the computing course.*

· · · · · · · · · · · · · ·

approximately /ə'prɒksəmətli/ *adverb* a little more or less than an exact number, amount etc → same meaning ABOUT: *It will take approximately 15 minutes to walk to the station.*

· · · · · · · · · · · · · ·

Arabic /'ærəbɪk/ *noun* [U] the language of Arab people and the religious language of Islam

· · · · · · · · · · · · · ·

architecture /'ɑːkətektʃə/ *noun* [U] the style and design of buildings: *The city has some beautiful architecture.*

· · · · · · · · · · · · · ·

area /'eəriə/ *noun* [C] plural **areas**
1 a part of a country, town, building etc: *Camden is my favourite area of London.* | *a room with an area for children to play*
2 a particular subject or type of activity: *The course covers three main subject areas.*

1 · · · · · · · · · · · · ·

2 · · · · · · · · · · · · ·

army /'ɑːmi/ *noun* [C] plural **armies** the part of a country's military force that is trained to fight on land: *My brother joined the army.*

· · · · · · · · · · · · · ·

arrival /ə'raɪvəl/ *noun* [U] when you get to a place you were going to: *Julie met Mike a few days after her arrival at college.*

· · · · · · · · · · · · · ·

arrive /ə'raɪv/ *verb* third person singular **arrives**, present participle **arriving**, past tense **arrived**, past participle **have arrived** to get to a place after a journey: *We arrived at the party just as Lee was leaving.* | *If the train is on time, we will arrive in Oxford by eight.*

· · · · · · · · · · · · · ·

art /ɑːt/ *noun* plural **arts**
1 [U] things that you can look at such as drawings or paintings, that are beautiful or express ideas: *Do you like modern art?*
2 the arts [C] art, music, theatre, film, literature etc: *I am interested in the arts.*

1 · · · · · · · · · · · · ·

2 · · · · · · · · · · · · ·

· · · · · · · · · · · · · ·

art gallery /'ɑːt ˌgæləri/ *noun* [C] plural **art galleries** a building where you go to see paintings, drawings etc: *The city has several important art galleries.*

artist /'ɑːtɪst/ *noun* [C] plural **artists** someone who draws or paints pictures: *It is hard to make money as an artist.*

atmosphere /'ætməsfɪə/ *noun* [singular] the kind of feeling that you get when you are in a place: *The town has a nice friendly atmosphere.*

attention /ə'tenʃən/ *noun* [U] when you watch, listen to, or think about something carefully: *You should* **pay** *more* **attention** *in class.*

attractive /ə'træktɪv/ *adjective* comparative **more attractive**, superlative **most attractive** pretty or pleasant to look at: *His new girlfriend is very attractive.*

aunt /ɑːnt/ *noun* [C] plural **aunts** the sister of your father or mother, or the wife of your UNCLE: *I'm going to stay with my aunt.* | *Aunt Mary is here.*

average¹ /'ævərɪdʒ/ *noun* [U] **on average** used for talking about what usually happens: *On average, men still earn more than women.*

average² *adjective*
1 the average amount is the amount you get when you add several figures together and then divide the result by the number of figures: *The average age of the students is 14.*
2 typical or normal: *The average person doesn't know much about computers.*

awful /'ɔːfəl/ *adjective* comparative **more awful**, superlative **most awful** very bad or unpleasant: *What awful food!*

B, b

B & B /ˌbiː ən 'biː/ *noun* [C] plural **B & Bs** a house or a small hotel where you pay to sleep and have breakfast: *We stayed at a small B & B in the Cotswolds.*

baby /'beɪbi/ *noun* [C] plural **babies** a very young child who has not learned to talk yet: *The baby's crying.*

backwards /'bækwədz/ *adverb* towards the direction that is behind you → opposite FORWARD: *He fell over backwards.*

bad /bæd/ *adjective* comparative **worse** /wɜːs/ superlative **worst** /wɜːst/
1 not enjoyable or pleasant → opposite GOOD: *bad weather* | *I've had a really bad day.* | *I've got some bad news for you.*
2 of a low standard or quality → opposite GOOD: *I've never read such a bad essay.* | *That was a really bad party.*

3 serious or severe: *Was the traffic bad this morning?*
4 not useful or suitable → opposite GOOD: *That's a bad idea.*
5 something that is bad for you is not healthy for your body or mind → opposite GOOD: *Smoking is bad for you.*
6 bad at not able to do something well → opposite GOOD: *Gary's really bad at maths.*
7 not bad fairly good: *'Was the food good?' 'Not bad.'*
8 feel bad to feel ill: *I felt bad the next morning.*

barbecue /'bɑːbɪkjuː/ *noun* [C] plural **barbecues** when you cook and eat hot food outdoors, on a fire or a special piece of equipment: *We had a barbecue on the beach.*

basement /'beɪsmənt/ *noun* [C] plural **basements** the rooms in a building that are below the level of the ground: *We keep our wine in the basement.*

beach /biːtʃ/ *noun* [C] plural **beaches** an area of sand next to the sea where people often go to relax or swim in the sea: *Shall we go to the beach?*

beard /bɪəd/ *noun* [C] plural **beards** the hair that grows on the bottom part of a man's face: *He has shaved his beard off.*

beautiful /'bjuːtəfəl/ *adjective* comparative **more beautiful**, superlative **most beautiful** very attractive or pleasant: *Some of the models were incredibly beautiful.* | *That's a beautiful picture.* | *The music was really beautiful.*

become /bɪ'kʌm/ *verb* third person singular **becomes**, present participle **becoming**, past tense **became** /bɪ'keɪm/ past participle **have become**
1 *formal* to start to be or do something → same meaning GET¹: *The weather had become colder.* | *It is becoming difficult to find a parking space.* | *Dad started to become angry.*
2 if someone becomes a doctor, teacher etc, they start to be a doctor, teacher etc: *At the age of only 35 he became a judge.*

begin /bɪ'gɪn/ *verb* third person singular **begins**, present participle **beginning**, past tense **began** /bɪ'gæn/ past participle **have begun** /bɪ'gʌn/
1 to start doing something, or to start to happen → same meaning START: *The exam will begin at 9:00.* | *She began to cry.*
2 begin with if a book, film, word etc begins with something, that is how it starts → same meaning START: *It begins with a description of the author's home.*

believe /bə'liːv/ *verb* third person singular **believes**, present participle **believing**, past tense **believed**, past participle **have believed**
1 to think that something is true: *I can't believe they're brothers.*
2 if you believe someone, you think that they are telling the truth: *I told her what happened, but she didn't believe me.*

belt /belt/ noun [C] plural **belts** a band of leather or cloth that you wear around your waist, for example to stop your trousers or skirt from falling down: *I tightened my belt.*

best¹ /best/ adjective
1 better than anyone or anything else: *This is the best Chinese restaurant in town.* | *Where's the best place to leave my bike?*
2 your best friend the friend you know and like the most: *Susan's my best friend.*

best² adverb most: *Which bit of the film did you* **like best**?

best³ noun [C] plural **best the best** the person or thing that is better than any others: *Which song is* **the best**?

between /bɪ'twiːn/ preposition
1 showing that a place is in the middle, with other places at a distance from it: *Oxford is between London and Birmingham.*
2 after one event or time and before another: *I didn't see my parents at all between Christmas and Easter.*
3 showing a range of amounts, by giving the largest and smallest: *My journey to school takes between 30 and 40 minutes.* | *children aged between 7 and 11*
4 showing who is involved in a relationship, agreement, fight etc: *There has always been a friendly relationship between these two countries.*
5 showing which two things or people you are comparing: *the contrast between town and country life*

big /bɪg/ adjective comparative **bigger**, superlative **biggest**
1 large → opposite SMALL: *the biggest city in the world*
2 important or serious → opposite SMALL: *It was the biggest mistake of my life.*
3 informal very successful: *His last film was a big hit.*

bill /bɪl/ noun [C] plural **bills** a list of things that you have bought or that someone has done for you, showing how much you have to pay for them: *Have you* **paid the electricity bill**?

bird /bɜːd/ noun [C] plural **birds** an animal with wings and feathers that can usually fly. Female birds produce eggs

blind¹ /blaɪnd/ adjective a blind person cannot see because their eyes are damaged: *She is going* (=becoming) **blind**.

blind² noun [plural] **the blind** people who cannot see: *special facilities for the blind*

blood /blʌd/ noun [U] the red liquid inside your body: *I cut my finger and there was blood everywhere!*

board /bɔːd/ *verb* third person singular **boards**, present participle **boarding**, past tense **boarded**, past participle **have boarded**
1 to get on a plane, ship, or train: *Passengers in rows 15 to 25 may now board.*
2 if a plane or ship is boarding, passengers are getting on it: *Flight 207 for Paris is now boarding.*

1 . . . .

2 . . . .

bored /bɔːd/ *adjective* comparative **more bored**, superlative **most bored** unhappy and impatient because something is not interesting or you have nothing to do: *Most of the students looked bored.*

. . . .

boring /ˈbɔːrɪŋ/ *adjective* comparative **more boring**, superlative **most boring** something that is boring makes you feel unhappy and impatient because it is not interesting in any way: *The programme was so boring she fell asleep.*

. . . .

born /bɔːn/ *adjective* **be born** to come out of your mother's body and start your life: *I was born in 1986.*

. . . .

boyfriend /ˈbɔɪfrend/ *noun* [C] plural **boyfriends** a boy or man who you have a special romantic relationship with: *Leo is Anya's boyfriend.*

. . . .

breakfast /ˈbrekfəst/ *noun* [C, U] plural **breakfasts** the meal that you eat in the morning: *I haven't **had breakfast** yet.*

. . . .

breed /briːd/ *noun* [C] plural **breeds** a particular type of dog, horse etc: *a rare breed of sheep*

. . . .

bridge /brɪdʒ/ *noun* [C] plural **bridges** a special road that is built over a river so that people, trains, or cars can cross it: *They are building a new bridge over the river.*

. . . .

brilliant /ˈbrɪljənt/ *adjective* comparative **more brilliant**, superlative **most brilliant** BrE informal very good or enjoyable: *We had a brilliant time!*

. . . .

brother /ˈbrʌðə/ *noun* [C] plural **brothers** a boy or man who has the same parents as you: *This is my brother Dave.*

. . . .

building /ˈbɪldɪŋ/ *noun* [C] plural **buildings** a place such as a house that has a roof and walls: *The science laboratory is in this building.*

. . . .

business /ˈbɪznəs/ *noun* [C, U] plural **businesses**
1 [U] making money by buying or selling things: *You need a lot of money to succeed **in business**.*
2 [C] an organization that produces or sells things: *a small **family business***
3 on business because of your work: *The next day, Tim went to Paris on business.*

1 . . . .

2 . . . .

3 . . . .

busy /'bɪzi/ *adjective* comparative **busier**, superlative **busiest**
1 if you are busy, you have a lot of things to do: *a busy mother of three small children*
2 a busy time is a time when you have a lot of things that you must do: *Christmas is always the busiest time of year*.
3 a busy place is full of people, cars etc: *We live on a very busy road*.

1 · · · · · · · · · · ·
2 · · · · · · · · · · ·
3 · · · · · · · · · · ·

buy /baɪ/ *verb* third person singular **buys**, present participle **buying**, past tense **bought** /bɔːt/ past participle **have bought** if you buy something, you give someone money and they give you the thing in return: *I buy my computer games from a shop in the high street.* | *Ken bought a box of chocolates.*

· · · · · · · · · · ·

C, c

call¹ /kɔːl/ *verb* third person singular **calls**, present participle **calling**, past tense **called**, past participle **have called**
1 to telephone someone → same meaning **PHONE**, **RING**: *I called Sue at her office in London.*
2 **to give someone or something a name**: *If my baby's a boy, I'm going to call him William.*
3 to describe someone or something using a particular word or phrase: *Critics have called his latest film a great success.*
4 to say something loudly because you want someone to hear you: *We could hear someone calling for help*.

1 · · · · · · · · · ·
2 · · · · · · · · · ·
3 · · · · · · · · · ·
4 · · · · · · · · · ·

call² *noun* [C] plural **calls**
1 when you speak to someone on the telephone: *Could I use your phone to make a call please?*
2 a message at an airport that a particular plane will soon leave: *This is the last call for flight BA872 to Moscow.*

1 · · · · · · · · · ·
2 · · · · · · · · · ·

calorie /'kæləri/ *noun* [C] plural **calories** an amount of energy that is in food: *An average potato has about 90 calories.*

· · · · · · · · · · ·

campsite /'kæmpsaɪt/ *noun* [C] plural **campsites** *BrE* a piece of land where you can stay in a tent: *We reached the campsite early in the evening.*

· · · · · · · · · · ·

canal /kə'næl/ *noun* [C] plural **canals** a long narrow area of water that has been cut into a piece of land so that boats can travel along it: *Venice is famous for its canals.*

· · · · · · · · · · ·

capital /'kæpətl/ *noun* [C] plural **capitals**
1 the most important city in a country, where the government and other big organizations are: *Paris is the capital of France.*
2 the large form of a letter of the alphabet, that you use at the beginning of a name or sentence: *The days of the week always begin with a capital.*

1 · · · · · · · · · ·
2 · · · · · · · · · ·

career /kə'rɪə/ noun [C] plural **careers** a job that you learn to do and work in for a long time: *careers in business and finance.*

carpet /'kɑːpɪt/ noun [C] plural **carpets** a thick piece of material that covers a floor

carry /'kæri/ verb third person singular **carries**, present participle **carrying**, past tense **carried**, past participle **have carried** to hold something in your hands or arms and take it somewhere: *Would you like me to carry your bag?*

cartoon /kɑː'tuːn/ noun [C] plural **cartoons**
1 a film that is made with characters that are drawn, rather than real actors: *a Walt Disney cartoon*
2 a drawing, especially in a newspaper or magazine, that makes a joke about something or tells a story: *a cartoon that appears in the Washington Post*

cash point /'kæʃpɔɪnt/ noun [C] plural **cash points** *BrE* a machine that you can use to get money from your bank account without going into the bank: *I can go to the cash point and get £50 out.*

castle /'kɑːsəl/ noun [C] plural **castles** a large strong building that was built in the past to keep the people inside safe from being attacked: *a 12th century castle*

casual /'kæʒuəl/ adjective comparative **more casual**, superlative **most casual** casual clothes are comfortable and you wear them in informal situations: *casual trousers*

catch /kætʃ/ third person singular **catches**, present participle **catching**, past tense **caught** /kɔːt/ past participle **have caught**
1 catch a bus, train etc to get on a bus, train etc: *I caught the 7.30 train to London.*
2 to stop a person or animal from running or moving away from you: *I caught a fish in the river today.*

cathedral /kə'θiːdrəl/ noun [C] plural **cathedrals** a very large church that is the most important one in a particular area: *Thousands of tourists visit the cathedral every year.*

centre /'sentə/ noun [C] plural **centres**
1 the part in the middle of a city or town where most of the shops, restaurants, clubs etc are: *We took a bus to **the centre of** Cairo.*
2 a building where people go for a particular purpose: *I have an appointment at the Health Centre this afternoon.*

century /'sentʃəri/ noun [C] plural **centuries** a period of 100 years, used especially for dates: *at the beginning of the last century*

cereal /'sɪəriəl/ noun
1 [U] a food you eat for breakfast that contains a mixture of wheat, rice, nuts etc, and that you usually mix with milk: *a bowl of cereal*

2 [C] a plant such as wheat or rice that is grown for food: *Other cereals are grown in this region too.*

chat[1] /tʃæt/ *noun* [C] plural **chats** when you talk in a friendly and informal way with someone: *Let's meet for coffee and a chat.*

chat[2] *verb* third person singular **chats**, present participle **chatting**, past tense **chatted**, past participle **have chatted** to talk in a friendly and informal way: *Pete and I were chatting in the bar.* | *What are you two chatting about?*

chat room /'tʃæt ruːm, rʊm/ *noun* [C] plural **chat rooms** a place on the Internet where you can have a conversation with other people by writing messages, usually about a particular subject: *Children should be taught to be careful about who they talk to in chat rooms.*

cheap /tʃiːp/ *adjective* comparative **cheaper**, superlative **cheapest** something that is cheap does not cost very much money, or costs less money than you expect → opposite **EXPENSIVE**: *cheap rail fares* | *CDs are much cheaper in the US.*

check /tʃek/ *verb* third person singular **checks**, present participle **checking**, past tense **checked**, past participle **have checked**
1 to do something in order to make sure that everything is safe, correct, or working properly: *The firemen check all the equipment daily.*
2 to ask someone's advice or permission before you do something: *I'm not authorized to give you a refund – I'll have to check first.*

check in /ˌtʃek 'ɪn/ *verb* third person singular **checks in**, present participle **checking in**, past tense **checked in**, past participle **have checked in** to go to the desk at an airport and say that you have arrived: *We have to check in an hour before the flight leaves.*

cheque book /'tʃekbʊk/ *noun* [C] plural **cheque books** a small book of containing pieces of paper that you write on and use to pay for things: *You need to report the loss of your cheque book immediately.*

chess /tʃes/ *noun* [U] a board game for two players in which you must catch your opponent's king in order to win: *a game of chess*

chew /tʃuː/ *verb* third person singular **chews**, present participle **chewing**, past tense **chewed**, past participle **have chewed** to bite something in your mouth many times in order to taste it: *He was chewing a piece of gum.*

chewing gum /'tʃuːɪŋ ˌɡʌm/ *noun* [U] a type of sweet that you chew for a long time, but do not swallow: *a stick of chewing gum*

childhood /'tʃaɪldhʊd/ *noun* [U] the time when you are a child: *I had a happy childhood.*

choose /tʃuːz/ *verb* third person singular **chooses**, present participle **choosing**, past tense **chose** /tʃəʊz/ past participle **have chosen** /ˈtʃəʊzən/ to decide to have or do the thing you like best: *It took us ages to choose a new carpet.*

church /tʃɜːtʃ/ *noun* [C, U] plural **churches** a building where people in the Christian religion go to pray: *We always **go to church** on Sundays.*

cinema /ˈsɪnəmə/ *noun* [C] plural **cinemas** *BrE* a building where you go to see a film: *Shall we go to the cinema tonight?*

city /ˈsɪti/ *noun* [C] plural **cities** a large important town: *Leeds is the third largest city in England.*

classical music /ˌklæsɪkəl ˈmjuːzɪk/ *noun* [U] music by people such as Beethoven and Mozart that is serious and important: *Do you like listening to classical music?*

clean¹ /kliːn/ *adjective* comparative **cleaner**, superlative **cleanest** not dirty: *The room looked very neat and clean.*

clean² *verb* third person singular **cleans**, present participle **cleaning**, past tense **cleaned**, past participle **have cleaned** to remove dirt from something, for example by washing it: *I need to clean my boots.*

cliff /klɪf/ *noun* [C] plural **cliffs** a high piece of land with a very steep side, usually next to the sea: *Don't go near the edge of the cliff.*

close /kləʊz/ *verb* third person singular **closes**, present participle **closing**, past tense **closed**, past participle **have closed**
1 to make something shut: *Please could you close the window?*
2 if a shop, bank etc closes, it is no longer open so you cannot use it: *The shops close at 5:30. | The school is closed for the summer.*

clothes /kləʊðz/ *plural noun* [U] the things such as shirts, skirts, or trousers that you wear: *She was wearing smart clothes. | He put on some clean clothes.*

coach /kəʊtʃ/ *verb* third person singular **coaches**, present participle **coaching**, past tense **coached**, past participle **have coached** to teach someone how to play a sport: *Who coaches your football team?*

coast /kəʊst/ *noun* [C] plural **coasts** the land next to the sea: *It gets quite cold on the coast.*

coin /kɔɪn/ *noun* [C] plural **coins** a piece of money made of metal: *He put a fifty pence coin into the drinks machine.*

come /kʌm/ *verb* third person singular **comes**, present participle **coming**, past tense **came** /keɪm/ past participle **have come**
1 to move towards a place or person: *It would be nice if Chris could come.*
2 to arrive at a place: *Jean was really tired when she came home. | Mum sent us a parcel, but it hasn't come yet.*
3 to have a position: *In the set '2, 4, 6, 8,' what number comes next?*

comedian /kə'miːdiən/ noun [C] plural **comedians** someone whose job is to tell jokes and make people laugh: *The show stars one of Britain's favourite comedians.*

comedy /'kɒmədi/ noun [C] plural **comedies** a funny film or play: *All my favourite films are comedies.*

come from /ˌkʌm frəm/ verb third person singular **comes from**, present participle **coming from**, past tense **came from** /keɪm/ past participle **have come from** where you come from is the place where you were born and usually live: *I come from London.*

comfortable /'kʌmftəbəl/ adjective comparative **more comfortable**, superlative **most comfortable** something that is comfortable is nice to wear, sit on, or be in → opposite UNCOMFORTABLE: *a comfortable bed*

communicate /kə'mjuːnəkeɪt/ verb third person singular **communicates**, present participle **communicating**, past tense **communicated**, past participle **have communicated** if people communicate with each other, they give each other information, for example by writing letters, speaking on the telephone etc: *It can be difficult to communicate with people if you don't speak their language.*

communication /kəˌmjuːnə'keɪʃən/ noun [U] when people talk to each other or give each other information using letters, telephones etc: *E-mail has made communication much quicker.*

community /kə'mjuːnəti/ noun [C] plural **communities** a group of people who are similar in some way, for example because they have the same religion or do the same job: *The city has quite a large Jewish community.*

company /'kʌmpəni/ noun [C] plural **companies** an organization that makes or sells things: *My father **runs** his own **company**.*

composer /kəm'pəuzə/ noun [C] plural **composers** someone who writes music, especially as a job: *My favourite composer is Beethoven.*

condition /kən'dɪʃən/ noun [C, U] plural **conditions**
1 in good condition if something is in good condition, it works and there is nothing wrong with it: *The car's engine is still in good condition.*
2 weather conditions [plural] what the weather is like on a particular day: *The weather conditions made the rescue difficult.*

contact /'kɒntækt/ verb third person singular **contacts**, present participle **contacting**, past tense **contacted**, past participle **have contacted** to telephone or write to someone: *In an emergency, you should contact the police immediately.*

contain /kən'teɪn/ verb third person singular **contains**, present participle **containing**, past tense **contained**, past participle **have contained** if something contains things, those things are in it: *The suitcase contained a lot of old clothes.*

continent /ˈkɒntənənt/ *noun* [C] plural **continents** one of the large areas of land in the world, such as Africa, Asia, or Europe: *the continents of Asia and Africa*

cook /kʊk/ *verb* third person singular **cooks**, present participle **cooking**, past tense **cooked**, past participle **have cooked** to make food ready to eat, by heating it, mixing things together etc: *You need to learn to cook.*

cooking /ˈkʊkɪŋ/ *noun* [U] making food ready to eat, by heating it, mixing things together etc: *I love cooking!*

cosmetics /kɒzˈmetɪks/ *noun* [plural] products that you put on your skin to improve your appearance: *She spends a lot on cosmetics, especially lipstick.*

cosmopolitan /ˌkɒzməˈpɒlɪtən/ *adjective* comparative **more cosmopolitan**, superlative **most cosmopolitan** a cosmopolitan place has people from many different parts of the world: *a vibrant, cosmopolitan city*

cost¹ /kɒst/ *noun* [C] plural **costs** the amount of money that you have to pay for something: ***The cost of** accommodation in the city centre is very high.*

cost² *verb* third person singular **costs**, present participle **costing**, past tense **cost**, past participle **have cost** if something costs a particular amount, that is the amount you have to pay for it: *How much do these jeans cost?*

course /kɔːs/ *noun* [C] plural **courses**
1 a set of lessons about a subject: *I'd like to **take** a **course in** business studies.*
2 a place where people play golf: *The course here is one of the most difficult in the world.*
3 of course spoken used to say 'yes' or in a strong way: *'Can I come in?' 'Of course! Please, sit down.'*

cousin /ˈkʌzən/ *noun* [C] plural **cousins** the son or daughter of your AUNT or UNCLE: *When I was little my cousin used to come over to my house.*

create /kriˈeɪt/ *verb* third person singular **creates**, present participle **creating**, past tense **created**, past participle **have created** to make something happen or exist: *The new rules will create a lot of problems.*

crisis /ˈkraɪsɪs/ *noun* [C] plural **crises** /ˈkraɪsiːz/ a situation in which someone or something has very bad problems: *He had to go and deal with a crisis at home.*

cross¹ /krɒs/ *verb* third person singular **crosses**, present participle **crossing**, past tense **crossed**, past participle **have crossed** to go from one side of a road, river, room etc to the other: *Hold Daddy's hand while we cross the road.* | *A small boy was waiting to cross, so I stopped the car.*

cross² *noun* [C] plural **crosses** *BrE* a mark (X) that you make on paper, especially to show that something that is written is not correct: *The teacher had put a cross by three of my answers.*

cross out /ˌkrɒs aʊt/ *verb* third person singular **crosses out**, present participle **crossing out**, past tense **crossed out**, past participle **have crossed out** to draw a line through something that you have written because it is wrong: *If you make a mistake, just cross it out.*

crowded /ˈkraʊdɪd/ *adjective* comparative **more crowded**, superlative **most crowded** a place that is crowded is full of people: *a crowded beach*

cruel /ˈkruːəl/ *adjective* comparative **crueller**, superlative **cruellest** someone who is cruel deliberately treats people or animals in a very unkind way: *I think it's cruel to keep wild animals in zoos.*

currency /ˈkʌrənsi/ *noun* [C] plural **currencies** the type of money that a country uses: *We need to get some of the local currency before we go on holiday.*

customer service /ˌkʌstəmə ˈsɜːvɪs/ *noun* [U] dealing with questions, problems etc that customers have: *the importance of good customer service*

customs officer /ˈkʌstəmz ˌɒfɪsə/ *noun* [C] plural **customs officers** someone whose job is to check goods coming into a country and collect any taxes on them for the government: *Police and customs officers seized stolen cars, cash, and weapons.*

cycling /ˈsaɪklɪŋ/ *noun* [U] riding a bicycle: *Cycling is good exercise for you.*

D, d

dark¹ /dɑːk/ *adjective* comparative **darker**, superlative **darkest**
1 a dark colour is strong and closer to black than to white: *I'd like a carpet that's a bit darker than this one.*
2 someone who is dark or who has dark hair or eyes has black or brown skin, hair, or eyes: *Tony's dad was dark, but his mother had blonde hair.*

dark² *noun* **the dark** when there is no light: *When I was little, I was afraid of the dark.*

daughter /ˈdɔːtə/ *noun* [C] plural **daughters** a girl child: *She's got two daughters and one son.*

December /dɪˈsembə/ *noun* [C, U] plural **Decembers** the twelfth month of the year: *War began in the middle of December.*

decide /dɪ'saɪd/ *verb* third person singular **decides**, present participle **deciding**, past tense **decided**, past participle **have decided** to choose what you are going to do after thinking about it: *Megan decided to go to Denise's party.* | *I can't decide which dress to wear.* | *We decided that we couldn't afford to go on holiday this year.*

decoration /,dekə'reɪʃən/ *noun* [C] plural **decorations** a pretty thing that you use to make something look more attractive: *The shop windows were full of Christmas decorations*

delay /dɪ'leɪ/ *verb* comparative **more delayed**, superlative **most delayed** late because of something that has happened: *Their flight's delayed.*

delicious /dɪ'lɪʃəs/ *adjective* comparative **more delicious**, superlative **most delicious** delicious food tastes very good: *This soup is delicious!*

deliver /dɪ'lɪvə/ *verb* third person singular **delivers**, present participle **delivering**, past tense **delivered**, past participle **have delivered** to take something such as a letter or a package to a place: *He got a job delivering pizzas.*

demonstrate /'demənstreɪt/ *verb* third person singular **demonstrates**, present participle **demonstrating**, past tense **demonstrated**, past participle **have demonstrated** to show someone how to do something or how a machine works: *The ski instructor demonstrated the correct way to turn.*

dentist /'dentɪst/ *noun* [C] plural **dentists** someone whose job is to look after and repair people's teeth: *I'm going to the dentist's* (=the place where a dentist works) *this afternoon*

department store /dɪ'pɑːtmənt ,stɔː/ *noun* [C] plural **department stores** a large shop that sells many different types of things: *She's a sales assistant in a department store.*

departure /dɪ'pɑːtʃə/ *noun* [C] plural **departures** when a person, plane, train etc leaves a place: *Our departure was delayed because of bad weather.*

desert /'dezət/ *noun* [C] plural **deserts** a large area of very hot dry land where few plants grow: *It took three days to cross the desert.*

design¹ /dɪ'zaɪn/ *noun* [C, U] plural **designs**
1 [U] making a drawing of something to show how you will make it or what it will look like: *Joe has a natural talent for design.*
2 [C] a pattern used to decorate something: *Each plate has a different design.*

design² *verb* third person singular **designs**, present participle **designing**, past tense **designed**, past participle **have designed** to draw or plan something that you will make, plan, or build: *The company is designing a golf course.*

development /dɪ'veləpmənt/ *noun* [U] the process of becoming bigger, better, stronger etc: *Vitamins are necessary for a child's growth and development.*

die[1] /daɪ/ *verb* third person singular **dies**, present participle **dying**, past tense **died**, past participle **have died** to stop living: *Grandmother died last year.*

die[2] *noun* [C] plural **dice** /daɪs/ a small block of wood, plastic etc that has six sides with a different number of spots on each side, used in games: *The die rolled off the table.*

different /'dɪfərənt/ *adjective* comparative **more different**, superlative **most different**
1 not the same as someone or something else: *Each colour was different.* | *Schools in Japan are different from schools in England.*
2 used to talk about two or more separate things: *I went to three different shops.*

difficult /'dɪfɪkəlt/ *adjective* comparative **more difficult**, superlative **most difficult** not easy to understand or do: *Philosophy is a difficult subject.* | *It's really difficult to find a cheap place to live in London.*

director /də'rektə/ *noun* [C] plural **directors** someone who gives instructions to actors in a film or play: *Who was the director of 'Star Wars'?*

dirt /dɜːt/ *noun* [U] dust, mud, or soil that makes things dirty: *Don't get any dirt on the carpet.*

dirty /'dɜːti/ *adjective* comparative **dirtier**, superlative **dirtiest** not clean: *Don't get your clothes dirty.*

do /duː/ *verb* third person singular **does** /dʌz/ present participle **doing** /'duːɪŋ/ past tense **did** /dɪd/ past participle **have done** /dʌn/
1 if you do an action or activity, you make it happen: *'What are you doing?' 'I'm making a cake.'* | *It's your turn to do the washing-up.*
2 used with another verb to form negative sentences: *They did not understand what he meant.*
3 used with another verb to form questions: *What did you say?*
4 used with another verb to tell someone not to do something: *Don't touch the iron – it's hot.*
5 used at the end of a sentence to ask a question or to ask someone to agree with you: *You didn't tell him what I said, did you?*
6 used when you do not want to repeat another verb: *She's only eight, but she eats more than I do* (=she eats more than I eat).

doll /dɒl/ *noun* [C] plural **dolls** a child's toy that looks like a very small person: *My little sister was playing with her dolls.*

drink[1] /drɪŋk/ *verb* third person singular **drinks**, present participle **drinking**, past tense **drank** /dræŋk/ past participle **have drunk** /drʌŋk/
1 to take liquid into your mouth and swallow it: *Rob was drinking a Coke.* | *Do you want something to drink?*
2 to drink alcohol, especially regularly: *Don't drink and drive.* | *I usually drink white wine.*

drink² *noun* plural **drinks**
1 [C] an amount of something such as water, juice etc that you drink: *Are you thirsty? Would you like a drink?*
2 [C] an amount of alcohol that you drink: *Do you want to go for a drink after work?*
3 [U] liquid that you can drink: *We stopped for some food and drink.*

drive /draɪv/ *verb* third person singular **drives**, present participle **driving**, past tense **drove** /drəʊv/ past participle **have driven** /'drɪvən/ to make a car move in the direction you want: *I learned to drive when I was seventeen.* | *I think the man was driving a red car.* | *Peggy drove to work as usual.*

driving /'draɪvɪŋ/ *noun* [U] the activity or skill of driving a car: *His driving is terrible sometimes.*

drug /drʌg/ *noun* [C] plural **drugs** something that people smoke, swallow etc in order to make themselves feel happy or excited. In many countries it is against the law to use drugs: *He has never taken drugs.*

during /'djʊərɪŋ/ *preposition*
1 all through a period of time: *Foxes sleep during the day and hunt at night.*
2 at one time in a period of time: *Their car was stolen during the night.*

E, e

early /'ɜːli/ *adjective, adverb* comparative **earlier**, superlative **earliest**
1 near the beginning of a period of time: *It snowed in early January.* | *The postman comes early in the morning.*
2 before the usual or expected time: *You're early – I wasn't expecting you till 2 o'clock.* | *I got there early and had to wait for Debbie.*

earn /ɜːn/ *verb* third person singular **earns**, present participle **earning**, past tense **earned**, past participle **have earned** to get money from the work that you do: *How much does he earn?*

Earth /ɜːθ/ *noun* [U] the PLANET that we live on: *People used to believe the Earth was flat, not round.* | *He saw Earth from space.*

east /iːst/ *noun* [U] one of the four points that tell you the direction of something. East is the direction from which the sun rises: *They live in the east of Ireland.*

easy /'iːzi/ *adjective* comparative **easier**, superlative **easiest** not difficult → opposite **DIFFICULT, HARD**: *some easy homework* | *The house is easy to find.*

eat /iːt/ *verb* third person singular **eats,** present participle **eating,** past tense **ate** /et, eɪt/ past participle **have eaten** /ˈiːtn/ to put food into your mouth, chew it, and swallow it: *Most of the children eat sandwiches for lunch.* | *Do you want to go and get something to eat* (=some food)?

economics /ˌekəˈnɒmɪks/ *noun* [U] the study of the way that a country produces money and things to sell: *I want to do economics at college.*

electrical /ɪˈlektrɪkəl/ *adjective* using or relating to electricity: *a store selling electrical equipment*

emergency /ɪˈmɜːdʒənsi/ *noun* [C] plural **emergencies** a dangerous situation that happens suddenly: *Make sure you know what to do in an emergency.*

engineering /ˌendʒəˈnɪərɪŋ/ *noun* [U] the work of designing roads, bridges, machines etc: *The course will introduce young people to engineering.*

English¹ /ˈɪŋglɪʃ/ *noun* [U]
1 the language that people speak in Britain, the US, Australia etc: *Do you speak English?*
2 the English the people of England: *The English are very polite.*

English² *adjective*
1 connected with the English language: *English lessons* | *some English verbs*
2 connected with or coming from England: *the English countryside*

enjoy /ɪnˈdʒɔɪ/ *verb* third person singular **enjoys,** present participle **enjoying,** past tense **enjoyed,** past participle **have enjoyed** to get pleasure from something: *I enjoyed our walk.* | *I enjoy cooking when I have time.*

enormous /ɪˈnɔːməs/ *adjective* comparative **more enormous,** superlative **most enormous** very big: *an enormous amount of money*

evening /ˈiːvnɪŋ/ *noun* [C] plural **evenings** the end of the day and the early part of the night: *We usually eat at around 7 in the evening.* | *Shall we meet tomorrow evening?*

every /ˈevri/ *determiner* **every day, every week, every year etc** on each day, in each week, in each year etc: *He phones his girlfriend every day.* | *They go skiing every winter.*

everything /ˈevriθɪŋ/ *pronoun* all the things: *Have you got everything you need?* | *He forgot about everything else* (=all other things) *when he was playing computer games.*

excellent /ˈeksələnt/ *adjective* comparative **more excellent,** superlative **most excellent** very good: *He's an excellent player.* | *That was an excellent film.*

exercise /ˈeksəsaɪz/ *noun* [U] physical activity such as sport that you do in order to stay strong and healthy: *You should take more exercise.* | *Walking up and down stairs is good exercise.*

exhibition /ˌeksəˈbɪʃən/ *noun* [C] plural **exhibitions** a collection of objects, paintings, photographs etc that are put in a public place so that people can enjoy looking at them: *We went to an exhibition of modern art.*

expensive /ɪkˈspensɪv/ *adjective* comparative **more expensive**, superlative **most expensive** something that is expensive costs a lot of money → opposite CHEAP, INEXPENSIVE: *That hotel is too expensive.* | *a very expensive car*

expert /ˈekspɜːt/ *noun* [C] plural **experts** someone with special skills or knowledge: *A bomb expert was called.* | *an expert in English history*

explain /ɪkˈspleɪn/ *verb* third person singular **explains**, present participle **explaining**, past tense **explained**, past participle **have explained** to tell someone about something so that they understand it: *I tried to explain how to play the game.* | *The teacher explained the question to me.* | *Please explain why you are late.*

extraordinary /ɪkˈstrɔːdənəri/ *adjective* comparative **more extraordinary**, superlative **most extraordinary** very unusual: *David told us an extraordinary story.* | *She is an extraordinary woman.*

F, f

fact /fækt/ *noun* [C] plural **facts**
1 something that you know is true or that you know has happened: *We won't make a decision until we know all the facts.* | *Children need to learn the facts about health.*
2 in fact say this when you are adding information to what you are saying: *His mother just got married again; in fact, this is her third marriage.*

fail /feɪl/ *verb* third person singular **fails**, present participle **failing**, past tense **failed**, past participle **have failed** to not pass a test or exam: *She failed all her exams.* | *If you fail, you can take the test again.*

fall /fɔːl/ *verb* third person singular **falls**, present participle **falling**, past tense **fell** /fel/ past participle **have fallen** /ˈfɔːlən/ **fall in love** to start to love someone in a romantic way: *They were falling in love.* | *She fell in love with her friend's boyfriend.*

fantastic /fænˈtæstɪk/ *adjective* comparative **more fantastic**, superlative **most fantastic** *informal* extremely good: *It's a fantastic film!* | *You look fantastic.*

 **fashion** /ˈfæʃən/ *noun* [U] the styles of clothes, hair etc that are new and popular at a particular time: *He's not at all interested in fashion.* | *a fashion magazine*

fashionable /ˈfæʃənəbəl/ *adjective* comparative **more fashionable**, superlative **most fashionable** something that is fashionable is popular at a particular time → opposite UNFASHIONABLE: *Long hair is fashionable for men now.*

fast¹ /fɑːst/ *adjective* comparative **faster**, superlative **fastest** moving or happening quickly → opposite SLOW: *He has always loved fast cars.* | *This computer is much faster than my old one.* | *He is the fastest runner in the world.*

fast² *adverb* quickly → opposite SLOWLY: *I can't run very fast.* | *You have to work faster.*

favourite¹ /ˈfeɪvərət/ *adjective* your favourite thing or person is the one that you like most: *We chose Joe's favorite music for the party.* | *She's my favourite teacher.*

favourite² *noun* [C] plural **favourites** the person or thing that you like more than all the others: *Which picture is your favourite?*

feature /ˈfiːtʃə/ *noun* [C] plural **features** a part or quality that something has: *This new software has some very useful features.* | *Airbags are a feature of most new cars.*

feed /fiːd/ *verb* third person singular **feeds**, present participle **feeding**, past tense **fed** /fed/ past participle **have fed** to give food to a person or animal: *Have you fed the cats this morning?* | *We fed apples to the horses.* | *The baby wants to feed herself.*

feel /fiːl/ *verb* third person singular **feels**, present participle **feeling**, past tense **felt** /felt/ past participle **have felt** to experience something such as anger, happiness, cold, hunger etc: *I felt cold and lonely.* | *He must feel very disappointed.* | *How did you feel when you saw her again?*

female /ˈfiːmeɪl/ *adjective* belonging to the sex that can have babies or produce eggs: *a female tiger*

fiction /ˈfɪkʃən/ *noun* [U] stories about people and events that are not real: *Most children enjoy reading fiction.* | *I didn't know whether what he was saying was fact or fiction.*

field /fiːld/ *noun* [C] plural **fields** an area of land that can be used for growing food or keeping animals: *There were cows in the field.* | *The children ran across the field.*

find /faɪnd/ *verb* third person singular **finds**, present participle **finding**, past tense **found** /faʊnd/ past participle **have found** to discover, see, or get something, especially after you have been looking for it: *The boys found a gold watch buried under a tree.* | *I can't find my socks!* | *Mark went outside to find us a taxi.*

finish /'fɪnɪʃ/ *verb* third person singular **finishes**, present participle **finishing**, past tense **finished**, past participle **have finished** to stop, or stop doing something: *What time did the party finish?* | *Just let me finish this letter.*

fitness /'fɪtnəs/ *noun* [U] good health, so that someone is able to run or do physical work without getting very tired: *He started to go running to improve his fitness.*

flat /flæt/ *noun* [C] plural **flats** a set of rooms for someone to live in that is part of a larger building: *His flat is near the city centre.* | *a block of flats*

flight /flaɪt/ *noun* [C] plural **flights** a journey in a plane: *What time is your flight?* | *She booked a flight to New York.*

float /fləʊt/ *verb* third person singular **floats**, present participle **floating**, past tense **floated**, past participle **have floated** to stay or move on the surface of a liquid → opposite SINK: *Does plastic float?* | *Little boats were floating on the river.*

floor /flɔː/ *noun* [C] plural **floors** one of the levels in a building: *The toilets are on the top floor.*

flower /'flaʊə/ *noun* [C] plural **flowers** the brightly coloured parts of plants and trees: *I gave Mum a bunch of flowers*

fly¹ /flaɪ/ *verb* third person singular **flies**, present participle **flying**, past tense **flew** /fluː/ past participle **have flown** /fləʊn/
1 to travel somewhere by plane: *Sam flew to New York for his brother's wedding.* | *We are now flying over the Alps.*
2 to move through the air using wings: *Penguins are birds, but they can't fly.*

fly² *noun* [C] plural **flies** a common small insect with two wings

flying /'flaɪ-ɪŋ/ *noun* [U] travelling by plane: *A lot of people are scared of flying.*

follow /'fɒləʊ/ *verb* third person singular **follows**, present participle **following**, past tense **followed**, past participle **have followed** to walk or drive behind someone or something: *I followed her into the house.* | *Sam had a feeling that someone was following him.*

foreign language /ˌfɒrən 'læŋgwɪdʒ/ *noun* [C] plural **foreign languages** a language that is not your own language or not from your own country: *Do you speak any foreign languages?*

forest /'fɒrɪst/ *noun* [C] plural **forests** a large area of land covered with trees: *He got lost in the forest.*

forget /fə'get/ *verb* third person singular **forgets**, present participle **forgetting**, past tense **forgot** /fə'gɒt/ past participle **have forgotten** /fə'gɒtn/ to not remember something: *I'll never forget the day I started school.* | *I've forgotten what her name is.* | *Don't forget to feed the cat.*

fork /fɔːk/ *noun* [C] plural **forks** a small tool with four points that you use for picking up food when you eat: *He put down his knife and fork.*

free /friː/ *adjective* comparative **freer**, superlative **freest**
1 something that is free does not cost any money: *a free gift in a magazine* | *Membership of the club is free.*
2 not busy doing things you have to do: *I'm free every evening this week.* | *What do you like doing in your free time?*
3 if something is free, it is not being used: *There's a free table over there.*

fresh /freʃ/ *adjective* comparative **fresher**, superlative **freshest** fresh food is good to eat because it has been produced or picked recently: *Eat plenty of fresh fruit and vegetables.*

friend /frend/ *noun* [C] plural **friends** someone that you know well and like: *She invited all her friends to the party.* | *Anna is a good friend of mine.*

friendly /'frendli/ *adjective* comparative **friendlier**, superlative **friendliest** someone who is friendly talks and behaves in a nice way towards other people → opposite UNFRIENDLY: *Everyone in the village was very friendly to us.*

frightened /'fraɪtnd/ *adjective* comparative **more frightened**, superlative **most frightened** afraid that something bad might happen: *Liz is really frightened of spiders.* | *I was frightened that someone would hurt themselves.*

frightening /'fraɪtn-ɪŋ/ *adjective* comparative **more frightening**, superlative **most frightening** something that is frightening makes you feel afraid: *It's a very frightening film.*

fruit /fruːt/ *noun* [C,U] plural **fruit, fruits** something such as an apple or orange which grows on a plant, tree, or bush, and contains seeds: *Bananas are my favourite fruit.* | *a basket of fruit*

full-time /ˌfʊl 'taɪm/ *adverb, adjective* if you work or study full-time, you work or study all day during the whole week: *I'm looking for a full-time job.* | *It's hard to study when you work full-time.*

fun /fʌn/ *noun* [U] if something is fun, you enjoy doing it or being involved in it: *The party was great fun.* | *Everyone had fun playing in the snow.*

funny /ˈfʌni/ *adjective* comparative **funnier**, superlative **funniest** if someone or something is funny, they make you laugh: *It was one of the funniest films I've ever seen.*

fur /fɜː/ *noun* [U] the thick soft hair that covers the bodies of some animals: *I stroked the rabbit's soft fur.*

furniture /ˈfɜːnɪtʃə/ *noun* [U] objects such as chairs, tables, and beds: *All our furniture is old.* | *Do you sell office furniture?*

G, g

game /ɡeɪm/ *noun* [C] plural **games** an activity or sport which has rules and which you do to have fun, with other people or by yourself: *The children were playing a game.* | *a card game* | *I got a new computer game for Christmas.* | *Would you like a game of tennis?*

garden /ˈɡɑːdn/ *noun* [C] plural **gardens**
1 a piece of land next to your house where you can grow grass and flowers: *The kids are playing in the garden.*
2 gardens a public park where there are a lot of flowers and plants: *Thousands of people visit the gardens each year.*

geography /dʒiˈɒɡrəfi/ *noun* [U] the study of the countries of the world, including their land, rivers, and cities

get /ɡet/ *verb* third person singular **gets**, present participle **getting**, past tense **got** /ɡɒt/ past participle **have got**
1 get married/angry/cold etc to become married, angry, cold etc: *They got married last year.* | *It gets very cold at night.* | *Be careful, or someone will get hurt.*
2 to take, find, or receive something: *He got a new job.* | *I get lots of emails.*
3 to buy something: *I'm going to get a newspaper.* | *What did you get your sister for her birthday?*
4 to move or travel somewhere: *How do you get to school?* | *He got home at about 11.* | *Get down from that ladder!*

get off /ɡet ˈɒf/ *verb* third person singular **gets off**, present participle **getting off**, past tense **got off** /ɡɒt/ past participle **have got off** to leave a bus, train, plane, or large boat: *She got off the bus.* | *I got off at Victoria Station.*

get on /get ˈɒn/ verb third person singular **gets on**, present participle **getting on**, past tense **got on** /gɒt/ past participle **have got on** to walk onto a bus, train, or plane: *I got on the wrong bus.* | *The train was so full I couldn't get on.*

· · · · · · · · ·

get up /get ˈʌp/ verb third person singular **gets up**, present participle **getting up**, past tense **got up** /gɒt/ past participle **have got up** to stop sleeping and move out of bed: *He gets up at six every morning.*

· · · · · · · · ·

gift /gɪft/ noun [C] plural **gifts** something that you give to someone as a present: *People give each other gifts at Christmas.* | *We got a beautiful clock as a wedding gift.*

· · · · · · · · ·

girlfriend /ˈgɜːlfrend/ noun [C] plural **girlfriends** a girl or woman with whom you have a romantic relationship: *Has Steve got a girlfriend?*

· · · · · · · · ·

give /gɪv/ verb third person singular **gives**, present participle **giving**, past tense **gave** /geɪv/ past participle **have given** /ˈgɪvən/
1 to let someone have something: *What did you give Sophie for her birthday?* | *Give me the keys and I'll open the door.* | *Ken gave the bags to Ellen.*

1 · · · · · · · · · ·

2 to tell someone something: *Please give your name to the secretary.* | *He gave me directions to his house.*

2 · · · · · · · · · ·

glass /glɑːs/ noun [C] plural **glasses** a cup with no handle that is made of a clear hard material called glass: *a wine glass* | *Could I have a glass of water?*

· · · · · · · · ·

glasses /ˈglɑːsɪz/ noun [plural] things that you wear in front of your eyes to help you see better: *Susan wears glasses.* | *a pair of glasses*

· · · · · · · · ·

global /ˈgləʊbəl/ adjective affecting or including the whole world: *Pollution is a global problem.*

· · · · · · · · ·

go /gəʊ/ verb third person singular **goes**, present participle **going**, past tense **went** /went/ past participle **have gone** /gɒn/
1 to leave one place and move to another place: *Are you going to Sam's party?* | *Jim's gone to buy some milk.* | *We're going camping at the weekend.*

1 · · · · · · · · · ·

2 go home to go back to your home from somewhere: *It's time to go home.*

2 · · · · · · · · · ·

3 go on a diet to start eating less food or only certain foods, in order to become thinner: *He needs to go on a diet.*

3 · · · · · · · · · ·

go away /ˌɡəʊ əˈweɪ/ *verb* third person singular **goes away**, present participle **going away**, past tense **went away** /went/ past participle **have gone away** /ɡɒn/ to spend time away from home, especially on holiday: *Let's go away for the weekend!*

go back /ˌɡəʊ ˈbæk/ *verb* third person singular **goes back**, present participle **going back**, past tense **went back** /went/ past participle **have gone back** /ɡɒn/ to return to a place: *I went back to get my bag.* | *We have to go back to school on Monday.*

go by /ˌɡəʊ ˈbaɪ/ *verb* third person singular **goes by**, present participle **going by**, past tense **went by** /went/ past participle **have gone by** /ɡɒn/ **go by car, go by train etc** to use a car, a train etc to travel somewhere: *It's quicker to go by car.* | *I went by bus to my friend's house.*

good /ɡʊd/ *adjective* comparative **better** /ˈbetə/ superlative **best** /best/
1 of a high standard or quality → opposite **BAD**: *good food* | *He had a really good idea.* | *This is the best hotel in the town.*
2 enjoyable or pleasant → opposite **BAD**: *Did you have a good holiday?* | *The party was really good.*
3 good at able to do something well → opposite **BAD AT**: *She's very good at her job.*

good-looking /ˌɡʊd ˈlʊkɪŋ/ *adjective* comparative **better-looking** /ˌbetə/ superlative **best-looking** /ˌbest/ attractive to look at: *a very good-looking man*

go out /ˌɡəʊ ˈaʊt/ *verb* third person singular **goes out**, present participle **going out**, past tense **went out** /went/ past participle **have gone out** /ɡɒn/ to leave your house, especially in order to enjoy yourself: *We always go out on Saturdays.* | *I went out to the cinema last night.*

graduate /ˈɡrædʒueɪt/ *verb* third person singular **graduates**, present participle **graduating**, past tense **graduated**, past participle **have graduated** to pass your final examinations at university: *Don graduated from York University in 2002.*

grandchild /ˈɡræntʃaɪld/ *noun* [C] plural **grandchildren** /ˈɡræntʃɪldrən/ the child of your son or daughter: *Rosa is his youngest grandchild.*

grandfather /ˈɡrænˈfɑːðə/ *noun* [C] plural **grandfathers** the father of one of your parents: *My grandfather gave me this book.*

grandmother /ˈɡrænˈmʌðə/ *noun* [C] plural **grandmothers** the mother of one of your parents: *This is a photograph of my grandmother.*

grandparent /ˈɡrænˈpeərənt/ *noun* [C] plural **grandparents** the parent of your mother or father: *We visited my grandparents at the weekend.*

grape /ɡreɪp/ *noun* [C] a small round juicy fruit that grows in bunches and is used to make wine: *a bunch of black grapes*

grass /grɑːs/ *noun* [U] the green plant that covers the ground in gardens and fields: *We lay on the grass by the river.*

great /greɪt/ *adjective* comparative **greater**, superlative **greatest** very good or enjoyable: *We had a great time at the beach.* | *It's really great to be home.*

great-grandson /ˌgreɪt ˈgrænsʌn/ *noun* [C] plural **great-grandsons** the son of your GRANDCHILD (=the child of your son or daughter)

grill /grɪl/ *verb* third person singular **grills**, present participle **grilling**, past tense **grilled**, past participle **have grilled** to cook meat, fish etc by putting it close to strong heat: *Grill the steak for about 4 minutes each side.*

ground floor /ˌgraʊnd ˈflɔː/ *noun* [C] plural **ground floors** the part of a building that is on the same level as the ground: *The men's clothing department is on the ground floor.*

group /gruːp/ *noun* [C] plural **groups**
1 several people or things that are together in the same place: *a group of islands* | *Please can the class get into groups of three* (=three people in each group).
2 several musicians who play and sing popular music together [= band]: *'Queen' is my favourite rock group.*

guess /ges/ *verb* third person singular **guesses**, present participle **guessing**, past tense **guessed**, past participle **have guessed** to answer a question or decide something without being sure whether you are right: *I guessed her age correctly.* | *Guess how much this dress cost.*

guitar /gɪˈtɑː/ *noun* [C] plural **guitars** a wooden musical instrument with strings and a long neck, that you play by pulling the strings: *an electric guitar*

gun /gʌn/ *noun* [C] plural **guns** a weapon that fires bullets: *The police here all carry guns.*

gym /dʒɪm/ *noun* [C] plural **gyms** a large room or a building containing equipment for doing physical exercise: *I go to the gym twice a week.*

H, h

haircut /ˈheəkʌt/ *noun* [C] plural **haircuts** an occasion when someone cuts your hair: *I'm going to have a haircut this week.*

hairdresser's /ˈheəˈdresəz/ *noun* [C] a place where you go to have your hair washed, cut, and arranged into a style: *I have an appointment at the hairdresser's this afternoon.*

hand /hænd/ *noun* **by hand** a letter that is delivered by hand is brought by the person who wrote it and not sent in the post: *I delivered her birthday card by hand.*

handsome /ˈhænsəm/ *adjective* comparative **more handsome**, superlative **most handsome** a handsome man is attractive: *He was tall, dark and handsome.*

happen /ˈhæpən/ *verb* third person singular **happens**, present participle **happening**, past tense **happened**, past participle **have happened** to start and continue for a period of time: *What happened today at work?* | *I couldn't see what was happening on the stage.* | *Thomas was afraid that something terrible had happened.*

happy /ˈhæpi/ *adjective* comparative **happier**, superlative **happiest** feeling pleased or cheerful → opposite UNHAPPY: *Sam was feeling happy because it was his birthday.*

hard /hɑːd/ *adjective* comparative **harder**, superlative **hardest**
1 difficult to cut, break, or bend → opposite SOFT: *The chairs were hard and uncomfortable.* | *a book with a hard cover*
2 difficult to do → opposite EASY: *That test was much harder than the one we had last week.* | *That's a very hard question to answer.*

hat /hæt/ *noun* [C] plural **hats** something that you wear on your head

hate /heɪt/ *verb* third person singular **hates**, present participle **hating**, past tense **hated**, past participle **have hated** to have a very strong feeling that you do not like someone or something → opposite LOVE[1]: *I hate my boss.* | *Anne hates cleaning the car.*

have /həv, hæv/ *verb* third person singular **have**, present participle **having**, past tense **had** /həd, hæd/ past participle **have had**
1 if you have something, it is yours: *Do you have a computer?* | *Philip has brown eyes.* | *She has a lot of friends.*
2 to eat or drink something: *What do you usually have for breakfast?* | *Let's have a cup of coffee.*

head /hed/ *noun* [C] plural **heads** the leader or most important person in a company or school: *He is the head of Sky Sports television.* | *Their school has got a new head.*

headphones /ˈhedfəʊnz/ *noun* [plural] a piece of equipment that you wear over your ears to listen to music, to the radio etc: *a pair of headphones*

health /helθ/ *noun* [U]
1 your health is how well or ill you are: *Exercise is good for your health.*

2 health and safety things that affect the health and safety of people in places where they work or in public places: *the officer responsible for health and safety in the factory*

healthy /ˈhelθi/ *adjective* comparative **healthier,** superlative **healthiest** healthy things are good for you and will help you stay well → opposite UNHEALTHY: *a healthy diet* | *It isn't healthy to go everywhere by car.*

hear /hɪə/ *verb* third person singular **hears,** present participle **hearing,** past tense **heard** /hɜːd/ past participle **have heard**
1 to notice or understand sounds: *Did you hear that noise?* | *I called him, but he didn't hear me.* | *I could hear my parents arguing.*
2 to get news or information about something: *I heard about the accident from Tom's mum.* | *Did you hear what happened at the party?*

heavy /ˈhevi/ *adjective* comparative **heavier,** superlative **heaviest** something that is heavy weighs a lot → opposite LIGHT: *She was carrying a heavy suitcase.* | *The box was too heavy for me to lift.*

heights /haɪts/ *noun* [plural] high places or tall buildings: *I'm afraid of heights.*

help /help/ *verb* third person singular **helps,** present participle **helping,** past tense **helped,** past participle **have helped** to do something useful for someone, for example to do some of their work with them: *Shall I help you clean the car?* | *Sarah helped me to carry the boxes upstairs.* | *Will you help me with my homework?*

herb /hɜːb/ *noun* [C] plural **herbs** a plant that you use in cooking to add more taste

high /haɪ/ *adjective* comparative **higher,** superlative **highest** tall or a long way above the ground: *a high wall* | *The shelf is too high for me to reach.* | *Our village is high in the mountains.*

hill /hɪl/ *noun* [C] plural **hills** an area of high land, like a small mountain: *We walked to the top of the hill.* | *The town is built on a hill.*

hire /haɪə/ *verb* third person singular **hire,** present participle **hiring,** past tense **hired,** past participle **have hired** to pay money to use something for a short time: *They hired a car for three days.*

historical /hɪˈstɒrɪkəl/ *adjective* from history or related to history: *The film is based on a historical event.*

history /ˈhɪstəri/ *noun* [U]
1 all the things that happened in the past: *She's studying history at university.*
2 the history of something is how it has developed and changed since it started: *the history of pop music*

hobby /ˈhɒbi/ *noun* [C] plural **hobbies** an activity that you enjoy doing in your free time: *My hobbies are playing the guitar and reading.*

holiday /ˈhɒlədi/ *noun* [C] plural **holidays**
1 a period of time when you go to another place for enjoyment: *Did you have a nice holiday? | Sam isn't here this week. He's on holiday in Italy.*
2 a day when you do not have to go to work or school: *Next Monday is a holiday.*

home¹ /həʊm/ *noun* [C] plural **homes**
1 the house or place where you usually live: *When are you moving into your new home? | This was always such a happy home for us.*
2 at home in the house or place where you usually live: *I'm going to stay at home this weekend. | I called, but he wasn't at home.*
3 the home of sth the place where something started or is based: *Hollywood is the home of the film industry.*

home² *adverb* if you go home, you go to the place where you live: *It's getting late. I think we ought to go home. | We got home at seven o'clock.*

hot /hɒt/ *adjective* comparative **hotter**, superlative **hottest** something that is hot has a high temperature → opposite COLD: *It was a very hot day. | You'll feel better after a hot bath. | My coffee is still too hot to drink.*

housework /ˈhaʊswɜːk/ *noun* [U] work that you do at home such as cleaning and washing: *I usually do the housework at weekends.*

human being /ˌhjuːmən ˈbiːɪŋ/ *noun* [C] plural **human beings** a man, woman, or child

hunter /ˈhʌntə/ *noun* [C] plural **hunters** an animal or person that catches and kills wild animals for food or sport

hunting /ˈhʌntɪŋ/ *noun* [U] the activity of catching and killing wild animals for food or sport

husband /ˈhʌzbənd/ *noun* [C] plural **husbands** the man that a woman is married to: *Her husband's name is John.*

I, i

idea /aɪˈdɪə/ *noun* [C] plural **ideas**
1 a plan, thought, or suggestion: *'Let's eat.' 'Good idea!' | Emily had a great idea for raising money.*
2 it's a good idea to used to tell someone that it is sensible to do something: *It's a good idea to get to the airport at least an hour early.*

ideal /ˌaɪˈdɪəl/ *adjective* the best that something can be: *What would be your ideal holiday?*

ill /ɪl/ *adjective* if you are ill, you do not feel well and are not healthy [= **sick**]: *Mrs. Jackson is not here today because she is ill.*

. . . .

important /ɪm'pɔːtənt/ *adjective* comparative **more important**, superlative **most important**
1 if something is important, you need to have it, do it, or think about it: *Love is more important than money.* | *It is important to exercise regularly.*
2 having a lot of power or influence: *an important businesswoman* | *This discovery was very important.*

1 . . . .

2 . . . .

impossible /ɪm'pɒsəbəl/ *adjective* comparative **more impossible**, superlative **most impossible** if something is impossible, it cannot happen or you cannot do it: *an impossible task* | *It was impossible to get tickets for the game.*

. . . .

improve /ɪm'pruːv/ *verb* third person singular **improves**, present participle **improving**, past tense **improved**, past participle **have improved**
1 to make something better: *I'm staying in London to improve my English.*
2 to become better: *The team is improving with every game.*

1 . . . .

2 . . . .

include /ɪn'kluːd/ *verb* third person singular **includes**, present participle **including**, past tense **included**, past participle **have included** if something includes a person or thing, it has that person or thing as one of its parts: *Does the price of a hotel room include breakfast?* | *My name had been included on the list.*

. . . .

industry /'ɪndəstri/ *noun* [C] plural **industries** all the companies that make or sell the same kind of thing: *the airline industry* | *the steel industry*

. . . .

information /ˌɪnfə'meɪʃən/ *noun* [U] facts or details about a situation, person, or event: *How can I get more information about the course?* | *That's a very useful piece of information.*

. . . .

information technology /ɪnfə'meɪʃən tek'nɒlədʒi/ *noun* [U] the use of computers to store and manage information

. . . .

insect /'ɪnsekt/ *noun* [C] plural **insects** any small creature that has six legs, for example a fly

. . . .

instrument /'ɪnstrəmənt/ *noun* [C] plural **instruments** something such as a piano that you play in order to make music: *Do you play any musical instruments?*

. . . .

interested /'ɪntrəstɪd/ *adjective* comparative **more interested**, superlative **most interested** feeling that you want to know more about something, do it more, or see it more: *Jo is very interested in animals.* | *I can show you some other books, if you're interested.*

. . . .

interesting /'ɪntrəstɪŋ/ *adjective* comparative **more interesting**, superlative **most interesting** unusual or exciting in a way that makes

. . . .

you think, and want to know more: *A good teacher can make any subject interesting.* | *an interesting TV programme*

international /ˌɪntəˈnæʃənəl/ *adjective* involving or existing in many countries: *international football matches* | *an international bank*

invent /ɪnˈvent/ *verb* third person singular **invents**, present participle **inventing**, past tense **invented**, past participle **have invented** to think of or make something completely new: *Who invented the first computer?*

invention /ɪnˈvenʃən/ *noun* plural **inventions**
1 [C] a completely new thing that someone invents: *The wind-up radio was a brilliant invention.*
2 [U] when someone invents something: *the invention of the telephone*

inventor /ɪnˈventə/ *noun* [C] plural **inventors** someone who thinks of or makes something completely new: *the inventor of the light bulb*

island /ˈaɪlənd/ *noun* [C] plural **islands** a piece of land that is completely surrounded by water: *Britain is an island.*

item /ˈaɪtəm/ *noun* [C] plural **items** a thing or object: *They sell hundreds of different items.*

J, j

jeans /dʒiːnz/ *noun* [plural] a popular type of trousers made from denim (=strong cloth that is usually blue): *He was wearing an old pair of jeans.* | *I like your jeans.*

jewellery /ˈdʒuːəlri/ *noun* [U] things that you wear for decoration, such as rings and necklaces: *She wears a lot of gold jewellery.*

job /dʒɒb/ *noun* [C] plural **jobs** your job is work that you do regularly in order to earn money: *Teaching is an interesting job.* | *He left school and got a job in a bank.* | *a well-paid job*

journey /ˈdʒɜːni/ *noun* [C] plural **journeys** a trip from one place to another, especially in a car or other vehicle: *How long does your journey to school take?* | *You need things to do when you're on a long journey.*

juice /dʒuːs/ *noun* [U] the liquid from fruit or vegetables: *a glass of orange juice*

jump /dʒʌmp/ *verb* third person singular **jumps**, present participle **jumping**, past tense **jumped**, past participle **have jumped** to push yourself off the ground using your legs: *Jordan jumped but the ball flew over his head.* | *Kangaroos can jump a long way.*

K, k

keep /kiːp/ *verb* third person singular **keeps**, present participle **keeping**, past tense **kept** /kept/ past participle **have kept**
1 to stay in the same state, or make something stay in the same state: *Try to keep calm.* | *Keep the door closed – it's cold.*
2 to continue to do something often or for a long time: *I keep losing my keys.* | *He kept saying the same thing over and over again.*
3 keep in touch to regularly speak or write to someone: *She lives in Australia, but we keep in touch by e-mail.*
4 keep a diary to regularly write in a book about things that have happened to you

keyboard /ˈkiːbɔːd/ *noun* [C] plural **keyboards** the keys on a computer that you press to make it work

kill /kɪl/ *verb* third person singular **kills**, present participle **killing**, past tense **killed**, past participle **have killed** to make a person or animal die: *They accused him of killing his wife.* | *He was killed in the accident.*

kind /kaɪnd/ *noun* [C] plural **kinds** a type of person or thing: *What kind of music do you like?* | *They sell all kinds of interesting things in the market.*

kitchenware /ˈkɪtʃənweə/ *noun* [U] things such as pans that are used in the kitchen for cooking

kitten /ˈkɪtn/ *noun* [C] plural **kittens** a young cat

knife /naɪf/ *noun* [C] plural **knives** /naɪvz/ a thing you use to cut food with: *a knife and fork* | *This knife is very sharp.*

know /nəʊ/ *verb* third person singular **knows**, present participle **knowing**, past tense **knew** /njuː/ past participle **have known** /nəʊn/
1 when you have learned something, you know it: *Look up the words you don't know in the dictionary.* | *Jan knows a lot about computers.*
2 when you know someone or something, you have met them or seen them before: *Do you know Rob Walker?* | *I know New York quite well.*

L, l

ladder /ˈlædə/ *noun* [C] plural **ladders** a thing for climbing up to high places. A ladder has two long bars that are connected by short bars that you use as steps

lake /leɪk/ *noun* [C] plural **lakes** a large area of water with land all around it: *There's an island in the middle of the lake.*

landing /ˈlændɪŋ/ *noun* [C] plural **landings** when a plane or space-ship comes down from the air onto the ground: *The pilot made an emergency landing.*

large /lɑːdʒ / *adjective* comparative **larger**, superlative **largest** big: *a large house* | *Have you got this coat in a larger size?*

last¹ /lɑːst/ *adjective*
1 most recent: *I loved her last book.* | *Where did you go last night?*
2 after all the other things or people: *It's my last day at school.* | *This is the last call for flight BA351.*

last² *verb* third person singular **lasts**, present participle **lasting**, past tense **lasted**, past participle **have lasted** to continue to happen or exist: *His first marriage lasted 10 years.* | *The rain lasted all day.*

late /leɪt/ *adjective* comparative **later**, superlative **latest** near the end of the day: *It's getting late and I'm tired.*

laugh /lɑːf/ *verb* third person singular **laughs**, present participle **laughing**, past tense **laughed**, past participle **have laughed** to make a sound with your voice when you think that something is funny: *We couldn't stop laughing.*

law /lɔː/ *noun* [U] all the rules that a government makes in a country, saying what people may and may not do: *Charles is studying law at university.*

lazy /ˈleɪzi/ *adjective* comparative **lazier**, superlative **laziest** not want-ing to work: *My sister's so lazy.*

leader /ˈliːdə/ *noun* [C] the person who is in charge of a country or group: *a meeting of world leaders*

learn /lɜːn/ *verb* third person singular **learns**, present participle **learning**, past tense **learned** or **learnt** /lɜːnt / past participle **have learned** or **have learnt** to get knowledge by studying: *How long have you been learning English?* | *I want to learn to drive.*

leather /ˈleðə/ *noun* [U] animal skin that is used to make shoes, clothes, bags etc: *a leather bag*

leave /liːv/ *verb* third person singular **leaves**, present participle **leaving**, past tense **left** /left/ past participle **have left**
1 to go away from a place: *When did you leave school?* | *'Is Sandra still there?' 'No, she left half an hour ago.'*
2 leave a message to speak on an answering machine so that someone can listen to it later: *Please leave a message after the tone.*

1 . . . .

2 . . . .

left¹ /left/ *noun* [singular] the opposite side to the hand that most people write with: *The school is on the left of the street.*

. . . .

left² the past tense and past participle of **LEAVE**

. . . .

life /laɪf/ *noun* plural **lives** /laɪvz/
1 [C, U] the period of time during which someone is alive: *I have lived in England all my life.*
2 [C, U] the state of being alive: *They filmed the baby's first moments of life.*
3 [U] living things such as people, animals, or plants: *Is there life on Mars?*

1 . . . .

2 . . . .

3 . . . .

link /lɪŋk/ *verb* third person singular **links**, present participle **linking**, past tense **linked**, past participle **have linked** to join one place or thing to another: *The bridge links the two sides of the town.* | *Computers in a network are linked.*

. . . .

listen to /ˈlɪsən tə/ *verb* third person singular **listens to**, present participle **listening to**, past tense **listened to**, past participle **have listened to** to use your ears to hear something: *I enjoy listening to music.* | *Listen to your teacher.*

. . . .

literature /ˈlɪtərətʃə/ *noun* [U] books, poems, and plays that people think are good and important: *I'm interested in French literature.*

. . . .

live¹ /lɪv/ *verb* third person singular **lives**, present participle **living**, past tense **lived**, past participle **have lived**
1 if you live in a place, that place is your home: *Where do you live?* | *I live in New York.*
2 to be alive: *How long can you live without water?* | *My grandfather lived until he was ninety.*

1 . . . .

2 . . . .

live² /laɪv/ *adjective* live music is perfomed for people who are watching and listening in the same place

. . . .

lively /ˈlaɪvli/ *adjective* comparative **livelier**, superlative **liveliest** interesting and exciting: *The student bar has a really lively atmosphere.*

. . . .

living /ˈlɪvɪŋ/ *noun* [singular] the way that you earn money in order to live: *She earns a living by giving music lessons.*

. . . .

long¹ /lɒŋ/ *adjective* comparative **longer**, superlative **longest**
1 something that is long measures a large distance from one end to the other → opposite **SHORT**: *She's tall and slim, with long legs.* | *a long piece of string*
2 continuing for a great amount of time → opposite **SHORT**: *The chemistry lesson seemed very long.* | *She works long hours.*

1 . . . .

2 . . . .

long² *adverb* a long time, or for a long time: *How long does it take to cook pasta?* | *Did you wait long for the bus?*

· · · · · · · · · · · · · · ·

look /lʊk/ *verb* third person singular **looks**, present participle **looking**, past tense **looked**, past participle **have looked** to use your eyes to see something: *She looked at her watch.*

· · · · · · · · · · · · · · ·

look for /'lʊk fə/ *verb* third person singular **looks for**, present participle **looking for**, past tense **looked for**, past participle **have looked for** to want particular types of things or a particular type of person: *We are looking for a strong person to do this job.*

· · · · · · · · · · · · · · ·

look up /ˌlʊk 'ʌp/ *verb* third person singular **looks up**, present participle **looking up**, past tense **looked up**, past participle **have looked up** to find a piece of information in a book: *Look the word up in the dictionary.*

· · · · · · · · · · · · · · ·

lose /luːz/ *verb* third person singular **loses**, present participle **losing**, past tense **lost** /lɒst/ past participle **have lost** to not know where something is: *I've lost my pen have you seen it anywhere?*

· · · · · · · · · · · · · · ·

love¹ /lʌv/ *verb* third person singular **loves**, present participle **loving**, past tense **loved**, past participle **have loved**
1 to like someone and care about them a lot: *I really love my mum and dad.*
2 to like something a lot: *I love that dress you're wearing!*
3 to enjoy doing something very much: *Adam loves playing computer games.*

1 · · · · · · · · · · · · · ·
2 · · · · · · · · · · · · · ·
3 · · · · · · · · · · · · · ·

love² *noun* [C, U] plural **loves** when you like or enjoy doing something very much: *Tom has a great love of travel.*

· · · · · · · · · · · · · · ·

lovely /'lʌvli/ *adjective* comparative **lovelier**, superlative **loveliest** very nice, attractive, or pleasant: *She has a lovely face.* | *I've had a lovely day.*

· · · · · · · · · · · · · · ·

M, m

magazine /ˌmægə'ziːn/ *noun* [C] a large thin book with a paper cover, that you can buy every week or every month: *I bought a magazine to read on the train.*

· · · · · · · · · · · · · · ·

magnificent /mæg'nɪfəsənt/ *adjective* comparative **more magnificent**, superlative **most magnificent** very good or beautiful: *a magnificent palace*

make¹ /meɪk/ *verb* third person singular **makes**, present participle **making**, past tense **made** /meɪd/ past participle **have made** to put things together in order to produce or create something: *I'm making a cake for Rose's birthday.* | *Steven Spielberg makes films.*

· · · · · · · · · · · · · · ·

make² /meɪk/ *noun* [C] plural **makes** a type of product made by a company: *'What make is your PC?' 'It's a Dell.'*

make-up /'meɪk ʌp/ *noun* [U] creams and powders that a woman puts on her face to make herself look more attractive: *Do you ever wear make-up?*

management /'mænɪdʒmənt/ *noun* [U] the job of organizing the work of a company or shop, and the people who work there: *The banks blamed the situation on bad management.*

many /'meni/ *determiner, pronoun, adjective*
1 a large number of people or things: *There aren't many tickets left.*
2 too many use this when the number of something is larger than you want or need: *You've eaten too many sweets.*

marital status /'mærɪtl ˌsteɪtəs/ *noun* [U] your marital status is whether you are married or not: *What is your marital status – single, married, or divorced?*

mark /mɑːk/ *noun* [C] plural **marks** a letter or number given by a teacher to show how good a student's work is: *If I get good marks in my exams, my dad will buy me a computer game.*

market /'mɑːkɪt/ *noun* [C] plural **markets** an area where people bring food and other things to sell. A market is usually outside: *I usually buy fruit and vegetables at the market.*

marketing /'mɑːkɪtɪŋ/ *noun* [U] the job of deciding how to advertise and sell a product: *Stella works in marketing.*

marriage /'mærɪdʒ/ *noun* [U] the relationship between a man and a woman who are legally married to each other: *We have a happy marriage.*

married /'mærid/ *adjective* someone who is married has a husband or a wife: *Alice and Garry are getting married.* | *a married couple*

match¹ /mætʃ/ *noun* [C] plural **matches** a game between two people or teams: *a football match* | *Who won the match?*

match² *verb* third person singular **matches**, present participle **matching**, past tense **matched**, past participle **have matched** to find something that is similar to another thing or belongs with another thing: *See if you can match the names to the voices you will hear.*

maths /mæθs/ *noun* [U] the study or science of numbers, shapes, and measuring things

meal /miːl/ *noun* [C] past tense **meals** food that you eat at a particular time: *We usually have a big meal in the evening.* | *Cara is going to cook her boyfriend a meal.*

mean /miːn/ *verb* third person singular **means**, present participle **meaning**, past tense **meant** /ment/ past participle **have meant** to have a particular meaning: *What does this sign mean?* | *I don't know what this means, it's in Spanish.*

meat /miːt/ *noun* [U] the parts of an animal that you can cook and eat: *I don't eat very much meat.*

media /'miːdiə/ *noun* [singular] **the media** television, radio, and newspapers: *The crime was reported by the media.* | *John wants to work in the media as a journalist.*

medical /'medɪkəl/ *adjective* related to medicine and the job of treating people who are ill: *She needs medical care.*

medicine /'medsən/ *noun* [C, U] a special pill or drink you have when you are ill that helps you to get better: *cough medicine* | *A lot of people are interested in natural medicines.*

meet /miːt/ *verb* third person singular **meets**, present participle **meeting**, past tense **met** /met/ past participle **have met**
1 to see and talk to someone for the first time: *They first met at university.* | *Have you ever met her husband?*
2 to go somewhere and wait for someone: *We'll meet at eight o'clock outside the theatre.*
3 to go somewhere and see and talk to people: *After work I often meet my friends for a drink.*

mend /mend/ *verb* third person singular **mends**, present participle **mending**, past tense **mended**, past participle **have mended** to repair or fix something that is broken or damaged: *If they can't mend the TV, we'll have to get a new one.*

message /'mesɪdʒ/ *noun* [C] plural **messages** something that you say or write and send to another person: *I've got a message for you from Sammy.* | *Bea was out when I phoned so I left a message.*

midday /ˌmɪd'deɪ/ *noun* [U] 12 o'clock in the middle of the day

middle /'mɪdl/ *noun* **the middle** the part of something that is in the centre, furthest from the edges: *The sun is hottest in the middle of the day.* | *He put the cake in the middle of the table.*

midnight /'mɪdnaɪt/ *noun* [U] 12 o'clock at night: *We stayed up until midnight.*

mile /maɪl/ *noun* [C] plural **miles** a measure of distance that people use in Britain and the USA that is equal to 1.6 kilometres.: *Our school is about three miles away.* | *Ten miles is 16 kilometres.*

mineral /'mɪnərəl/ *noun* [C] plural **minerals** a natural substance such as iron or salt that is in the earth and some foods

miss /mɪs/ *verb* third person singular **misses**, present participle **missing**, past tense **missed**, past participle **have missed** to feel sad because someone that you like is not with you, or because you are no longer in a place you enjoyed in the past: *I really miss Mum and Dad now I'm at university.*

modern /ˈmɒdn/ *adjective* comparative **more modern,** superlative **most modern** something that is modern is made or designed using new ideas or styles: *a modern transport system for the 21st century* | *Everything in their house is very modern.*

money /ˈmʌni/ *noun* [U] the coins and paper notes that you use to buy things: *Billy spent lots of money in town today.* | *How much money did that CD cost?*

morning /ˈmɔːnɪŋ/ *noun* [C] plural **mornings** the time from the beginning until the middle of the day: *I saw Steve this morning.* | *I start work at six o'clock in the morning.*

mosque /mɒsk/ *noun* [C] plural **mosques** a building where Muslims go to pray

mountain /ˈmaʊntən/ *noun* [C] plural **mountains** a very high hill that is difficult to get to the top of: *The Matterhorn is the highest mountain in Switzerland.*

move /muːv/ *verb* third person singular **moves,** present participle **moving,** past tense **moved,** past participle **have moved** to go from one position or place to another: *The dog moved slowly towards us.*

multi-millionaire /ˌmʌlti ˌmɪljəˈneə/ *noun* [C] plural **multi-millionaires** someone who is very rich and has several million pounds or several million dollars

museum /mjuːˈziːəm/ *noun* [C] plural **museums** a building where people can go and look at important objects from the past or works of art: *The museum is free for children and students.* | *London is full of interesting museums.*

music /ˈmjuːzɪk/ *noun* [U] the pleasant sounds that people make by singing or playing musical instruments: *Do you like this music?* | *They were playing very loud music.*

N, n

natural /ˈnætʃərəl/ *adjective* comparative **more natural,** superlative **most natural** natural things are found in nature rather than being made by humans: *A lot of people are interested in natural medicines made from plants and herbs.*

nature /ˈneɪtʃə/ *noun* [U] everything in the world that is not made or caused by humans, for example animals and plants

near /nɪə/ *adjective, adverb* comparative **nearer**, superlative **nearest** close to another place: *Mike's school is very near his house.* | *We went to a pub near the river.* | *Where is the nearest underground station?*

necessary /ˈnesəsəri/ *adjective* comparative **more necessary**, superlative **most necessary** if something is necessary, you need it: *It is necessary to have a passport if you want to travel to another country.*

need /niːd/ *verb* third person singular **needs**, present participle **needing**, past tense **needed**, past participle **have needed**
1 if you need something, you must have it: *I live in the city, so I don't really need a car.*
2 need to do sth if you need to do something, it is necessary for you to do it: *I need to speak to Mike urgently.*

network /ˈnetwɜːk/ *noun* [C] plural **networks** a large group of things that are connected to each other across a city, country, etc: *a network of computers* | *France has a very efficient train network.*

new /njuː/ *adjective* comparative **newer**, superlative **newest**
1 if something is new, someone has just made it, bought it etc: *Have you seen Jake's new car.* | *I want a new pair of jeans.*
2 if something is new, you have not had it, seen it, or learned it before: *Her new boyfriend is much nicer than her old one.* | *Do you like their new apartment?*

newspaper /ˈnjuːsˌpeɪpə/ *noun* [C] plural **newspapers** large folded pieces of paper that are printed with news and articles: *I read about it in the newspaper.*

noisy /ˈnɔɪzi/ *adjective* comparative **noisier**, superlative **noisiest** making a lot of noise or full of noise: *You're being too noisy.* | *a noisy city street*

notebook /ˈnəʊtbʊk/ *noun* [C] plural **notebooks** a small book in which you can write things that you need to remember

O, o

obey /əʊˈbeɪ/ *verb* third person singular **obeys**, present participle **obeying**, past tense **obeyed**, past participle **have obeyed** to do what a person or rule tells you to do → opposite DISOBEY: *Students must obey the school rules.*

office /ˈɒfɪs/ *noun* [C] plural **offices** a room in a building where people work: *Oliver doesn't like to work in an office, he likes to work outside.* | *Mary is an office worker* (=she works in an office).

official /əˈfɪʃəl/ *adjective* comparative **more official**, superlative **most official** done or given by someone in power: *The official report will be published next month.* | *Canada has two official languages – English and French.*

old /əʊld/ *adjective* comparative **older**, superlative **oldest**
1 someone who is old has lived a long time: *an old woman* | *He was very old when he died.*
2 used when talking or asking about the age of a person or thing: *My sister's three years old.* | *How old are you?*
3 not modern or new: *We lived in an old house in the country.* | *Brian drives an old car.*

open¹ /ˈəʊpən/ *adjective*
1 not closed: *The door was open, so I went in.* | *An open book lay on the desk.*
2 if a shop, restaurant etc is open, people can come into it and use it: *The Indian restaurant is only open in the evening.* | *The bank opens at 9 o'clock in the morning.*

open² *verb* third person singular **opens**, present participle **opening**, past tense **opened**, past participle **have opened**
1 to move something so that it is open: *She opened her bag and took out some money.* | *Ella opened her book.*
2 when a shop, bank etc opens, people can go in and use it: *Most shops open at 9.30 on Saturday.* | *The new hospital will open in September.*

opera /ˈɒpərə/ *noun* [C, U] plural **operas** a musical play in which the actors since the words to music: *We went to an opera last night.* | *an opera singer*

order¹ /ˈɔːdə/ *noun* plural **orders**
1 [U] the way in which you arrange things so that they follow each other in a particular way: *Put the pictures in the correct order.*
2 [C] the food and drink that you ask for in a restaurant: *Can I take your order now, please?*

order² *verb* third person singular **orders**, present participle **ordering**, past tense **ordered**, past participle **have ordered** to ask for food or drink in a restaurant: *I ordered a cup of coffee and a sandwich.*

ordinary /ˈɔːdənəri/ *adjective* normal or usual, and not different from other people or things: *He was just an ordinary person but he suddenly became famous.*

originally /ə'rɪdʒɪnəli/ *adverb* in the beginning: *My family are originally from Ireland.*

own[1] /əʊn/ *adjective* belonging to a particular person: *He has his own company.*

own[2] *verb* third person singular **owns**, present participle **owning**, past tense **owned**, past participle **have owned** if you own something, it belongs to you: *He was the only person I knew who owned a van.*

P, p

packet /'pækɪt/ *noun* [C] plural **packets** a small bag or box that has food, cigarettes etc inside: *a packet of pasta*

palace /'pælɪs/ *noun* [C] plural **palaces** a very large house where a king or queen lives: *The Queen of England lives in Buckingham Palace.*

parcel /'pɑːsəl/ *noun* [C] plural **parcels** something that you wrap in paper so that it can be sent somewhere

parent /'peərənt/ *noun* [C] plural **parents** your parents are your father and mother: *Do you live with your parents?*

passenger /'pæsəndʒə/ *noun* [C] plural **passengers** someone who is travelling in a vehicle: *There were ten passengers on the bus.*

patent office /'peɪtnt ˌɒfɪs/ *noun* [C, usually singular] plural **patent offices** a place where someone who invents something can get an official piece of paper to say that he or she can make the invention and sell it, and no one else can copy it

pay /peɪ/ *verb* third person singular **pays**, present participle **paying**, past tense **paid** /peɪd/ past participle **have paid** to give someone money for something that you are buying from them: *Matt paid for the meal.* | *Can I pay by credit card?* | *Children under 16 don't have to pay.*

peaceful /'piːsfəl/ *adjective* comparative **more peaceful**, superlative **most peaceful** calm and quiet: *I just want a peaceful weekend with my family.*

people /'piːpəl/ *plural noun* men, women, and children. 'People' is the plural of 'person': *There are too many people in this room.* | *Jan knows lots of nice people.*

perfect /'pɜːfɪkt/ *adjective* something that is perfect is so good that it could not be any better: *She speaks perfect English.* | *This flat is perfect for us – it has everything that we need.*

person /'pɜːsən/ *noun* [C] plural **people** /'piːpəl/ a man, woman, or child: *Diana is a very kind person.*

personal /'pɜːsənəl/ *adjective* something that is personal is for only one person to use or is connected with one person's life: *Fill in your personal details on the application form.* | *My diary is personal, I don't want anyone to read it.*

pet /pet/ *noun* [C] plural **pets** an animal that you keep at home, for example a dog or a cat: *Do you have any pets?* | *We have a pet – a dog called Lucky.*

phone /fəʊn/ *verb* third person singular **phones**, present participle **phoning**, past tense **phoned**, past participle **have phoned** to speak to someone using a telephone: *Steve phoned me seven times last week* | *You can* **phone up** *and book tickets*

place /pleɪs/ *noun* [C] plural **places** a building, a town, or a country: *London is an exciting place to live.*

planet /'plænət/ *noun* [C] plural **planets** one of the large objects in space like the Earth that moves around the sun or a star: *Mercury is the smallest planet in our solar system.*

plant /plɑːnt/ *noun* [C] plural **plants** anything with green leaves that grows in the earth: *Plants need water and light to live.*

platform /'plætfɔːm/ *noun* [C] plural **platforms** a long flat area in a station where you get on and off a train: *The train for Brighton leaves from Platform 4.*

play¹ /pleɪ/ *verb* third person singular **plays**, present participle **playing**, past tense **played**, past participle **have played**
1 to put a tape or CD into a cassette player or a CD player so you can listen to it: *Let's play my new CD.*
2 to make music with a musical instrument: *I'm learning to play the guitar.*
3 to do a game or sport: *Sam hates playing football.* | *Jennifer plays golf every week.*

play² *noun* [C] plural **plays** a story that is performed by actors in a theatre, on the radio etc: *'Hamlet' is a play by Shakespeare.*

Poland /'pəʊlənd/ *noun* [singular] a country in Europe

political leader /pə'lɪtɪkəl 'liːdə/ *noun* [C] plural **political leaders** someone who is in charge of a group in politics or the government of a country

politician /ˌpɒləˈtɪʃən/ noun [C] plural **politicians** someone who works in politics: *Jeremy is a politician.*

politics /ˈpɒlətɪks/ noun [U] ideas and activities that are concerned with government and power in a country or area: *Are you interested in politics?* | *She wanted a career in politics.*

poor /pʊə/ adjective comparative **poorer**, superlative **poorest**
1 not having very much money → opposite RICH: *My family was very poor.*
2 something that is poor is not as good as it should be: *His school-work has been poor recently.*

popular /ˈpɒpjələ/ adjective liked by a lot of people → opposite UNPOPULAR: *He's one of the most popular boys in the school.* | *Which actors are popular in your country?*

post¹ /pəʊst/ noun [U]
1 the system of sending and receiving letters and parcels to and from people: *A big parcel arrived by post.*
2 letters etc that people send each other: *The post arrives at about eight o'clock in the morning.*

post² verb third person singular **posts**, present participle **posting**, past tense **posted**, past participle **have posted** to send a letter or parcel to someone by post: *Don't forget to post that letter to Mum.*

prefer /prɪˈfɜː/ verb third person singular **prefers**, present participle **preferring**, past tense **preferred**, past participle **have preferred** to like someone or something more than someone or something else: *I prefer football to cricket.* | *I'd prefer to stay at home today.*

pregnant /ˈpregnənt/ adjective if a woman or female animal is pregnant, she has a baby growing in her body: *How long is a cat pregnant for?*

present /ˈprezənt/ noun [C] plural **presents** a nice thing that you give to someone on a special occasion: *Mum got some lovely presents on her birthday.* | *I went into town to buy a present for my dad.*

primary school /ˈpraɪməri ˌskuːl/ noun [C] plural **primary schools** a school for children between the ages of 5 and 11

prison /ˈprɪzən/ noun [C, U] plural **prisons** a building where criminals are kept as a punishment: *He's been in prison for two years.*

problem /ˈprɒbləm/ noun [C] plural **problems** something that makes a situation difficult: *There are a lot of traffic problems in the city.* | *I had a problem with my computer this morning.*

proceed /prəˈsiːd/ verb third person singular **proceeds**, present participle **proceeding**, past tense **proceeded**, past participle **have proceeded** formal to continue: *The police have decided not to proceed with the case.*

professional /prəˈfeʃənəl/ *adjective* a professional musician, football player etc plays music, football etc as their job and gets paid for it: *a professional photographer*

professor /prəˈfesə/ *noun* [C] plural **professors** a teacher with the highest job in a university department: *Professor Sinclair*

protein /ˈprəʊtiːn/ *noun* [U] a substance in food such as meat and eggs, which helps your body to grow and be healthy

pub /pʌb/ *noun* [C] plural **pubs** a place where you can buy alcoholic drinks, and sometimes food, especially in Britain: *I'll meet you at the pub for a drink.*

publish /ˈpʌblɪʃ/ *verb* third person singular **publishes**, present participle **publishing**, past tense **published**, past participle **have published** to print a book or information for people to read: *a company that publishes children's books*

put /pʊt/ *verb* third person singular **puts**, present participle **putting**, past tense **put**, past participle **have put** to move something to a place and leave it there: *Where did I put my keys?* | *Harry put the pen in his pocket.*

put up /ˌpʊt ˈʌp/ *verb* third person singular **puts up**, present participle **putting up**, past tense **put up**, past participle **have put up** to put something on a wall or in a high position: *The teachers had put the children's paintings up on the walls.*

Q, q

qualification /ˌkwɒləfəˈkeɪʃən/ *noun* [C] plural **qualifications** you get qualifications after you complete a course of study and pass exams: *What qualifications do you need to be a teacher?* | *He has a qualification in Information Technology.*

queue¹ /kjuː/ *noun* [C] plural **queues** a line of people or vehicles that are waiting for something: *I joined the back of the queue.* | *There's a long queue in the post office this morning.*

queue² *verb* third person singular **queues**, present participle **queueing**, past tense **queued**, past participle **have queued** to wait in a line of people: *How long have you been queueing for tickets?*

quiet /'kwaɪət/ *adjective* comparative **quieter**, superlative **quietest**
1 without a lot of noise → opposite LOUD: *She spoke in a quiet voice.* | *I'm trying to study, please be quiet.*
2 not busy and without a lot of things happening: *We had a quiet, relaxing weekend at home.*

R, r

racing /'reɪsɪŋ/ *noun* [U] a sport in which horses or dogs run in a competition to see which is the fastest: *horse racing*

rain /reɪn/ *verb* third person singular **rains**, present participle **raining**, past tense **rained**, past participle **have rained** when it rains, small drops of water fall from the sky: *If it's raining, we'll have to do something indoors.*

read /riːd/ *verb* third person singular **reads**, present participle **reading**, past tense **read** /red/ past participle **have read** /red/ to look at something that is written down and understand what it means: *Dad sat in his chair, reading the paper.* | *My little brother is learning to read.* | *I like reading.*

receive /rɪ'siːv/ *verb* third person singular **receives**, present participle **receiving**, past tense **received**, past participle **have received** to get something that is given or sent to you: *You should receive the package by Saturday.* | *I received Tanya's email this morning.*

reception /rɪ'sepʃən/ *noun* [U] the part of a hotel or office near the entrance, where visitors or customers go when they arrive: *Please sign your name at reception when you arrive.* | *All visitors please report to reception* (=tell someone in reception that you are there).

recommend /ˌrekə'mend/ *verb* third person singular **recommends**, present participle **recommending**, past tense **recommended**, past participle **have recommended** to suggest to someone that they should do something, go somewhere, buy something etc: *Can you recommend a good Italian restaurant?* | *This is a good cheap airline, I recommend it.*

register /'redʒəstə/ *verb* third person singular **registers**, present participle **registering**, past tense **registered**, past participle **have registered** to put a name on an official list: *How many students have registered for the course, so far?*

relatives /'relətɪvz/ *noun* [plural] people who are part of your family, but not the people who live with you like your parents or brothers and sisters: *He is visiting some relatives in Yorkshire.*

relax /rɪ'læks/ *verb* third person singular **relaxes**, present participle **relaxing**, past tense **relaxed**, past participle **have relaxed** to rest and become calm, and stop thinking about your work or your problems: *I decided just to stay home and relax.*

. . . .

relaxing /rɪ'læksɪŋ/ *adjective* comparative **more relaxing**, superlative **most relaxing** something that is relaxing makes you feel calm and rested and not worried about anything: *We're going away for a relaxing weekend in the country.*

. . . .

religious /rɪ'lɪdʒəs/ *adjective* connected with a religion (=the belief that there is a God, for example Christianity, Islam, Buddhism)

. . . .

remember /rɪ'membə/ *verb* third person singular **remembers**, present participle **remembering**, past tense **remembered**, past participle **have remembered** to keep something in your mind, or to bring something back into your mind and not forget it: *What's your brother's name, I can't remember.* | *Do you remember your dreams?*

. . . .

rent /rent/ *verb* third person singular **rents**, present participle **renting**, past tense **rented**, past participle **have rented** to pay money to use something such as a car or video: *We can rent a video tonight.* | *We rented bicycles and rode along the beach.*

. . . .

replace /rɪ'pleɪs/ *verb* third person singular **replaces**, present participle **replacing**, past tense **replaced**, past participle **have replaced**
1 to take something away and use another thing instead: *When the TV broke, we didn't replace it.* | *Replace the words in brackets with a word that means the opposite.*
2 to be used instead of something else: *Will electronic books ever replace paper books?*

1 . . . .

2 . . . .

return /rɪ'tɜːn/ *noun* [C] plural **returns** a ticket for a journey to a place and back again → opposite SINGLE: *How much is a return to London?*

. . . .

revolution /ˌrevə'luːʃən/ *noun* [C] plural **revolutions**
1 when the people of a country change the political system completely, using force: *the French Revolution*
2 a complete change in the way people do something: *a revolution in scientific thinking*

1 . . . .

2 . . . .

ride /raɪd/ *verb* third person singular **rides**, present participle **riding**, past tense **rode** /rəʊd/ past participle **have ridden** /'rɪdn/ to move along on a bicycle or horse: *I learnt to ride a bike when I was five.* | *Have you ever ridden a horse?*

. . . .

right¹ /raɪt/ *adjective*
1 the right side is the side nearest your right hand, which is the hand most people write with → opposite LEFT: *Dan's broken his right leg.*
2 correct → opposite WRONG: *In the test, all my answers were right.* | *Are you sure this is the right way?* | *You're right – it is raining.*

1 . . . .

2 . . . .

right² *adverb* towards the right side → opposite LEFT: *Turn right by the traffic lights.*

right³ *noun* [singular] the right side → opposite LEFT: *That's him on the right.* | *In France they drive on the right.*

romantic /rəʊˈmæntɪk/ *adjective* comparative **more romantic**, superlative **most romantic** connected with love and with treating the person you love in a special way: *a romantic film* | *I wish my boyfriend was more romantic.*

rug /rʌɡ/ *noun* [C] plural **rugs** a piece of thick material that you put on the floor: *a beautiful Turkish rug*

rugby /ˈrʌɡbi/ *noun* [U] a game played by two teams who carry and kick a ball that is the shape of a large egg

run /rʌn/ *verb* third person singular **runs**, present participle **running**, past tense **ran** /ræn/ past participle **have run** to move quickly, going faster than when you walk: *I can run faster than Tom.* | *A boy was running down the road.* | *They had to run to catch the bus.*

S, s

safely /ˈseɪfli/ *adverb* in a way that is not harmful or dangerous: *Drive safely!*

safety /ˈseɪfti/ *noun* [U] **health and safety** → HEALTH

sailing /ˈseɪlɪŋ/ *noun* [U] the sport of sailing boats: *Do you like sailing?*

Saturday /ˈsætədi/ *noun* [C,U] plural **Saturdays** the day of the week between Friday and Sunday: *What are you doing on Saturday?*

say /seɪ/ *verb* third person singular **says** /sez/ present participle **saying**, past tense **said** /sed/ past participle **have said** to speak words in order to give information or show your thoughts, feelings etc: *What did you say? I didn't hear you.* | *'Wait,' said Laura.* | *She said that she wasn't feeling well.* | *How do you say 'friend' in Spanish?*

scenery /ˈsiːnəri/ *noun* [U] the natural things such as woods and rivers that you see around you in the countryside: *the spectacular scenery of the Alps*

science /'saɪəns/ *noun* [U] the study of natural and physical things, and the knowledge we get by testing and proving facts: *Science made great progress in the17th century.* I *We've been learning about electricity in our science lessons.*

scientist /'saɪəntɪst/ *noun* [C] plural **scientists** someone who studies science

season /'siːzən/ *noun* [C] plural **seasons** the seasons are the periods of time into which a year is divided, based on changes in the weather. In Britain, the seasons are spring, summer, autumn, and winter: *Spring is my favorite season.*

secondary school /'sekəndəri ˌskuːl/ *noun* [C] plural **secondary schools** a school for children between the ages of 11 and 18. A school for children under 11 is a primary school

secretary /'sekrətəri/ *noun* [C] plural **secretaries** someone whose job is to write letters, arrange meetings, answer telephone calls etc in an office

see /siː/ *verb* third person singular **sees**, present participle **seeing**, past tense **saw** /sɔː/ past participle **have seen** /siːn/
1 to use your eyes: *It was too dark to see anything.* I *I saw two policemen knocking at her door.*
2 to meet or visit someone: *I see Pam every Saturday.* I *I haven't seen Bob for months.*
3 to understand: *Do you see how it works?* I *'Then you just add these two numbers together.' 'Oh, I see.'*
4 to see a film, concert, television programme: *Let's go and see a movie.* I *Did you see the game last night?*
5 to find out information or facts: *Alison, can you see who is at the door?* I *See Chapter 3 for more information.*

sell /sel/ *verb* third person singular **sells**, present participle **selling**, past tense **sold** /səʊld/ past participle **have sold**
1 to offer something for people to buy: *The shop sells computer games.*
2 to be bought by people: *The book has sold millions of copies.*

share /ʃeə/ *verb* third person singular **shares**, present participle **sharing**, past tense **shared**, past participle **have shared** if two people share something, they both have it or use it: *The two secretaries share an office.* I *He shares a bedroom with his brother.*

shave /ʃeɪv/ *verb* third person singular **shaves**, present participle **shaving**, past tense **shaved**, past participle **have shaved** to cut off the hair on your face or body: *He washed and shaved.*

shop assistant /'ʃɒp əˈsɪstənt/ *noun* [C] plural **shop assistants** someone who works in a shop selling things and helping customers

shopping /'ʃɒpɪŋ/ *noun* [U]
1 when you go to shops to buy things: *Her boyfriend hates shopping.* | *I did the shopping for her when she was sick.* | *I'm going shopping for some new shoes.*
2 things that you have just bought: *Maggie was carrying bags of shopping.*

1 . . . .

2 . . . .

short /ʃɔːt/ *adjective* comparative **shorter**, superlative **shortest**
1 a short distance or length is not long → opposite **LONG**[1]: *His hair is short and black.* | *It's only a short walk to my school.*
2 happening for only a little time → opposite **LONG**[1]: *The film is quite short.* | *We made a short visit to his parents.*
3 a short person is not tall → opposite **TALL**: *Her father was a short fat man.* | *Louise is shorter than me.*

1 . . . .

2 . . . .

3 . . . .

shorts /ʃɔːts/ *noun* [plural] short trousers that only reach to your knees: *Jack was wearing shorts and a T-shirt.* | *I put on a pair of shorts.*

. . . .

show /ʃəʊ/ *verb* third person singular **shows**, present participle **showing**, past tense **showed**, past participle **have shown** /ʃəʊn/ to put on a film or programme at a cinema or on television, so that people are able to see it: *They are showing 'Star Wars' on TV on Saturday.*

. . . .

shower /'ʃaʊə/ *noun* [C] plural **showers**
1 a flow of water that you stand under to wash your whole body: *a bedroom with a private shower*
2 when you wash your body in a shower: *I'm going to have a shower before dinner.*

1 . . . .

2 . . . .

silly /'sɪli/ *adjective* comparative **sillier**, superlative **silliest** funny or stupid, and not serious or sensible: *a silly joke* | *Stop being silly and get on with your work.*

. . . .

similar /'sɪmələ/ *adjective* things that are similar are almost the same: *Martine and her sister look very similar.* | *Your taste in music is similar to mine.*

. . . .

simple /'sɪmpəl/ *adjective* comparative **simpler**, superlative **simplest** plain and ordinary, without anything extra or special added → opposite **COMPLICATED**: *I made a simple tomato soup.* | *He explained his ideas in a very simple way.*

. . . .

singer /'sɪŋə/ *noun* [C] plural **singers** someone who sings, especially as a job: *a pop singer*

. . . .

single[1] /'sɪŋgəl/ *adjective* not married or in a serious relationship: *Brad's gorgeous. Is he single?* | *a single woman in her thirties*

. . . .

single[2] *noun* [C] plural **singles**
1 a musical record, CD etc with only one or two songs on it: *Have you heard the new U2 single?*
2 a ticket to travel to a place but not back again → opposite **RETURN**: *a single to London*

1 . . . .

2 . . . .

sister /'sɪstə/ *noun* [C] plural **sisters** a girl or woman who has the same parents as you: *I share a bedroom with my sister.* | *Do you have any brothers or sisters?*

sit /sɪt/ *verb* third person singular **sits**, present participle **sitting**, past tense **sat** /sæt/ past participle **have sat** if you are sitting somewhere, you are resting there with your weight on your bottom: *The children were all sitting on the floor.* | *Who is that sitting next to Mary?*

situation /ˌsɪtʃu'eɪʃən/ *noun* [C] plural **situations** the particular things that are happening at one time and place: *We are in a very difficult situation.* | *There are some situations when it's better not to tell the truth.*

size /saɪz/ *noun* [C] plural **sizes**
1 how big or small something is: *Nicolas and I are about the same size.* | *The animal was about the size of a cat.*
2 a number, letter etc that shows how big clothes and shoes are: *What size shoes do you take?* | *Do you have this shirt in a bigger size?*

ski resort /'skiː rɪ'zɔːt/ *noun* [C] plural **ski resorts** a place in the mountains where a lot of people go to ski: *a ski resort in the French Alps*

sleep¹ /sliːp/ *verb* third person singular **sleeps**, present participle **sleeping**, past tense **slept** /slept/ past participle **have slept** if you are sleeping, you are resting with your eyes closed and your mind and body are not active: *Tom is sleeping. Don't wake him.* | *Did you sleep well last night?*

sleep² *noun* [U] time when you are sleeping: *I only had five hours' sleep last night.*

slim /slɪm/ *adjective* comparative **slimmer**, superlative **slimmest** thin in an attractive way: *a slim pretty girl* | *I wish I was a bit slimmer.*

slow /sləʊ/ *adjective* comparative **slower**, superlative **slowest** not moving or happening quickly → opposite FAST, QUICK: *This computer's very slow!* | *It was a slow journey because the roads were very busy.* | *Jamie's a very slow worker.*

slowly /'sləʊli/ *adverb* at a slow speed → opposite QUICKLY: *I drove slowly along the track.* | *Can you speak more slowly?*

small /smɔːl/ *adjective* comparative **smaller**, superlative **smallest** not big [= little] → opposite BIG: *There's a small hole in the roof.* | *A small number of students behaved badly.* | *My mom is smaller than me.*

smart /smɑːt/ *adjective* comparative **smarter**, superlative **smartest**
1 intelligent: *John's much smarter than his brother.* | *Lucy is a smart kid.*
2 fashionable: *It is one of London's smartest restaurants.*

smoke /sməʊk/ *verb* third person singular **smokes**, present participle **smoking**, past tense **smoked**, past participle **have smoked** to breathe in smoke from a cigarette or pipe: *Are you allowed to smoke at work?* | *a man who smokes 30 cigarettes a day*

snack /snæk/ *noun* [C] plural **snacks** food that you eat between your main meals, for example some fruit or a sandwich

son /sʌn/ *noun* [C] plural **sons** someone's boy child: *I have two sons and a daughter.*

sort /sɔːt/ *noun* [C] plural **sorts** a type of thing: *What sort of car are you going to buy?* | *'Do you like this band?' 'No, I don't really like that sort of music.'*

sound¹ /saʊnd/ *noun* [C, U] plural **sounds** something that you hear: *We could hear the sound of traffic outside.* | *Listen to these sounds.*

sound² *verb* third person singular **sounds**, present participle **sounding**, past tense **sounded**, past participle **have sounded** the way something sounds is how it seems to you when you listen to it: *The band sounded really good tonight.*

south /saʊθ/ *noun* [U] the direction towards the bottom of a map

souvenir /ˌsuːvəˈnɪə/ *noun* [C] plural **souvenirs** something you buy when you go on holiday, that will make you think about the place you have visited: *I bought a model of the Empire State Building as a souvenir of New York.*

speak /spiːk/ *verb* third person singular **speaks**, present participle **speaking**, past tense **spoke** /spəʊk/ past participle **have spoken** /ˈspəʊkən/
1 to talk to someone or to people about something: *I was speaking to Jane.*
2 to be able to say and understand words in a particular language: *Do you speak Russian?*

speed limit /ˈspiːd ˌlɪmɪt/ *noun* [C] plural **speed limits** the fastest speed that you are legally allowed to drive at: *a 40 mph speed limit*

spend /spend/ *verb* third person singular **spends**, present participle **spending**, past tense **spent** /spent/ past participle **have spent** to use your money to pay for something: *I spent all my money.* | *Brendan spent over £600 on his new bike.*

spoon /spuːn/ *noun* [C] plural **spoons** something that you use for eating food, shaped like a small bowl with a long handle

spoonful /ˈspuːnfʊl/ *noun* [C] plural **spoonfuls** the amount that a spoon can hold: *a spoonful of medicine*

sports stadium /ˈspɔːts ˌsteɪdiəm/ *noun* [C] plural **sports stadiums** a place with lots of seats all around it where you can watch sports games

square
/skweə/ *noun* [C] plural **squares** an open area with buildings around it in the middle of a town: *The Police Station is in the main square.*

star /stɑː/ *noun* [C] plural **stars** a famous actor, singer, sports player etc: *a movie star*

start /stɑːt/ *verb* third person singular **starts**, present participle **starting**, past tense **started**, past participle **have started**
1 to begin doing something: *My brother is starting school in September.*
2 to begin happening: *What time does the party start?*

stationery /'steɪʃənəri/ *noun* [U] things such as paper and envelopes that you use for writing: *Go to the stationery department in the store to buy a new pen.*

statue /'stætʃuː/ *noun* [C] plural **statues** a model of a person, made out of stone, metal etc, and often put in a public place so that people can look at it

stay /steɪ/ *verb* third person singular **stays**, present participle **staying**, past tense **stayed**, past participle **have stayed**
1 to live in a place for a short time: *How long are you going to stay in Japan? | They went to stay with Ed's parents.*
2 to continue to be open and not closed: *The supermarket stays open all night.*
3 to not go out in the evening, but stay at home: *I'm too tired to go out – I'm staying in tonight to watch TV.*

steal /stiːl/ *verb* third person singular **steals**, present participle **stealing**, past tense **stole** /stəʊl/ past participle **have stolen** /'stəʊlən/ to take something that belongs to someone else: *Someone stole my bike.*

stop /stɒp/ *verb* third person singular **stops**, present participle **stopping**, past tense **stopped**, past participle **have stopped**
1 to not do something any more: *Stop making so much noise! | I stopped smoking several years ago.*
2 to finish moving, working, or doing something: *Let's stop for a cup of coffee. | It's stopped raining now.*
3 to make something or someone stop: *Please stop the car – I feel sick.*

straight /streɪt/ *adverb*
1 in a straight line: *Walk straight on for about 500 metres – the police station is on the left. | The museum is straight ahead.*

2 without stopping: *I'm not going straight home after school, I'm going to the park with Jake.* | *She went straight to bed when she got home.*

strange /streɪndʒ/ *adjective* a strange place is a place where you have never been before: *She was all alone in a strange city.*

street life /'striːt laɪf/ *noun* [U] the things that are happening on a street

study¹ /'stʌdi/ *noun* [U] when you learn about a subject: *Biology is the study of living things.*

study² *verb* third person singular **studies**, present participle **studying**, past tense **studied**, past participle **have studied** to learn about a subject: *She wants to study law at university.*

successful /sək'sesfəl/ *adjective* comparative **more successful**, superlative **most successful**
1 if you are successful, you achieve what you have been trying to do: *a successful Hollywood actress*
2 something that is successful is liked by many people and makes a lot of money: *He has written two successful books.* | *a successful movie*

sugary /'ʃʊgəri/ *adjective* comparative **more sugary**, superlative **most sugary** containing sugar or tasting like sugar: *sugary drinks*

sunglasses /'sʌnglɑːsɪz/ *noun* [plural] dark glasses that you wear to protect your eyes from the sun: *She was wearing sunglasses.*

surname /'sɜːneɪm/ *noun* [C] plural **surnames** the name you share with your parents and brothers and sisters: *Her surname is Smith.*

surprising /sə'praɪzɪŋ/ *adjective* comparative **more surprising**, superlative **most surprising** if something is surprising, you did not expect it to happen: *This is a very surprising result.* | *It's not surprising* (=it doesn't make you surprised) *that Sherrie is good at swimming – all her family play a lot of sports.*

swim /swɪm/ *verb* third person singular **swims**, present participle **swimming**, past tense **swam** /swæm/ past participle **have swum** /swʌm/ to move through water using your arms and legs: *We swam in the lake.* | *George is just learning to swim.*

swimming pool /'swɪmɪŋ puːl/ *noun* [C] plural **swimming pools** a large hole full of water that is built for swimming in

T, t

take /teɪk/ *verb* third person singular **takes**, present participle **taking**, past tense **took** /tʊk/ past participle have **taken** /'teɪkən/
1 to move or carry something to a place: *Don't forget to take your bag with you.*
2 to go with someone: *Dad took me with him to the football game.* | *I'm taking the dog for a walk.*
3 to travel in a bus, train etc: *We took a train to London.* | *I'll take the bus home.*
4 if something takes a particular amount of time, you need that amount of time to do it: *It takes me ten minutes to get to school.* | *This chicken recipe only takes twenty minutes to make.*
5 take a photograph to use a camera to photograph someone or something: *I took lots of photos at the party.*
6 take turns if people take turns to do something, first one person does it, then another does: *We took turns to do the driving.*

1 . . . .

2 . . . .

3 . . . .

4 . . . .

5 . . . .

6 . . . .

teacher /'tiːtʃə/ *noun* [C] plural **teachers** someone whose job is to teach: *Miss Lind is my English teacher.*

. . . .

temperature /'tempərətʃə/ *noun* [C, U] plural **temperatures** how hot or cold something is: *The temperature drops at night to 2·°C.*

. . . .

temple /'tempəl/ *noun* [C] plural **temples** a building where people in some religions go to pray: *a Hindu temple*

. . . .

tennis /'tenɪs/ *noun* [U] a game played by two or four people in which you hit a ball over the net

. . . .

theatre /'θɪətə/ *noun* plural **theatres**
1 [C] a building where plays and other kinds of entertainment are performed on a stage: *Would you like to go to the theatre?*
2 [U] plays that are performed

1 . . . .

2 . . . .

thin /θɪn/ *adjective* comparative **thinner**, superlative **thinnest** someone who is thin has very little fat on their body → opposite FAT: *a tall thin man* | *Her face was thin and pale.*

. . . .

thirsty /'θɜːsti/ *adjective* comparative **thirstier**, superlative **thirstiest** if you are thirsty, you need to drink something: *I'm thirsty. Can I have a glass of water?*

. . . .

ticket office /ˈtɪkɪt ˌɒfɪs/ *noun*
[C] plural **ticket offices** the place
where you go to buy a ticket from
someone: *Mary bought her train
ticket at the ticket office.*

tidy /ˈtaɪdi/ *adjective* comparative
tidier, superlative **tidiest** arranged
in a neat and careful way → oppo-
site UNTIDY: *Your grandmother's coming, so make sure your room is
tidy!* | *Please leave the house tidy when you go.*

tired /taɪəd/ *adjective* comparative **more tired**, superlative **most tired**
someone who is tired feels that they want to sleep or rest: *By the end
of the day, I felt so tired that I had to lie down.* | *Young children get
tired very quickly.*

tiring /ˈtaɪərɪŋ/ *adjective* comparative **more tiring**, superlative **most
tiring** making you feel tired: *a long, tiring journey*

toothpaste /ˈtuːθpeɪst/
noun [U] a soft substance
that you use to clean your
teeth: *Use a small amount
of toothpaste.*

top /tɒp/ *noun* [C] plural **tops**
1 the highest part of something → opposite BOTTOM: *I'm going to try
and climb to the top of that tree.* | *Her name was at the top of the list.*
2 a piece of clothing that you wear on the top part of your body: *I've
bought a blue top to wear with this skirt.*

touch /tʌtʃ/ *noun*
1 get in touch to write to someone or telephone them: *George
decided to get in touch with an old friend of his.*
2 keep in touch to continue to speak or write to someone who does
not live near you: *Jane and I have kept in touch since we left school.*

tourist /ˈtʊərɪst/ *noun* [C] plural **tourists** someone who visits a place
for enjoyment or interest, esepecially when they are on holiday: *a
group of Japanese tourists*

toy /tɔɪ/ *noun* [C] plural **toys** a thing for children to play with: *Polly
was playing with her toys upstairs.*

traditional /trəˈdɪʃənəl/ *adjective* comparative **more traditional**,
superlative **most traditional** traditional beliefs or activities have
existed for a long time among a group of people: *traditional folk
music* | *It's traditional for the bride's father to pay for her wedding.*

traffic /ˈtræfɪk/ *noun* [U] cars etc that are moving on the roads: *The
traffic's really bad* (=busy and slow) *in the morning.*

traffic jam /ˈtræfɪk ˌdʒæm/ *noun* [C] plural **traffic jams** a long line of
cars etc on the road, moving very slowly or not moving at all: *We got
stuck in a traffic jam.*

train[1] /treɪn/ *noun* [C] plural **trains** a line of vehicles that are connected together, which travels along a railway and carries people or things: *I caught the nine o'clock **train to** Boston.* | *Shall we drive or **go by train**?*

train[2] *verb* third person singular **trains**, present participle **training**, past tense **trained**, past participle **have trained**
1 to teach someone the skills that they need to do something difficult: *We could **train** nurses **to** do these tests on patients.*
2 to learn how to do something that needs a particular skill: *Jeff **trained as** a pilot when he left school.* | *I'd like to **train to** become a teacher.*
3 to prepare for a sports competition by exercising and practising: *Vicky's been **training for** the race for the past nine months.*

trainers /ˈtreɪnəz/ *noun* [plural] *BrE* shoes that are made for running or playing sports but which many people wear as ordinary shoes: *a pair of new trainers*

training /ˈtreɪnɪŋ/ *noun* [U] activities that help you learn how to do a job or play a sport: *On the course we received training in every aspect of the job.* | *She was injured while in training for the Olympics.*

transit /ˈtrænsɪt, -zɪt/ *noun* [U] when goods or people are moved from one place to another: *Goods often get lost **in transit**.*

transport /ˈtrænspɔːt/ *noun* [U] *BrE* vehicles that people use to travel from one place to another: *Bicycles are the best form of transport in the city centre.* | *It's a poor country, with very little **public transport** (=buses, trains etc that everyone can use).*

travel[1] /ˈtrævəl/ *verb* third person singular **travels**, present participle **travelling**, past tense **travelled**, past participle **have travelled** to go from one place to another, usually in a vehicle: *I've been travelling all day and I'm exhausted!* | *It's quicker if you **travel by** train.*

travel[2] *noun* [U] when you travel: *Air travel is safe and cheap.*

trendy /ˈtrendi/ *adjective* comparative **trendier**, superlative **trendiest** *informal* modern and fashionable: *trendy shoes*

tropical /ˈtrɒpɪkəl/ *adjective* from the hottest and wettest parts of the world: *tropical rainforests*

true /truː/ *adjective* comparative **truer**, superlative **truest**
1 correct and based on facts or things that really happened → opposite FALSE: *The film was based on a **true** story.* | *Is it **true that** she's only 30 years old?*
2 real: *true love* | *a true friend*
3 come true if your dream or wish comes true, what you hope for actually happens: *She had hoped for a place at college, and now her dream had **come true**.*

try /traɪ/ *verb* third person singular **tries**, present participle **trying**, past tense **tried**, past participle **have tried**
1 if you try to do something, you make an effort to do it: *I've been **trying to** remember where I left my jacket.*

2 to do, use, or taste something in order to find out whether it is successful or good: *Would you like to try some of this soup?*
3 to go to a place or person, or call them, in order to find someone or something: *Sorry, he's not in. Would you like to try again later? | Let's try Mouncy Street. He could be there.*

2 . . . .

3 . . . .

U, u

ugly /ˈʌgli/ *adjective* comparative **uglier**, superlative **ugliest** very unattractive or unpleasant to look at: *an ugly animal with a fat body and short legs*

. . . .

uncle /ˈʌŋkəl/ *noun* [C] plural **uncles** the brother of your mother or father, or the husband of your **AUNT**: *I went to stay with my uncle and aunt for a few days. | Uncle Mike always visits us at Christmas.*

. . . .

understand /ˌʌndəˈstænd/ third person singular **understands**, present participle **understanding**, past tense **understood** /ˌʌndəˈstʊd/ past participle **have understood** if you understand something that is spoken or written, you know what it means: *Does Jim understand Spanish? | I couldn't understand what the men were saying.*

. . . .

unemployed /ˌʌnɪmˈplɔɪd/ *adjective* someone who is unemployed does not have a job → same meaning OUT OF WORK: *I'm unemployed at the moment, but I'm looking for work*

. . . .

unfortunately /ʌnˈfɔːtʃənətli/ *adverb* used to say that you feel sad or disappointed about something: *Unfortunately, we had to go home early.*

. . . .

uniform /ˈjuːnəfɔːm/ *noun* [C, U] plural **uniforms** a special set of clothes that people wear so that they all look the same when they work in some jobs or go to some schools: *Our school uniform is green and white. | The soliders were in uniform (=wearing their uniforms).*

. . . .

urgently /ˈɜːdʒəntli/ *adverb* if something is needed urgently, it is important and someone must deal with it immediately: *Food and medicine are needed urgently | I need that report urgently*

. . . .

use¹ /juːz/ *verb* third person singular **uses**, present participle **using**, past tense **used**, past participle **have used**
1 if you use something, you do something with it: *Can I use your phone? | Neil used his cigarette lighter to start the fire.*
2 to say or write a particular word or phrase: *Why did you use the word 'if'?*

1 . . . .

2 . . . .

use² /juːs/ *noun* [U] when people use something: *The use of sun-screens can help prevent skin cancer.*

. . . .

useful /'juːsfəl/ *adjective* comparative **more useful**, superlative **most useful** a useful thing helps you do or get what you want: *a useful map of the town centre*

V, v

value /'væljuː/ *noun* [U] used to say that something is worth the amount you pay for it: *At only £45 a night, it's great value for money.*

vegetarian /ˌvedʒə'teəriən/ *noun* [C] plural **vegetarians** someone who does not eat meat or fish: *Do you have any dishes that are suitable for vegetarians?*

video /'vɪdiəʊ/ *noun* [C] plural **videos**
1 a tape on which a film or television programme has been recorded: *Have you got a video of 'Robocop 3'?*
2 *BrE* a machine for recording and watching videos: *Did you remember to set the video?*

view /vjuː/ *noun* [C] plural **views** everything that you can see from a place, especially when this is very beautiful or interesting: *We bought a house with a view of the beach.* | *There are great views from the mountain.*

virus /'vaɪərəs/ *noun* [C] plural **viruses** a computer program that can destroy or damage information stored in the computer: *Many viruses are spread by software downloaded from the Internet.*

visit /'vɪzɪt/ *verb* [T] third person singular **visits**, present participle **visiting**, past tense **visited**, past participle **have visited** to go and spend time with someone: *Granny is visiting us next weekend.* | *I went to visit Simon in hospital.* | *You must come and visit me sometime.*

vitamin /'vɪtəmən/ *noun* [C] plural **vitamins** a natural chemical in food that keeps you healthy: *Try to eat foods that are rich in vitamins and minerals.* | *Oranges contain a lot of Vitamin C.*

W, w

wait /weɪt/ *verb* third person singular **waits**, present participle **waiting**, past tense **waited**, past participle **have waited** to stay in a place or not do anything until something happens or someone arrives: *Hurry up! Everyone's waiting.* | *We had to **wait** 45 minutes for a train.*

wake /weɪk/ *verb* third person singular **wakes**, present participle **waking**, past tense **woke** /wəʊk/ past participle **have woken** /'wəʊkən/ if you wake, or if someone or something wakes you, you stop sleeping: *Guy was woken by a loud noise.* | *I woke really early this morning.*

wake up /ˌweɪk 'ʌp/ *verb* third person singular **wakes up**, present participle **waking up**, past tense **woke up** /wəʊk/ past participle **have woken up** /'wəʊkən/ if you wake up, or if someone or something wakes you up, you stop sleeping: *Wake up, Sam! Your breakfast is ready.* | *Can you wake me up at 7.00 tomorrow?*

walk¹ /wɔːk/ *verb* third person singular **walks**, present participle **walking**, past tense **walked**, past participle **have walked** to move forwards by putting one foot in front of the other: *I usually **walk to** college.*

walk² *noun* [C] plural **walks**
1 a journey that you make by walking: *We always **go for a walk** on Sundays.* | *The children **took** Ben **for a walk** along the river.* | *The hotel is a 10-minute walk away* (=it takes 10 minutes to walk there).
2 a path that people can walk along for pleasure: *There are some lovely walks in the area.*

watch /wɒtʃ/ *verb* third person singular **watches**, present participle **watching**, past tense **watched**, past participle **have watched** to look for a period of time at someone doing something or something that is happening: *We watched a film on TV.* | *Do you want to play too, or just sit and watch?*

way /weɪ/ *noun* plural **ways**
1 [C] how you do or make something: *Can you think of a **good way** of raising money for the school?*
2 [C] how someone behaves, talks, feels etc: *Marge was looking at him **in a strange way**.*
3 [C] the road, path etc that you must go on in order to get to a place:

*Excuse me, is this the **way** to the station?*
4 [singular] the distance between two places: *People don't always realize that San Francisco is **a long way** from Los Angeles.*
5 on the way when you are going somewhere: *Guess who I saw on the way home.*

wear /weə/ *verb* third person singular **wears**, present participle **wearing**, past tense **wore** /wɔː/ past participle **worn** /wɔːn/ if you wear clothes, shoes, glasses etc, you have them on your body: *I decided to wear my blue dress.* | *Do you ever wear lipstick?*

weather /ˈweðə/ *noun* [U] how hot or cold it is and how much sun, rain, or wind there is in a place at a particular time: *Did you have **good weather** on your trip?* | *We had a week of lovely **hot weather**.*

wedding /ˈwedɪŋ/ *noun* [C] plural **weddings** when two people get married: *I've been invited to Janet and Peter's wedding.*

weigh /weɪ/ *verb* third person singular **weighs**, present participle **weighing**, past tense **weighed**, past participle **have weighed** if something weighs a particular amount, that is how heavy it is: *How much does she weigh?* | *My suitcase weighed 20 kilos.*

west[1] /west/ *noun* [U] **the west** the part of a country or area that is nearest to where the sun goes down in the evening: *Rain is expected in the west.*

west[2] *adjective* the west part of a country or area is nearest to where the sun goes down in the evening: *Los Angeles is on the west coast.*

west[3] *adverb* towards the direction that you look in to see the sun go down in the evening: *The house faces west.*

wife /waɪf/ *noun* [C] plural **wives** /waɪvz/ the woman that a man is married to: *My brother and his wife came to visit us last week.*

win /wɪn/ third person singular **wins**, present participle **winning**, past tense **won** /wʌn/ past participle **have won**
1 to be the best or first in a game, competition, or fight → opposite LOSE: *Mark's team won the basketball tournament.* | *We always knew we would win the war.*
2 to get a prize in a game or competition: *I won a free trip to New York!*

woman /ˈwʊmən/ *noun* [C] plural **women** /ˈwɪmɪn/ an adult female person: *Diana was a very beautiful woman.*

won /wʌn/ the past tense and past participle of **WIN**

woods /wʊdz/ *noun* [plural] a small **FOREST**: *We got lost in the woods*

work¹ /wɜːk/ *verb* third person singular **works**, present participle **working**, past tense **worked**, past participle **have worked**
1 to do a job in order to earn money: *Where do you work?* | *I work in a bank?* | *Do you like working for your father?* | *Steve now works as an engineer.* | *Skip is a working dog* (=a dog that works) – *he helps the police to find drugs.*
2 to do something that needs effort in order to achieve a result: *You have to work hard to pass your exams.*

1 . . . .

2 . . . .

work² *noun* [U]
1 something that you do in order to earn money: *What kind of work would you like to do when you leave school?*
2 the place where you do your job: *Paul isn't here – he's at work.* | *I go to work at eight o'clock.* | *She comes to work by bus.*
3 the time when you are doing your job: *I'll meet you after work.*

1 . . . .

2 . . . .

3 . . . .

write /raɪt/ *verb* third person singular **writes**, present participle **writing**, past tense **wrote** /rəʊt/ past participle **have written** /'rɪtn/
1 to make letters or words on paper, using a pen or pencil: *We teach children how to read and write.* | *Write your name on this piece of paper.*
2 to produce a letter to send to someone: *Will you write to me when you've gone?* | *I'm writing a letter to my mother.*
3 to produce a book, song etc: *He wrote several books and many poems.*

1 . . . .

2 . . . .

3 . . . .

writer /'raɪtə/ *noun* [C] plural **writers** someone who writes books or stories, or for newspapers etc: *a writer of children's stories*

. . . .

Y, y

young /jʌŋ/ *adjective* comparative **younger**, superlative **youngest** a young person has not yet lived for a long time: *Young people from all over the world come here to study English.*

. . . .